Under a Double Headed Eagle: Józef Mianowski

# Central and Eastern Europe

*Regional Perspectives in Global Context*

*Series Editors*

Constantin Iordachi (Central European University, Budapest)
Maciej Janowski (Polish Academy of Sciences, Warsaw)
Balázs Trencsényi (Central European University, Budapest)

VOLUME 13

# Under a Double Headed Eagle: Józef Mianowski

*Biography of a Conservative*

by

Leszek Zasztowt

*Translated from Polish by*

Konrad Brodziński

BRILL | SCHÖNINGH

The Author: Leszek Zasztowt is a historian, ordinary professor and a former director of the Ludwik & Aleksander Birkenmajer Institute for the History of Science (2007–2015), Polish Academy of Sciences, and professor at the University of Warsaw at the Center for East European Studies. President of the Józef Mianowski Fund – A Foundation for the Promotion of Science –, vice president of the Warsaw Scientific Society.

Cover image: Joseph Mianowski (1804–1879). Source: From the collection of the Polish Academy of Sciences Archives in Warsaw, reference number ZF, IV-10.

Reviewers:
Dr hab. Joanna Schiller-Walicka, PAS
Dr hab. Jacek Soszyński, PAS

Bibliographic information published by the Deutsche Nationalbibliothek

The Deutsche Nationalbibliothek lists this publication in the Deutsche Nationalbibliografie; detailed bibliographic data available online: http://dnb.d-nb.de

All rights reserved. No part of this publication may be reproduced, translated, stored in a retrieval system, or transmitted in any form or by any means, electronic, mechanical, photocopying, recording or otherwise, without prior written permission from the publisher.

© 2024 by Brill Schöningh, Wollmarktstraße 115, 33098 Paderborn, Germany, an imprint of the Brill-Group (Koninklijke Brill BV, Leiden, The Netherlands; Brill USA Inc., Boston MA, USA; Brill Asia Pte Ltd, Singapore; Brill Deutschland GmbH, Paderborn, Germany; Brill Österreich GmbH, Vienna, Austria) Koninklijke Brill BV incorporates the imprints Brill, Brill Nijhoff, Brill Schöningh, Brill Fink, Brill mentis, Brill Wageningen Academic, Vandenhoeck & Ruprecht, Böhlau and V&R unipress.

www.brill.com

Cover design: Celine van Hoek, Leiden
Production: Brill Deutschland GmbH, Paderborn

ISSN 1877-8550
ISBN 978-3-506-79472-7 (hardback)
ISBN 978-3-657-79472-0 (e-book)

# Table of Contents

Preface to the English Language Edition .............................. VII

Preface ........................................................... XI

1. Ukraine – The Mianowski Family – Uman' ........................ 1

2. Lithuania – Vilnius – University of Vilnius – The Medical-Surgical
   Academy – The Konarski Affair ................................. 19

3. Russia – Petersburg ........................................... 49

4. Polish Kingdom – Warsaw ....................................... 61

5. Italy – Senigallia ............................................ 85

Epilogue .......................................................... 89

Bibliography ...................................................... 93

Annexes ........................................................... 105

Index of Names .................................................... 121

List of Figures ................................................... 129

Figures ........................................................... 133

# Preface to the English Language Edition

In 1795 the Polish state (to give it the narrowest of its descriptions) ceased to exist. This occurred after the third partition. The first two partitions of 1772 and 1793 had merely pruned its territory on all four sides: from the west, east, south, and north. It was a strange entity. Formally defined as Poland, it was de facto generally known as the Commonwealth of Both Nations, and also as the Polish-Lithuanian Republic. It was composed of the Crown of the Polish Kingdom, with a capital first in Cracow and then in Warsaw, and the Grand Duchy of Lithuania whose capital was Vilnius. But the biggest peculiarity of all was that despite those two names the state comprised not just Poland and Lithuania: its other key components were Ukraine and Belarus. An attempt was made in the 17th century to create a Commonwealth of Three Nations through the formation of a Grand Duchy of Rus (Ukraine) with its capital in Kyiv (the Treaty of Hadiach in 1658). Unfortunately, it ended in failure.

Throughout the 15th and 16th centuries, and in the first half of the 17th, this state was one of the mightiest in Central-Eastern Europe. It was seen as being extremely liberal, enamoured of liberties and freedom. Why was that? Probably, on the one hand, because of its broad tolerance of all faiths. In addition to the Catholics and Orthodox who constituted the majority, the republic's citizens encompassed Muslims, Judaists, and many Protestants of all shades, with naturally a predominance of Lutherans and Calvinists. On the other hand, it was a monarchy of the nobility, scrupulously safeguarding its rights, though one in which only the nobles and the clergy were privileged estates. The nobility often constituted as much as 10% of the population. As a result, some historians today even see it as an embryo of the future European Union.

Not only was the position of peasants, the middle class and of all social categories – which could be broken down in unusual detail even in the 18th century – not markedly different from that of their counterparts in the west of the European peninsula – it was worse. This concerned the liberties and social status of the middle class. And that without even mentioning the situation of the peasant population. Furthermore, the state was a mix of ethnicities. In addition to Poles and Lithuanians (in 1618, respectively four and a half million and 750.000 inhabitants), it had a population of Ruthenians (Ukrainians and Belarusians) totalling five million. In the first half of the 17th century, some 6–8% of the inhabitants were Jews. The remaining minorities, to use a modern term – Tatars, Armenians, Karaites, but also Dutch, Scots,

Germans, French and English – did not in total exceed one percent. All were termed Poles.

After the final partition, a large part of the state found itself ruled by the Russian Empire. It covered all the territories to the east of the rivers Niemen and Bug: a total of 120.000 square kilometres, as against about a million square kilometres of the entire area of the state in the first half of the 17th century. We might note that the expanse of land annexed by Russia was just short of three times the size of contemporary Netherlands, and larger by a quarter than the present territory of Portugal.

The republic of the nobles could not withstand the competition and coercion of its neighbouring absolute monarchies. The republican polity, brought in – rather late in the day, as it turned out – by the Constitution of 3 May 1791, did not favour the restoration of the state's earlier power. It is generally acknowledged that this was the first constitution in Europe, and the second in the world after the American one. Aside from Russia, large swathes of the Republic were shared out between Habsburg Austria and Hohenzollern Prussia.

It is worth emphasising that the social changes which made inroads into 18th century Europe also encompassed the Republic. However, attempts at its modernisation ultimately ended in failure. Absolutism was at the time – some would argue, even today – the most effective form of government. First and foremost, it guaranteed the state's military strength. The Republic, on the other hand, was constantly racked by financial problems, difficulties with recovering taxes and the wilfulness of a nobility averse to centralisation of the state and reform. In the 17th century, it was still an equal or even dominant player in this part of Europe. A century later, it was only a pale reflection of its former power.

What befell the Republic's inhabitants after the partitions? They became subjects of Russia, Austria, and Prussia. In the 123 years of what was termed *zabory*, 'the occupations' – from 1796 to 1918 – there were numerous attempts at restoration in diverse guises: from the Napoleonic Duchy of Warsaw (1807–1815), covering former central territories inhabited mostly by ethnic Poles, to the Polish Kingdom, established at the Congress of Vienna (and lasting till 1915), with a similar ethnic composition. But there was no *de facto* Polish state. Despite its enticing name, the Polish Kingdom was subservient to the Russian Empire, and its crowned kings were Russian tsars.

Underpinning this state of things was loyalism. Many inhabitants of the former Republic strove to live and function as loyal subjects of the Romanovs, Habsburgs, or Hohenzollerns. They were also known as 'realists', i.e., people who believed that no change whatever in the political situation was possible and it was necessary to adapt to the status quo. That they were right was confirmed by successive insurrections, all ending in defeat. Directed primarily against Russia, the two largest took place in 1830–31 (this was known as the November Uprising and was a Polish-Russian war which came close to victory) and in 1863–64 (known as the January Uprising, with the participation not only of Poles but also of Lithuanians, Belarusians, Ukrainians and indeed Jews). In the wake of these insurrections and numerous other anti-Russian conspiracies, scores of Poles, Lithuanians, Belarusians, and Ukrainians ended up as émigrés, primarily in France (Paris) and Great Britain (London). The headcount of what is known as the great emigration in France is estimated to be at least 30.000, mainly from the military and all men. After the January Uprising of 1863–64 there was a further exodus to the West, but around 62.000 fetched up in what is broadly known as Siberia. The latest estimates are of 38.000 exiled to or re-settled in Siberia, and 24.000 relocated in the northern regions of European Russia.

What was life like in the territories annexed by Russia in the 19th century? What were the views and attitudes of the Poles living in lands belonging to the Russian Empire: the vassal Polish Kingdom, Lithuania, Belarus, and a sub-stantial part of the former crown Ukraine? How did people arrange their lives when they did not take up revolutionary action and foreswore an open struggle with the Tsarist regime? Could one be a Polish patriot without fighting gun in hand for independence? The Russians believed that Poles were genetically pre-ordained to be anti-Russian. Even in the west of Europe this charge of morbid Russophobia was taken to be the rule, and an incurable state of mind. It seems that this was one of the greatest falsehoods that Russian imperial propaganda managed to incubate in the continent's West. The tale that unfolds below is an attempt to show the reality from the inside, through the life story of a man who served Russia and loved Poland. It also seeks to salvage a photograph of the fast-disappearing traces of the old Republic under Russian rule – seen through the prism of Polish conservatism at a time when the United Kingdom of Great Britain was ruled by George III and George IV, William IV and, finally, Queen Victoria.

Leszek Zasztowt

# Preface

> *Splendid star, so happy, like an angel of youth!*
> *You carry the summer on a golden ray.*
> *Then, like its hope, in darkness you rest.*
> *In mist-covered autumn you're shrouded today.*
> *How achingly you leave the Ukrainian skies,*
> *Whose beauty is mirrored in a damsel's eyes!*
> *Where the air, like her visage, wafts by calm and serene,*
> *Casting a spell, its breath with magic laden.*
> *Where her glance is reflected in her waters' sheen,*
> *Where hills are enticing, like the breast of a maiden,*
> *Where harmoniously her song floats along in the breeze,*
> *With her sex in the flowers, her freshness in the trees!*
> Seweryn G o s z c z y ń s k i, *Prophetic books of Father Mark*[1]

> *Our margrave's still walking the tightrope,*
> *Though he's clumsy and shaped like a boar,*
> *When he's fallen, he won't get a statue,*
> *He'll be branded a traitorous whore.*
> *Wielopolski, you'll fall to the bottom,*
> *With Poland it's always the case,*
> *But by that time, you will have forgotten*
> *Even falling should be done with some grace.*[2]
> Jerzy C z e c h, *The Margrave Wielopolski*

Józef Mianowski is a constant presence in the history of Polish scholarship of the 19th and 20th centuries. This is thanks mainly to the Fund of assistance for people working in the field of science named after Józef Mianowski, Doctor of Medicine, and set up in memory of the only rector of Warsaw's Main School. The Fund was an institution which before the First World War replaced the non-existent Polish ministry of science and education under Russian

---

1 S. G o s z c z y ń s k i, *Pieśni prorocze ks. Marka*, [w:] Z. W a s i l e w s k i, *Z życia poety romantycznego. Seweryn Goszczyński w Galicji: nieznane pamiętniki, utwory i listy 1832–1842*, Lwów 1910, pp. 44–45.
2 J. C z e c h, *Margrabia Wielopolski*, composed and performed by Przemysław Gintrowski. https://www.piosenkaztekstem.pl/opracowanie/przemyslaw-gintrowski-margrabia-wielopolski/.

occupation. Later, too, it played a significant role in supporting the development of learning in independent Poland[3].

The Mianowski Fund embedded itself in the memory of generations not only thanks to its financing of research, founding of scholarships and supporting publications. It also grew into an exemplary social institution which embraced almost all prominent Polish scholars and writers, especially at the end of the 19th century and the first half of the 20th – involving not just the elite of the Warsaw intelligentsia of the period but essentially the whole community of Poland's scholars. This was not particularly numerous, at least until the end of the 2nd Republic[4], and it would be harder to draw up a list of those who did not avail themselves of the assistance of the Mianowski Fund than to name those whom it helped as they made their way in scholarship and literature. And it needs to be added that even at the turn of the 20th century literary writing was still generally regarded as being on a par with scholarly research.

The memory of Mianowski persists. There are traces of it in the public arena, such as the hall bearing his name on the ground floor of the Kazimierzowski (Casimir) Palace, now housing the University rectorate, and the memorial inscription in the building of the former Main School being a quotation from his speech (unfortunately after refurbishment this inscription has disappeared); there is also the Mianowski street in Warsaw's Ochota district, near Narutowicz square. Mention of Mianowski is made in nearly all papers dealing with scholarship in the second half of the 19th century and to the growth of disciplines of that period, from the *belles-lettres* mentioned earlier to mathematical-nature sciences. Reactivated in 1991, the Mianowski Fund now exists as a foundation for the support of learning.

When however, we make a closer scrutiny of the sources, in search of information about the rector of the Main School and his personal life journey before taking up the position, it turns out that despite the plethora of memorial articles, all kinds of literary oddments, various *silva rerum* and *miscellanea*, there has been no single work which would present Mianowski's biography. What is

---

3 *Kasa Mianowskiego 1881–2011*, ed. L. Zasztowt, Warsaw 2011; P. Hübner, J. Piskurewicz, J. Soszyński, L. Zasztowt, *A History of the Józef Mianowski Fund*, transl. and ed. by J. Soszyński, Warsaw 2013; Z. Szweykowski, *Zarys historii Kasy im. Mianowskiego*, 'Nauka Polska' 1932, vol. 15, pp. 1–202; S. Fita, *Pokolenie Szkoły Głównej w życiu społecznym i kulturze polskiej*, Warsaw 1980; M. Brykalska, *Aleksander Świętochowski. Biografia*, vol. 1–2, Warsaw 1981–1987.

4 I.e. the period between the two world wars.

PREFACE                                                                                    XIII

still the most reliable and irreplaceable summary is Stefan Kieniewicz's profile of Mianowski in the *Polish Biographical Dictionary*[5].

As Grzegorz Bąbiak observed in the latest, comprehensive edition of materials regarding the history of the Main School:

Józef Mianowski has survived only because his grateful alumni decided to erect a statue to him which was more long-lasting than bronze. Instead of a figure on a pedestal they set up a Fund which supported (and supports) the development of scholarship. But were you to ask who Mianowski was, even putting the question to the capital's university students themselves – few would be able to give an answer. The common factor for all concerned was the Warsaw Main School, mentioned above all in the biographies of its most famous graduates from the Positivist generation[6].

Mianowski was a colourful and remarkable figure. An outstanding medical practitioner, with a modest body of scholarly work, he remained in his contemporaries' memory above all thanks to his character traits – everyone emphasised his extraordinary kindness, modesty, disinterested demonstrations of help and love of people – and thanks also to a certain sentimentality and an exceptional, if rather involuntary – one might say intuitive – patriotism.

Investigating Mianowski's life story, I wondered: which was his dominant personality and character trait? Which single attribute can one pick which would define his views, his attitude in life or his world outlook? And what immediately came to my mind was the title of what is still probably the best-known book by Professor Andrzej Walicki: *In the Circle of Conservative Utopia*[7]. I asked myself: could Mianowski be in some way included in the circle of 'Russian Slavophiles' with Polish roots? But I abandoned that thought, since, firstly, Mianowski was undeniably a Polish patriot, and so if he belonged to any circle, it would be that of radical Polish Slavophiles, émigrés grouped around Joachim Lelewel or Józef Hoene-Wroński: but for them it was the Poland of the past that was the heartland of Slavism, while Russia was its negation. Secondly, at the time when Mianowski lived and worked Russian Slavophilism

---

5   S. Kieniewicz, *Mianowski Józef (1804–1879)*, [in:] *Polski Słownik Biograficzny* [PSB], Wrocław 1974, vol. 19, p. 523–525. Cf. Earlier biographical notes on Mianowskiego: *Encyklopedia Powszechna S. Orgelbranda*, Warsaw 1864, vol. 18, p. 452; *Encyklopedia Ogólna Wiedzy Ludzkiej, Redakcji "Tygodnika Illustrowanego"*, Warsaw 1875, vol. 9, p. 227; *Encyklopedia Powszechna S. Orgelbranda*, Warsaw 1884, vol. 7, p. 441; *Enciklopedičeskij Slovar' F. Brokgauza, I.A. Efrona*, St. Peterburg 1897, vol. 20, p. 362.

6   The Polish Positivists were a literary, philosophical, and social movement of the second half of the 19th century which eschewed revolutionary fervour and concentrated on civil society and working 'from the ground up'.

7   A. Walicki, *W kręgu konserwatywnej utopii. Struktura i przemiany rosyjskiego słowianofilstwa*, Warsaw 1964, 2nd ed. Warsaw 2002.

was first at its peak and then declined, only gaining wider social resonance in the second half of the 19th century. Furthermore, I found hardly any convincing source-based evidence that he personally knew any of the Russian Slavophiles, although they were almost all peers of his in terms of age, like Mikhail P. Pogodin (1800–1875), not to mention Alexey S. Khomiakov (1804–1860), Ivan V. Kireyevsky (1806–1856), the elder Sergey T. Aksakov (1791–1859) and the younger Ivan (1823–1886). They were indeed of the same generation as our protagonist. But their milieu was far removed from the circles that Mianowski moved in. His connections were first and foremost with Petersburg and its aristocratic elite, quite different in its thinking – at least in the first half of the 19th century – from the Russian intelligentsia of Moscow. There were some Slavophile tendencies in Petersburg too, but perhaps because their advocates were connected with the aristocracy, they did not find fertile ground. In addition, Mianowski had few acquaintances in Moscow, which was the main point of reference for the Slavophiles. The fact remains that while Mianowski served as a link man between Russian Slavophiles from aristocratic circles and Polish émigrés – also Slavophile, but in a different way – and leading members of the Polish aristocracy, there is no trace of any specific outcomes resulting from such liaisons. All we are left with, therefore, is conservatism.

Similarly, I found no source materials that would indicate that Józef Mianowski had contacts with Ukraine's Dnieper-based intelligentsia, linked to the Brotherhood of Cyril and Methodius which existed in Kyiv in 1845–1847[8]. Here, though, we are dealing with a generation that is ten to 20 years younger than our protagonist. Moreover, all of them – Taras Szevchenko, Mykola (Nikolay) Kostomarov, Panteleymon Kulish, Mykola Hulak, Vasil Bilozersky – were based in Kyiv, which Mianowski rarely visited. During the time when they were active in the Brotherhood, they professed views which even then might have been too radical for Mianowski. While envisaging a future Ukraine that was in close alliance with Russia, they demanded – or at least that was their vision of the future – greater cultural freedom and, above all, an autonomous, separate space for the literary Ukrainian language that was taking shape at the time. The only member of that circle of Dnieper-based intellectuals whom Mianowski had every likelihood of knowing was Panteleymon Kulish, who in 1864–1869 worked as a clerk in Warsaw. Kulish was on good terms with several Poles, including some whom Mianowski knew well: the poet Michał Grabowski, Archbishop Ignacy Hołowiński and Józef Ignacy Kraszewski.

---

8   J. Gołąbek, *Bractwo św. Cyryla i Metodego w Kijowie*, Warsaw 1935; S. Kozak, *Ukraińscy spiskowcy i mesjaniści: Bractwo Cyryla i Metodego*, Warsaw 1990; J. Remy, *Brothers or Enemies: the Ukrainian National Movement and Russia, 1840s to the 1870s*, Toronto 2016.

PREFACE XV

Mianowski might even have met Kulish earlier on in the Aleksandrówka of the Grabowskis, though probably, due to the difference in age (Kulish having been born in 1819), a first meeting would have taken place in Warsaw. There is also nothing to point to any interest on Mianowski's part in the nascent separatist aspirations which at that time were gaining traction in Ukraine, and in Kyiv especially.

Mianowski's conservatism was of the liberal type: its points of reference were the ideas of such thinkers as Alexis de Tocqueville or Edmund Burke. Accordingly, it concerned itself particularly with the sphere of social values, involving a mistrust of revolution and a profound respect for family, property, religion, and nation, while broadly leaving free the economic and business area. Freedom, strictly defined, was for Mianowski the paramount value.

Mianowski was a conservative, with everything this entailed. His ideology was typical of 19th century thinking in the former Polish-Lithuanian Commonwealth. The doctor aspired to be a loyal subject of the Russian emperor. At the same time, he had very close links with the leading lights of academia, aristocracy, and finance, and the upper echelons of the Roman Catholic church. Fate dictated that on a few occasions he had to manoeuvre in politically awkward situations. In essence, his problem was the need to choose between toeing the line and being loyal on the one hand, and on the other veering on the side of a dangerous Polish patriotism which in practical terms could have resulted in exile to Siberia and the end of his career. Despite the naivety sometimes ascribed to him he was able on such perilous occasions to rise to the challenge, and indeed to demonstrate personal courage. His conservatism was thus – in my opinion – less restrictive and more open to others, especially to so-called 'ordinary people', than that of Prince Jan Tadeusz Lubomirski or Margrave Aleksander Wielopolski. To some extent his compassionate attitude to people from the lower social orders found its reflection in the entire Positivist movement in Warsaw. Among the eulogists of the memory of the rector of Warsaw's Main School was none other than 'the Pope of Polish Positivism', Aleksander Świętochowski[9]. Mianowski had close friends, or people that he cared about, both in the homeland and abroad. But they included rebellious and radical students from Vilnius, Petersburg or Warsaw who could not in any way be deemed to have been supporters of compromise and realpolitik. They were certainly not conservatives: rather, they belonged with the progressive radicals of their time.

How did it happen that a man respected by the Tsar's family, personally appreciated and singled out by Nicholas I himself – known to be ill-disposed

---

9   Many instances of this can be found in the biography of Świętochowski by Maria Brykalska.

to Poles – and by his successor, Alexander II, a man who was liked by the elite of Petersburg aristocracy – a man, in brief, who was a typical loyalist of his time – has remained in Polish memory as a model of patriotism and national virtues, almost the equal of Romuald Traugutt, the dictator of the 1863 uprising who was executed on the hillside of Alexander's Warsaw Citadel? Why has Mianowski remained so loved, while another Pole with a similar attitude to Russia and Russians, Margrave Aleksander Wielopolski, has been condemned to eternal opprobrium in the pantheon of collective memory? Józef Mianowski's case brought into sharp relief particular Polish imponderables: organic work versus armed struggle, loyalism versus patriotism, conservatism and concession versus an intransigent stance towards the occupying power. The sensitive and emotive Mianowski, with a sentimentalism characteristic of his compatriots from the Uman' region and Ukraine, apparently acted on impulse, on the need of the moment. That he did not end his life exiled to Siberia was probably thanks to quite unusual luck, including the good fortune of finding people, Poles, and Russians, to help him along his way. Poland – as also, significantly, Russia – were his 'adopted fatherlands', although his real *'petite patrie'* was undoubtedly Ukraine, and to a lesser extent Lithuania.

In relation to Poland, a country which was then non-existent on the maps of Europe, Mianowski's stance was rather typical and characteristic of people coming from the eastern territories of the First Republic. He did not know Poland. He did not know Mazovia or Małopolska (Lesser Poland), or Wielkopolska (Greater Poland). He saw Pomerania and Silesia more as districts of the Prussian partition than – in fragments at least – historical parts of the Crown. He did not perceive Poland as an ethnographic entity. Rather, it represented to him an ideal of a lost country: the historical Commonwealth. That perception quite likely allowed him to forget that the Commonwealth was the Commonwealth of Both Nations: he would have referred to it simply as Poland. Undoubtedly, however, pride of place in his picture of that country would have been occupied by Ruthenia and the Grand Duchy of Lithuania, lands which he knew from his childhood and youth. Warsaw, Kraków and Lviv, in contrast, appeared in the imagination primarily as patriotic points of reference. The reality was Uman', Vilnius and Krzemieniec, and Polish landed estates around Vilnius and in the Podole, Volhynia and Kyiv regions.

It so happened that his life journey took him to many pivotal moments in the history of Polish-Russian relations, in places were the fate of Poland and the Poles was being decided in the vast territories of the Russian partition. He studied and worked in Vilnius when it was still flourishing, but also after the closure of the city's university. It was there that he lived through both the November Uprising of 1830–1831 and the Szymon Konarski affair. It was in

PREFACE                                                                                        XVII

Vilnius too that he witnessed the liquidation of the union of churches and the subordination of the Greek Catholic Church to the Orthodox Church in 1839.

In the 1840s and 1850s he lived in Petersburg, where he belonged to the Polish conservative elite connected with the Russian aristocracy and Tsarist establishment. From that vantage point he bore witness to the harshest repressions at the tail end of the rule of Nicolas I, but also to the first reforms introduced by the new tsar, Alexander II.

In the 1860s he created and then managed Warsaw's Main School. He also played a minor role in the events of the January Uprising of 1863–1864[10] in the Polish Kingdom. It was in Warsaw that he witnessed and experienced the repressions that followed the insurrection, the dissolution of the Main School and burgeoning Russification. In short, then, Mianowski's story mirrors the typical experiences not so much of the Polish landed gentry of the period as the travails of the Polish intelligentsia, making a living out of intellectual work. Yes, Józef Mianowski was first and foremost a member of the Polish intelligentsia: not an outstanding intellectual, perhaps, but a representative of the 'thinking class'[11]. Though he came from a family of impoverished gentry and belonged to the Polish and Russian elite, his advancement to that elite was due in large part to his own effort and perseverance.

Though not naturally inclined towards politics, he was on at least two occasions involved in political activity, though in both cases this was more by chance than by personal choice. He spent his last years as a *de facto* émigré, though remaining to the end of his life a loyal Russian subject.

It is worth pointing out one feature of Mianowski's biography. In generational terms, he belonged with the Romantics. Many of his friends and colleagues were driven by their literary work, and especially their engagement in the struggle against Russia, and the tumultuous events of the post-partition Republic, to emigrate. A whole gallery of poets and writers presents itself here, Juliusz Słowacki being the most important. From the outset, however, Mianowski was more of a Positivist. This stemmed from his profession as a doctor, but also from his character. While fascinated by literature and poetry, as were most of his contemporaries, he elected from the very start of his career to tread the path of organic work. By a strange quirk of fate he became, in

---

10    Named 'January' after the month in which it began, this insurrection, ultimately a failure, was a key event in 19th century Polish history.

11    An expression coined by Ryszarda Czepulis-Rastenis. See R. Czepulis-Rastenis, "*Klassa umysłowa*": *inteligencja Królestwa Polskiego 1832–1862*, Warsaw 1973. Cf. J. Jedlicki, *Błędne koło. Dzieje inteligencji polskiej do roku 1918*, ed. J. Jedlicki, vol. 2, Warsaw 2008, p. 169, 258; M. Micińska, *Inteligencja na rozdrożach 1864–1918. Dzieje inteligencji polskiej do roku 1918*, ed. J. Jedlicki, vol. 3, Warsaw 2008, pp. 64, 66.

the 1860s, the spiritual father of the entire Positivist movement in Warsaw, becoming the undisputed authority to Bolesław Prus, Henryk Sienkiewicz, Aleksander Świętochowski and the whole generation of the Main School. In this way his life story also holds a mirror, on a micro scale, to the history of Polish social thought and national philosophy in the 19th century. This allows to see the Poles' way of thinking in that period, and the transformation it underwent under the hammer-blows of successive national defeats. In Mianowski's case it is clear, that he bemoaned the tragic fate of his friends and colleagues, prevented from the possibility of returning to their homeland. On the other hand, he believed that for the good of the country it was necessary to remain in place and build from the foundations upwards. Although we lack convincing and unequivocal source materials to confirm this, he probably disapproved of many of their decisions regarding political activity and commitment to fighting the Tsarist empire.

Mianowski's life story has in a sense dictated the structure of this book, whose five main sections correspond to his geographical peregrinations. The first covers his Ukrainian period – particularly his schooling in Uman', but also a short and far from complete genealogy of the Mianowski family. The second, and most substantial, concerns Lithuania, and in particular Vilnius, in which Mianowski attained general acclaim and professional success. The third part is an account of Mianowski's situation in Russia, living in the Empire's capital, Petersburg. It was there that the medical practitioner earned the permanent gratitude not only of the imperial family and the aristocratic elite of the city but also of countless Poles whom he helped in a variety of ways through difficult times. Petersburg also proved, contrary to his own expectations, to be a springboard that took him to the next phase of his career – in Warsaw, in the Polish Kingdom. The fourth section relates Mianowski's activities there, principally in the city's Main School. The fifth deals with the least known part of his life: he moved to Italy to spend his last years there, in Senigallia on the Adriatic coast.

The book draws on a broad database of sources which is ample but not homogeneous, and, is rather uneven in tracing the life journey of Józef Mianowski. Thus, details on his final years are scarce while the previous periods of Uman', Vilnius, Petersburg and Warsaw are reasonably well documented. Materials that have been accessed come from the Russian State Historical Archives in Petersburg, the Lithuanian State Historical Archives in Vilnius and the State Archives of the Capital City of Warsaw; use has also been made of small compilations of letters to be found in the collections of unpublished correspondence of the National Library in Warsaw, the Jagiellonian Library in Kraków, the Polish Academy of Sciences (PAN) Archives in Warsaw and the PAN and

PREFACE          XIX

Polish Academy of Sciences and Letters (PAU) Archives in Kraków, the National Ossoliński Institute in Wrocław and the Kórnik and Rapperswil libraries.

Much use has also been made of materials in print: numerous memoirs, and correspondence, in particular that of Hersylia née Bécu; Teofil of the Januszewskis; and Juliusz Słowacki, Seweryn Goszczyński and Józef Bohdan Zaleski. Other sources include papers on the history of institutions: of the Uman' county Basilian school, the University of Vilnius, the Vilnius Medical-Surgical Academy, the Medical-Surgical Academy in Warsaw, and Warsaw's Main School. An important source of information was provided by the various articles dispersed among the 19th century periodicals of Vilnius, Warsaw, and Petersburg, and of Lviv and Kraków. It would be useful at this point to emphasise the contribution of the Warsaw lawyer, bibliophile, and philanthropist Leopold Méyet, who was the first to take up the task of researching the biography of our protagonist.

.:.

In 1868 – the year before the Main School was dissolved – Mianowski was rector and full professor of the Main School, permanent member council of the curator of the Warsaw Scientific Circle (of the Ministry of Education), member of the Medical Council of the Polish Kingdom. He was vice-president of the Zachęta Society of Fine Arts in the Kingdom, as well as chairman of the private board of Warsaw's Hospital of the Baby Jesus. He had been awarded class IV – one of the highest – ranks of a councillor state. He was Knight of the Order of St Anne 1st Class, St Stanislae 1st Class and St Vladimir 2nd class. He had been distinguished for 25 years of exemplary service and had two dark bronze medals: one for achievements in the 1853–1856 Turkish war and the other in recognition of his help in suppressing the 'Polish rebellion'[12] of 1863–1864. Seven years after the abolition of the Main School, in 1876, he also received the order of St Vladimir, 2nd Class, and a 12-year stipend amounting to 2500 roubles per year[13]. Those last distinctions, which were awarded to him some three years before his death, he owed to the protection of Field Marshal Prince Alexander I. Bariatynsky, the personal intervention of the minister of public goods Piotr A. Valuyev, and the good will of two Warsaw governors – the former one, Fyodor F. Berg and the incumbent, Pavel J. Kotzebue.

---

12    Rossijskij Gosudarstvennyj Istoričeskij Arhiv v Sankt Peterburgie [RGIA], fond [f.] 733, opis' [op.] 147, edinica hranenă [e.hr.] 752, Formulărnyj spisok o službe, sheet (k.) 3.

13    S. K i e n i e w i c z, *Mianowski Józef (1804–1879)*, p. 524.

XX                                                                                    PREFACE

So how did Mianowski, 72 years of age at the time, manage to hold on to such influence in Petersburg and yet not lose hold of his popular support in Warsaw?

Was he really a typical loyalist, as appears from the archives about his service along the successive steps up the ladder of imperial hierarchy of officialdom? Or did he do everything to conceal his Polish patriotism and, as many of his compatriots, was one more example of 'Wallenrodyzm'[14]? He loved and understood the Poland of the past, or more precisely what remained of the heritage of the former Commonwealth. What, though, was his real attitude towards Russia? Did he hate it, or love it? Or did he perhaps simply use his Petersburg prism to treat it as a cosmopolis, a perfect place to further his career and enjoy financial success? Might Russia for him have been Petersburg – a city of glitter and opportunities, like Paris? Such questions unfold themselves as we ask them. Perhaps we can answer at least a few.

---

14    After the hero of *Konrad Wallenrod* – a novel in verse by Poland's leading romantic poet Adam Mickiewicz – who employs deceit and subterfuge in pursuit of noble aims.

CHAPTER 1

# Ukraine – The Mianowski Family – Uman'

## Ukraine

*Splendid star, so happy, like an angel of youth!*
*You carry the summer on a golden ray.*
*Then, like its hope, in darkness you rest.*
*In mist-covered autumn you're shrouded today.*
*How achingly you leave the Ukrainian skies,*
*Whose beauty is mirrored in a damsel's eyes!*
*Where the air, like her visage, wafts by calm and serene,*
*Casting a spell, its breath with magic laden.*
*Where her glance is reflected in her waters' sheen,*
*Where hills are enticing, like the breast of a maiden,*
*Where harmoniously her song floats along in the breeze,*
*With her sex in the flowers, her freshness in the trees!*[1]

## The Mianowski Family

Józef Mianowski, son of Ignacy, was born towards the end of 1803[2] in the parish of Smila, deanery of Fastiv (previously Khvastiv, later Zvenihorodka) and the county previously described as Kievian, then Umanian (and later Cherkassian) within the Kyiv governorship. Baptised there in 1804, he was the son of Ignacy Mianowski[3]. From 1633 onwards Smila was owned by the Koniecpolski clan; after the second partition it belonged to the Russian Empire. The small town was located nearly 200 km south of Kyiv; 30 km to its northeast lay Cherkassy on the Dnieper, while some 150 km to the west was the town of Uman'.

We do not know today which branch of the family the Uman' Mianowskis belonged to. Some members of the family also inhabited the nearby Zhytomyr

---

1 S. G o s z c z y ń s k i, *Zamek kaniowski*, Warsaw 1874, p. 15 (seventh canto).
2 According to the leaving certificate from his Uman' school he was aged 19 in 1822. In the view of Leopold Méyet, it is not certain that Smila was his birthplace. What is sure, however, is that it was there that Mianowski was baptised in 1804. Biblioteka Narodowa [BN], Reference no. BN 7321, L. M é y e t, *Przyczynki historyczno-literackie*, sheet (k.) 3, 6. Some biographical notes on Mianowski claim that he was born in Uman', an obvious error.
3 L. M é y e t, *Przyczynki historyczno-literackie*, sheet (k.) 3.

© BRILL SCHÖNINGH, 2024 | DOI:10.30965/9783657794720_002

2 CHAPTER 1

region[4], the region of Vilnius[5], and Eastern Prussia, western Galicia[6] and what was later the territory of the Polish Kingdom. In Warsaw their graves are to be found in the Powązki Cemetery – they include that of Antoni Wincenty Mianowski (1743–1822), clerk of the Main Court of the City of Warsaw and a civic activist, and of his descendant Aleksander Mianowski (1899–1969), hydrotechnical engineer and co-creator of the largest hydrotechnical structures, including barriers on the rivers Oder, Vistula (including one in Włocławek) and Narew[7].

In 19th century the so-called Congress Kingdom of Poland they bore one of two coats of arms: *Przerowa* and *Tępa Podkowa* (Blunt Horseshoe)[8]. The oldest branch of the family, known as the Orlikowski, came from Mianowo near Ostrów Mazowiecka and Orlikowo on the Wis of Mazovian lands, and their seal bore the crest of Abdank. In 1443 the Mazovian prince Władysław granted Janusz and Piotr of Mianowo privileged rights to the estate of Orlikowo, confirmed in Płock in 1459 when Mazovian prince Ziemowit conferred the rights on Mateusz of Mianowo[9].

According to Czesław Malewski, Józef Mianowski (born c.1802) was the son of Ignacy and Antonina Micewicz. The source of these data is the Lithuanian State Historical Archives in Vilnius, according to which the Mianowski family had relatives in the estate of Šalčininkėliai (Soleczniki) near Vilnius and used the seals of Nowina and Ślepowron[10]. It seems highly likely that there

---

4   T. Epsztajn, *Edukacja dzieci i młodzieży w polskich rodzinach ziemiańskich na Wołyniu, Podolu i Ukrainie w II połowie XIX wieku*, Warsaw 1998, p. 189. It references Henryk Mianowski, later to be a military doctor. Cf. J. Korczyński, *Trochę wspomnień z Zytomieizra (lata uczniowskie 1897–1908)*, 'Pamiętnik Kijowski' 1963 (London), vol. 2, p. 241. Cf. also 'Pamiętnik Kijowski' 1966 (London), vol. 3, p. 252.

5   This included the family of Mikołaj Mianowski, professor of the University of Vilnius. Cf. S. Mianowski, *Świat, który odszedł: wspomnienia Wilnianina 1895–1945*, Warsaw 1997; D. Szpoper, A. Bielecki, *Aleksander Meysztowicz – portret polityczny konserwatysty*, Gdańsk 2001, pp. 131, 158–160.

6   For instance, another Józef Mianowski, from the Kraków region; a medical practitioner in Kuyavian Brześć, he died there in 1860. Cf. J. Bieliński, *Stan nauk lekarskich za czasów Akademii Medyko-Chirurgicznej Wileńskiej bibliograficznie przedstawiony. Przyczynek do dziejów medycyny*, Warsaw 1889, p. 678.

7   S. Szenic, *Cmentarz Powązkowski 1790–1850. Zmarli i ich rodziny*, Warsaw 1979, pp. 156–157.

8   *Spis szlachty Królestwa Polskiego z dodaniem krótkiej informacji o dowodach szlachectwa*, Warsaw 1851, p. 149 and Appendix II, p. 30.

9   *Herbarz Ignacego Kapicy Milewskiego (dopełnienie Niesieckiego)*, Sieniawa–Kraków 1870, p. 274, item 336; p. 311, item 384; J.S. Dunin-Borkowski, *Spis nazwisk szlachty polskiej*, Lviv 1887, p. 244.

10  Cz. Malewski, *Rodziny szlacheckie na Litwie w XIX wieku*, Warsaw 2016, p. 654.

UKRAINE – THE MIANOWSKI FAMILY – UMAN'

were links of kinship between the Mianowskis of Šalčininkėliai and Uman'. But there is no source-based evidence to show that Józef Mianowski was related to Professor Mikołaj Mianowski (1780–1843), likewise an obstetrician connected with the University of Vilnius, rector of the university (1831–1832) and co-founder of the Vilnius Medical-Surgical Academy of which he was president in 1840–1842[11]. In 1834 the Mianowskis purchased the Šalčininkėliai estate from the Chodkiewicz family. There, in around 1849, Mikołaj Mianowski built an impressive timber-built manor house which survived until the Second World War. In 1834 he replaced the old place of worship with the timber-built church of St. George[12]. Interred in what are known as the 'Tomblets of Their Lordships' in the Šalčininkėliai cemetery are Professor Mikołaj Mianowski, his wife Antonina, and their sons, Aleksander Mianowski (died at the age of 70 with the rank of court councillor) and Konstanty Mianowski (20 September 1819–23 February 1892)[13].

The question that remains open is the exact date of Józef Mianowski's birth. Personally, I have no doubt that this was in the late autumn or December of 1803. However, since there is no confirmation of this in the source materials, we will accept, after Stefan Kieniewicz, that Józef Mianowski was born in 1804. Which is what he stated in most of his documents.

A part of the Mianowski clan relocated from northern Mazovia to Volhynia, probably in the 18th century or not much earlier than that. By the 19th century their domiciles had spread beyond Zhytomir and Lutsk to Ostroh, Uman', the former Bratslav voivodship and the county of Lipovets in the Kyiv governorship[14].

We know from the published correspondence between the Januszewskis and Mianowski in the years 1829–1837 that Józef had a younger brother who caused him some problems, and a sister[15]. There is no information, unfortunately, as to their names. Nor is it clear what the issues were with his

---

11  *Encyklopedia Ziemi Wileńskiej. Wileński słownik biograficzny*, ed. H. Dubowik, L.J. Malinowski, vol. 1, Bydgoszcz 2002, p. 226.

12  A.K., *Odnowione groby, odnowiona pamięć*, 'Tygodnik Wileńszczyzny'. http://www.tygodnik.lt/200645/wiesci6.html.

13  *Ibidem*.

14  A different, older Józef Mianowski, of the Tępa Podkowa crest, son of Michała of Żorniszcze. Lawyer in Kamieniec Podolski and Balta. Wołyniak [J.M. Gozdawa-Giżycki], *O bazylianach w Humaniu*, 'Przewodnik Naukowy i Literacki' 1899, vol. 27, p. 1173.

15  [T. i H. Januszewscy], *Listy Teofila i Hersylii (z domu Bécu) Januszewskich do Józefa Mianowskiego (1829–1837)*, letters edited with an introduction and comments by L. Méyet, Warsaw 1897 (Library of 'Wiek'), pp. 118–119, 123 (information about younger brother: letters dated 20 October and 10 November 1833), pp. 137–138 (information about sister: letter of 11 November 1834).

brother – but Józef must have taken some drastic decisions, and as a result of which he had pangs of conscience. Teofil Januszewski assured him in a letter that the measures he had taken were indispensable. These must indeed have been very strict, but – wrote Januszewski, there was no other way of setting the junior brother on the straight and narrow.

By the 1830s Mianowski had developed strong ties with his wife's side of the family – and, in particular – following her untimely death, with Aleksandra's sister Hersylia and her husband Teofil. At the time the Januszewskis – Hersylia in particular, but also the mother of the poet Juliusz Słowacki, Salomea Bécu – felt guilty that Mianowski was showering them with gifts and in his own way acted as the Vilnius broker for the interests of the Januszewskis and Bécus. A letter from Hersylia reminds her readers that after all 'our dear Józef' does have a sister who also needs to be taken care of.

Some information concerning the Mianowskis can be found in the Petersburg archives' collection of documents from 1851 in which the Petersburg Heraldic Office confirms his status as nobleman. These are sufficiently interesting to warrant citing their provisions[16] – with the caveat that at the present stage of research there are no other sources to corroborate this evidence.

The cited document reveals that Józef had two brothers. The elder one, Mikołaj, son of Ignacy and Aleksandra, domiciled in the Ostroh district of the Volyhn governorship was, according to a transcript of the certificate issued by the Mohylev clerical consistory, baptised on 10 February 1793. His marriage to Anna produced a son, Ignacy, born in 1826, as confirmed by a transcript taken from the registry documents of the clerical consistory of Lutsk-Zhytomir. The marriage also produced a second son, Faustyn. Mikołaj died probably in early 1830s. Józef's second, younger brother, Szymon Wincenty, had two sons, Leon and Stanisław[17]. According to Artur Kijas, Szymon Wincenty died in 1892 in Ulusoy in Siberia ('Kraj' 1892, no. 6)[18].

The father of Józef and the other two brothers – Ignacy – had a brother, Adam. Their father, and therefore Józef's grandfather, was Piotr Mianowski. As mentioned earlier, the documents were compiled in connection with the confirmation of noble status, and thus naturally concerned themselves solely

---

16    RGIA, f. 1405, op. 49, e.hr. 3752, *O dvorănskom dostoinstve roda Mianovskogo* (*10 fevrală 1851–4 aprelă 1851*), sheets (k.) 1–12.

17    Wincenty Mianowski was in his sixth, final year of the county school in Uman' in the academic year 1829–30. He could therefore have been the younger brother of Józef, who was born around 1812 and completed that stage of his education in 1822. Wołyniak, *O bazylianach w Humaniu*, p. 1144.

18    A. Kijas, *Mianowski Józef – МЯНОВСКИЙ ОСИП ИГНАТЬЕВИЧ*, webpage 'Polski Petersburg': http://www.polskipetersburg.pl/hasla/mianowski-jozef.

UKRAINE – THE MIANOWSKI FAMILY – UMAN'

with the male lineage of the Mianowskis. Hence, they contain no information regarding Ignacy's sister and female descendants.

Smila, Mianowski's birthplace, was along with its adjoining properties in the hands of the Koniecpolski and Wyhowski families; with time, it passed into the possession of the Lubomirskis. In 1787 Prince Franciszek Ksawery Lubomirski sold the whole estate for two million roubles to Prince Grigory A. Potemkin. After his death, the huge estate was divided among his eight heirs. The ownership of Smila itself fell to Count Aleksandr N. Samoylov, who moved in permanently. In 1838 the Count sold the property to his sister's husband, Count Aleksey A. Bobrinsky[19]. Both the Samoylov and the Bobrinsky families employed numerous Poles, some as administrators of the estate; in a later period, when Smila became an important industrial centre, producing and refining sugar and growing sugar beet[20], the employment extended to engineers, technicians, and accountants. It is a reasonable guess, therefore, that Józef's father – not a wealthy man, as his son's education path indicates – was a nobleman of limited personal means who was employed in those estates.

## Uman'

> The news spread in Kaniów like wildfire:
> All Ukraine was burning with ire:
> Gonta's treason had done for Uman'.
> So much slaughter and blood to a man,
> Hell, itself on the Poles was let loose.
> No escaping the savage hordes' noose[21].

Uman', whose gradual decline began during the 1792 war and was exacerbated under the rule of Targowica and the second partition of Poland, experienced a substantial rebirth at the turn of the 19th century. For a brief period, the town, along with its Basilian monastery of John the Baptist and its school had lost the support and care of its benefactor, Szczęsny Potocki; but moved by feelings of remorse Potocki restored his patronage and encouraged a process of regeneration. There were three functioning Uniate Orthodox churches –

---

19    *Śmiła*, [in:] *Słownik geograficzny Królestwa Polskiego i innych krajów słowiańskich*, Warsaw 1889, vol. 10, p. 883.

20    M. W i s z n i c k i, *Moje lata gimnazjalne w Kijowie 1881–1889*, 'Pamiętnik Kijowski' 1980 (London), vol. 4, p. 93.

21    S. G o s z c z y ń s k i, *Zamek kaniowski*, p. 38 (Canto 13).

6                                                                                          CHAPTER 1

St. Michael Archangel, Bishop St. Nicolas, and the Ascension of the Blessed
Virgin Mary – the last serving as the place of worship of the Basilian school[22].
Still alive in the community was the tradition of the martyrdom of Father
Herakliusz Kostecki, murdered *in odore sanctitatis* by rebellious haydamaks
in 1768 as – so the story was handed down – he was carrying the Most Holy
Sacrament during a procession in the marketplace[23]. In the wake of the
Uman' massacre of the same year, chroniclers agree that the monks played an
important role in restraining further violence:

> The Basilian fathers furnished excellent proof of the assiduousness of their
> work, rallying great numbers of the young from the entire district and the fur-
> thest borderlands, and if they were not fully successful in reversing the fatal
> scourge [of the haydamaks] it is certain that their missions did effectively con-
> tain their spread in the villages, so that many settlements of the Uman' region
> such as Podwysokie, Leszczynówka and others prevented the haydamaks from
> accessing their borders[24].

Between 1817 and 1822 Mianowski attended the Basilian priests' district school
for the gentry in Uman', which had been established in 1766 by the voivod of
Kyiv Franciszek Salezy Potocki, father of Stanisław Szczęsny. Along with the
Basilian monastery the school was maintained through an endowment from the
Potocki real estate, specifically the village of Grodzenówka (or Gredzanówka)
and the farming estate of Monasterek by Mańkówka, also known as Monasterek
Mańkowski or Mańkóweczka. The Basilian priests, brought into Uman' from
Chervonohrad, received these domains together with the subjects living there,
and were granted the leasehold on the inns, mills, ponds, fields, gardens, and
woods[25].

The endowment was incorporated into the statute of 1768. In June 1768,
during the Uman' massacre, the school and Basilian monastery were severely
damaged. After the establishment of the Commission for National Education
the Uman' school received the status of Basilian sub-departmental school of
the Ukrainian department of the Commission. Construction of the stone monastery building, and boarding school had begun before the massacre under the

---

22    W. Kołbuk, *Kościoły Wschodnie w Rzeczypospolitej około 1772 roku. Struktury administra-
      cyjne*, Lublin 1998, p. 109, items 515, 516, 517.
23    [J.] Krechowiecki, *Księża bazylianie na Wołyniu, Podolu i Ukrainie, rzecz historyczna,
      przez* [...], 'Przegląd Lwowski' 1871, vol. 2, p. 149.
24    *Ibidem.*
25    Wołyniak, *O bazylianach w Humaniu*, pp. 657–664; [J.] Krechowiecki, *Księża bazyli-
      anie na Wołyniu, Podolu i Ukrainie, rzecz historyczna, przez* [...], [cont.] 'Przegląd Lwowski'
      1872, vol. 3, p. 766 & following.

UKRAINE – THE MIANOWSKI FAMILY – UMAN'

high steward and knight Młodanowicz and was completed by the Basilians in 1789[26]. According to an inspection in 1804 the monastery was stone-built in three lines and two storeys; two of the lines contained monastic cells, the third housed the chapel and schools:

> Four-apartment cells 2, three-apartment cells 1, two-apartment 2, single 12, in addition a 'triple' guest room; also, a kitchen, larder and various household buildings. The whole edifice was 366 yards long and 42 wides[27].

Adjacent to the monastery were stables, a coach house, bakery, belfry, and warden's lodge[28].

Uman' in Mianowski's time was a shabby, dilapidated provincial town, with a predominately local Jewish population – although in the same period the Potocki dynasty funded the construction of the church of the Ascension of the Blessed Virgin Mary, completed in 1826 (i.e., after Mianowski had completed his schooling).

In 1793, after the second partition, Uman' had become part of Russia. From the end of the 18th century to the turn of the 20th there was a rapid growth in the Jewish population. 1,895 Jews (including six merchants) lived there in 1801; this rose to 4,333 in 1847, to 17,945 in 1897 (accounting for 57.9% of all inhabitants) and to 28,267 in 1914 (56.2% of the total). On 17 October 1810 the renowned Hassidic rabbi Nachman of Bratslav died in Uman' – the great grandson of Izrael Baal Shem Tove, one of the principal founders of 18th century Hassidism. His grave was already the destination of mass pilgrimages, of Hassidic Jews of the Bratslav movement. In Mianowski's time, the 1820s, Uman' became one of Ukraine's first centres of the Jewish Haskalah. The town was also home to Natan Sternhartz, who continued and led the movement after Nachman's death. In 1822 Hirsh-Ber (Herman Bernard) Gurvich, the son of a timber merchant, known for his popular translation into Yiddish of Joachim Kampe's *Die Entdeckung von Amerika*, set up Russia's first Jewish school of general education, 'based on the principles of Mendelssohn' (Moses Mendelssohn – a precursor of the Haskalah). Opposition to the project by

---

26    Bolesław znad Dniepru, *Humań*, 'Kłosy' 1872, vol. 15, no. 381, p. 259; [J.] Krechowiecki, *Księża bazylianie*, 'Przegląd Lwowski' 1872, vol. 2, p. 149. Probably Rafał Despot Młodanowski *vel* Mładanowicz, according to Krechowiecki. Cf. *Urzędnicy Wielkiego Księstwa Litewskiego. Ziemia Smoleńska i województwo smoleńskie XIV–XVIII w.*, ed. A. Rachuba, Warsaw 2003, p. 156, item 1016.

27    Approximately 220 metres in length (probably joint length). In that case each of the three buildings would be approximately 74 metres long and 25 metres wide, as measured in the old Polish yards of the First Republic – 59.6 cm.

28    Wołyniak, *O bazylianach w Humaniu*, pp. 1034–1035.

8 CHAPTER 1

Orthodox Jews meant that the school lasted only a few years; in 1835 Bernard Abrahamsohn attempted to revive it, to no avail[29].

The whole town was eclipsed by extensive parkland nearby – the Sofiówka. This landscape, one of the most beautiful in Europe, was a gift made in 1796 by Stanisław Szczęsny Potocki to his wife Zofia – his 'beautiful Bitynka' (because of her Greek origin). A poem dedicated to the estate was written in 1804 by Stanisław Trembecki[30]. With time Uman's status and appearance improved somewhat; by the 1890s it had become, after Kamieniec Podolski, the second largest city in Podolia.

The Basilian school boasted a well-stocked library, containing, in addition to books, educational aids including an electrical machine, barometers, globes and collections of coins. It subscribed to the 'Lithuanian Courier', 'Warsaw Journal', 'Warsaw Daily' and 'Warsaw Historical-Political Journal', along with the Russian periodicals *Syn Otiechestva, Peterburskiye Viedomosti* and *Viestnik Yevropy*[31]. In 1816 its inventory included number of physical tools, including a pneumatic and electrical machine, microscope, and perspective. It also held two copies of herbal of homegrown plants compiled and catalogued by pupils, a collection of minerals (500 items) donated by Ludwik Metzel, and models of machines and mills employed in agriculture[32].

In the second half of the 1790s the Uman' school was given the status of a county school for nobles, continuing under the tutelage of the Basilians. In 1797 it employed six teachers, with a pupil count of 324. On the formation in 1803 of the Vilnius Educational Region (with Adam Jerzy Czartoryski at its head) it was placed under the aegis of the University. That year there were five teachers instructing 291 pupils. Soon, however, the school grew. By 1816 it had 448 pupils, by 1819, 504. In 1830 the number had reached 600. Aside from the boarding school the pupils also took lodgings in a nearby suburb named Turek, where they constituted a separate student colony[33].

In September 1818, i.e., one year after Mianowski began learning there, the Uman' school was formally brought under the aegis of the University in Kharkiv since the Kievan governorship was now separated from the Vilnius

---

29 *Uman', Eliektronnaja Jewriejskaja Encikłopiedija* [online:] 1996, http://jewishencyclopedia. ru/?mode=article&id=14213. Cited in https://sztetl.org.pl/pl/miejscowosci/h/1833-human/ 99--historia-spolecznosci/139509-historia-spolecznosci.

30 S. Trembecki, *Sofiówka i wybór poeazji*, ed. W. Jankowski, Kraków 1925. Cf. R. Aftanazy, *Dzieje rezydencji na dawnych kresach Rzeczypospolitej*, vol. 10, Wrocław 1996, pp. 110–131.

31 Wołyniak, *O bazylianach w Humaniu*, pp. 1035, 1039.

32 *Ibidem*, p. 1039.

33 [J.] Krechowiecki, *Księża bazylianie*, vol. 3, p. 769.

UKRAINE – THE MIANOWSKI FAMILY – UMAN' 9

Region. Initially, this administrative decision changed nothing: the school continued to have links with Vilnius University. In 1822, just as Mianowski was completing his education at the school, Czartoryski strove to raise its status to that of gymnasium (high school), which *de facto* was what it was already in an informal way. Actually – most Basilian schools were in that situation, being judged by the curator to be exemplary. The Uman' school even used the term 'gymnasium' in its official documents.

On two occasions, in 1804 and 1812[34], the school was visited by Tadeusz Czacki; after his death, visits were made by Marcinkowski (in 1813) and by Jan Rudomina in 1816[35]. In the last years of its existence the school hosted Filip Plater and Jan Nepomucen Wyleżyński, marshal of the nobility of Zviahel county[36]. Apart from inspections by supervisors from the Vilnius Educational District there were canonical visits by delegates of the authorities of the Basilian priests. The latter included the provincial Fr. Floryan Szaszkiewicz, in July 1809, and, in May 1815 Fr. Pachomij Lewicki[37].

It was one of the best and most popular schools in the area, teaching in Mianowski's time, as mentioned earlier, some 500 pupils – mainly those who could not afford to be educated in Kyiv[38].

In former times the school year began in the last days of September and ended on 15 July. When Mianowski was there courses started earlier, on 8 September, and ended on the day of the holy apostles Peter and Paul – 29 June. That was also the day when the ceremonial public examination took place[39]. In addition, there was a long-standing tradition of school theatre. Plays were performed as part of the official celebrations of the end of the school year; comedies, however, were permitted by decree of Provincial Szaszkiewicz only once a year, at carnival time. Teachers were not allowed to take part in such frivolous shows.

In that period the school was led by rector Fr. Gracyan Mikuliński, and prefect Fr. Leon Skibowski. The latter – in particular, played an important if ultimately sad role in the annals of the school. He taught at Uman' from 1810; in 1818 he became the prefect, and then followed Mikuliński to be the school's last rector in 1826–1830.

---

34    Wołyniak, *O bazylianach w Humaniu*, p. 1031 & following.
35    *Ibidem*, p. 1038.
36    [J.] Krechowiecki, *Księża bazylianie*, t. 3, s. 770.
37    Wołyniak, *O bazylianach w Humaniu*, p. 1042.
38    L. Zasztowt, *Kresy 1832–1864. Szkolnictwo na ziemiach litewskich i ruskich dawnej Rzeczypospolitej*, Warsaw 1997, p. 222.
39    [J.] Krechowiecki, *Księża bazylianie*, vol. 3, p. 769.

He came from Galicia, where he was born around 1784. He attended Basilian schools in Lyubar and Uman', and Vilnius University, where he was awarded the degree of candidate of sciences in 1807. He lectured mainly in mathematics and natural history, but also in elocution and law, while at the same time holding various monastic posts: procurator, secretary of the province and consultant. Skibowski was a man of integrity, as well as being talented and a fine teacher. He was considered a patriot and held in great esteem by local landowners and the Potocki family. He lost that respect in 1839, having become an obedient instrument in the hands of the Uniate metropolitan Józef Siemaszko. As the *ihumen* of the Tryhory monastery he contributed to the effective 'conversion' to the Orthodox church of over 3000 Uniates in the decanate of Ovruch[40].

A year after commencing his education Mianowski was awarded a prize for *great* progress in his learning, especially in the areas of human history, law, law, elocution, and general literature, and also in calligraphy and the Russian language. According to Leopold Méyet, before Mianowski enrolled at the Uman' school he received his initial upbringing and education at home. At that time his family was already domiciled in Haisyn county, governorship of Podolia. He must have been well prepared for his studies, since he was enrolled in the fourth year (in fact, the second year) and from the start displayed diligence in his learning, while in his behaviour he was 'made of steel' [sic!], as testified by his school report from 1818:

### The County School of Uman'

*Certifies that Master Mianowski Józef enrolled in Year Four and registered as incoming pupil No. 363 on the 20th day of September in the year 1817 displayed in his studies the following progress:*

*– in the study of religion – –*
*– moral studies – –*
*– geography – good*
*– arithmetic – good*
*– geometry – good*
*– physics and natural history – considerable*
*– human history – great*
*– law – great*
*– elocution and general literature – great*
*– Greek – –*
*– Latin – good*
*– Russian – great*
*– German – good*

---

40    Wołyniak, *O bazylianach w Humaniu*, pp. 1040, 1152–1154.

*– French – good*
*– calligraphy – great*
*– drawing – average*
*In his comportment he was – made of steel. He was absent from 15 hours of lessons.*
*Homework – –.*
*Dated this day of 28 June 1818. Prefect of the school X. Skibowski[41].*

He successfully passed his examinations, while an individually addressed commendation dated 16 September 1818 in Vilnius was signed in person by the university's rector, Szymon Malewski[42]:

Department of National Education
University of Vilnius
No. 2588
16th September 1818
From Vilnius

To the Pupil of the Uman' School Józef Mianowski, Esq.

The inspector of schools of the Volhyn, Podolia and Kyiv governorships, His Excellency Wyleżyński, has reported that at the examination taken at the county school of Uman' you, Sir, displayed excellent progress in your learning and received praise from your teachers regarding your good comportment and assiduousness in your studies. It is a pleasure for the school authorities to receive reports of virtues that can truly embellish a pupil of the public schools, and in recognition of your diligence the University Governors have resolved to place a commendation for you in their records and to inform you of this by means of this letter.

Szymon Malewski, Rector
Secretary, Feliks Mierzejewski

It augured well for Mianowski's future studies at the University of Vilnius. He also received a distinction on completing his third year in 1819. Others in his class who received distinctions included Mikołaj Wróblewski, Gabryel Halicki, Zygmunt Prockiewicz, Mikołaj Podoski and Józef Hromowicz[43].

---

41    L. M é y e t, *Przyczynki historyczno-literackie*, sheet (k.) 4.
42    All dates in the text are rendered in the old style, i.e., following the Julian calendar, which in the 19th century differed from the Gregorian calendar, in force in western Europe, by 12 days. The old-style 1st September was thus the 13th of September by the Gregorian calendar. L. M é y e t, *Przyczynki historyczno-literackie*, sheet (k.); idem, *Z życia Mianowskiego. Trochę faktów i dokumentów*, 'Tygodnik Ilustrowany' 1903, no. 24, p. 465–466; *J. Mianowski* (biography), 'Tygodnik Ilustrowany' 1903, no. 23, p. 457; *J. Mianowski*, 'Tygodnik Ilustrowany' 1865, no. 286, pp. 97–98.
43    W o ł y n i a k, *O bazylianach w Humaniu*, p. 1039.

What kind of curriculum did the Uman' school follow? From 1818 onwards, it was once again somewhat curtailed. Political economy was no longer a taught subject; Polish literature was less prominent in the elocution lectures which were part of the course on rhetoric and poetics. The Polish language, however, remained one of the core subjects. Lectures in natural law continued as before. Elocution was taught with attention, drawing on the history of literature of ancient Greece and Rome and the history of ancient philosophy. Greek was no longer taught, though later it was restored as an optional subject. But particularly thorough attention was paid to general history, the natural sciences and mathematics. The lectures covered physics, botany, zoology, mineralogy, and geography, as well as elementary mathematics, algebra, geometry, and trigonometry.

Also retained in the curriculum was the emphasis on modern languages and Latin. Russian, German, and French were taught from the inception through reading, grammar, written exercises of many sorts, up to selected examples of the history of the literature of those languages. Logic was dropped from the programme, but ethics remained. Drawing and music were optional[44].

By the end of the second decade of the 19th century, under the rectorate of Gracyan Mikuliński – who, though a teacher of mathematics, no longer lectured in the subject – it was Leon Skibowski who taught elocution and history. In his rhetoric lectures he took over from his predecessor, considered to be an eminent 'man of literature and philologist', the priest Klemens Hryniewiecki, who 'has a healthy opinion of the art of beautiful speech and a learning adorned with true modesty'[45]. Law and general history, also taught earlier by Hryniewiecki, were taken over by Fr. Emilian Lewiński, who later – in 1827 – was to become prefect in Liubar. Lectures in physics and natural history, initially delivered by Skibowski, were taken over by Fr. Bartłomiej Lityński; the subject of mathematics was handed down from Fr. Julian Lubczański, who had also taught physics, to Fr. Nazariusz Zatthier. His successor, in turn – but still in the period when Mianowski was attending the school – was Father Justynian Tymanowicz, Master of Philosophy from Vilnius University, formerly prefect of the Basilian school in Lyubar, and from 1829 onwards prefect at Uman'; he was an expert mathematician and was appointed by the government to examine artillery officers seeking promotion[46].

---

44    *Ibidem*, p. 1037–1038.

45    'Dziennik Wileński' 1817, nr 25. Cited in Wołyniak, *O bazylianach w Humaniu*, p. 1040. See also [J.] Krechowiecki, *Księża bazylianie*, vol. 3, p. 770.

46    Wołyniak, *O bazylianach w Humaniu*, p. 1145; Bolesław znad Dniepru, *Humań*, p. 259. S. Goszczyński, *Podróż mojego życia. Urywki wspomnień i zapiski do pamiętnika 1801–1842*, ed. S. Pigoń, Vilnius 1924, p. 17.

UKRAINE – THE MIANOWSKI FAMILY – UMAN'

From his school years in Uman' Mianowski retained a long-standing friendship with Seweryn Goszczyński, later to be a poet and author of *Kaniów Castle* who emigrated to Paris in 1841, as well as close links with other compatriots, such as Seweryn Gałęzowski, Bohdan Zaleski, Michał Grabowski, Jan Krechowiecki, and the Korzeniowski, Chaborski and Krechowiecki families[47]. Goszczyński, Krechowiecki, Mianowski and Zaleski were classmates. In the penultimate, fifth year they were joined by Grabowski, whose father, Antoni, a major in the Russian army, inherited a shareholding from Tadeusz Brzozowski in Aleksandrówka in the county of Chyhyryn.

His closest school friend, Seweryn Goszczyński, arrived in Uman' in 1816[48], having previously attended school in Vinnytsia. He was admitted to the second year in the Basilian school. This is how he described it in his memoirs:

> At the beginning of 1816 I make my journey to the schools of Uman'. I stop at a suburb called Turek, on the estate of Huczyński, a tallower. I have a printed certificate, awarded as a letter of congratulations to me, one of the top pupils in the first year at Vinnytsia. This resulted in the prefect, Fr. Skibowski, admitting me without examinations to the second year, where I sat in the second place at the front desk next to Józef Mianowski, today an eminent physician in Petersburg. From that moment sprang a close friendship between us, lasting all through our school years and continuing unsevered to this day[49].

Among the closest friends of Goszczyński and Mianowski in their first year at the school were Józef Chrząszczewski, Józef Hromowicz and Józef Szumakowicz. In subsequent years relationships grew stronger with colleagues living in the boarding house.

> Over those few months – wrote Goszczyński – I made considerable progress in French. In my class I was one of the best pupils of Lens, who was our teacher of that language. This brought me close to Józef Chrząszczewski. Two others I was close to were Józef Hromowicz and Józef Szumakowicz. With them and Józef Mianowski we constituted a group of the four leading pupils every year, because we attended together year in year out[50].

In the boarding house Goszczyński and Mianowski became acquainted with other pupils: Julian Zaleski, Zygmunt Trodkiewicz, Janem Krechowiecki,

---

47  [J. F a l k o w s k i], *Wspomnienia z roku 1848–1849 przez autora 'Obrazów z życia kilku ostatnich pokoleń w Polsce'*, Poznań 1879, p. 264.

48  Though it may have been in 1817, as indicated by Mianowski's testimony cited earlier.

49  S. G o s z c z y ń s k i, *Podróż mojego życia*, p. 15.

50  *Ibidem*, p. 16. The wife of Mr Lens, teacher of French, was the landlady of a renowned boarding house for women in Uman'. L. Z a s z t o w t, *Kresy*, p. 223.

14                                                                                     CHAPTER 1

Ignacy Sarnecki and the Zbyszewski brothers. The director of the house was
Jan Tomaszewski. Goszczyński shared a dormitory with Augustyn and Pius
Groza and Hieronim and Fortunat Tarkowski[51].

In the Christmas holidays of 1819 Mianowski and Goszczyński left Umań:
Severyn went to stay with the Newlińskis in Hordaszówka, while Mianowski
went to his family near Haisyn. They parted ways near the small town of
Talne, known for its wooden church of the Holy Trinity, at that time still Greek
Catholic[52].

As mentioned earlier, Goszczyński's closest ties, beside Mianowski, were
with z Bohdan Zaleski, Jan Krechowiecki, Józef Chrząszczewski and Michał
Grabowski. Nurturing a common literary interest, Zaleski, Goszczyński and
Grabowski set up a triumvirate known in the school as 'Za-Go-Gra'[53]. It was a
kind of unofficial literary club. They read the 'Warsaw Journal' and subscribed
to the 'Vilnius Daily'. Bohdan Zaleski already had two of his dumkas published
in one of those periodicals. They collected their output on a monthly or quar-
terly basis in workbooks titled 'Exercises of the Mind', modelled on the 'Mental
Exercises' of Krzemieniec. According to Krechowiecki, two of Goszczyński's
works are from that period: *Duma about Stefan Czarniecki* and *Reveries of
Zofiówka*[54]. Their close alliance, but also a certain rivalry, was reflected in
Bohdan Zaleski's poem *Three Contemporaries*, written at a time – in Władysław
Nehring's account – when all three had already earned their first literary spurs
and acquired a certain fame:

> *Bohdan, Seweryn, Michał, we writers three*
> *Are playing a kind of separate poetry.*
> *All of one age, and from the same nest,*
> *We've started soaring high, to see who is best.*
> *A single star shines some light on earth's blizzard below,*
> *But we make our own circles, at our own pleasure,*
> *Each with different sounds, movement, force and coloured*
> *feathers over the flurries of snow – but always*
> *weighing the others up in fair and equal measure.*
> *So, who is better? Who'll last longer? Fly the highest?*

---

51  S. Goszczyński, *Podróż mojego życia*, p. 16.
52  *Ibidem*, pp. 28, 33. W. Kołbuk, *Kościoły Wschodnie w Rzeczypospolitej*, p. 142.
53  *Dzieła zbiorowe Seweryna Goszczyńskiego*, published by Z. Wasilewski, vol. 1, Lviv
    [1911], pp. XI, XIII.
54  J. Krechowiecki, *Wiadomość o życiu i pismach Michała Grabowskiego*, Kraków 1868,
    p. 5; W. Nehring, *Z młodych lat Bohdana Zaleskiego*, Warsaw 1887 (Copied out of
    'Biblioteka Warszawska' 1887, vol. 3, p. 185). Cf. S. Sierotwiński, *Goszczyński Seweryn
    (1801–1876)*, PSB, vol. 8, Wrocław 1959–1960, p. 375.

UKRAINE – THE MIANOWSKI FAMILY – UMAN'

*Which two will ultimately trail behind?*
*We have no way of knowing – and to be honest ...*
*We don't mind!*[55]

Goszczyński was bursting with a need for action. He decided to set up a secret pupils' union in the school, one of a political nature. It was a dangerous undertaking, but it came to fruition. Unfortunately, because of excessive candour on Mianowski's part the organisation was uncovered by the prefect, Fr. Skibowski. This was probably the reason why Goszczyński was obliged to leave school at the start of 1822, before completing the final, sixth year. This is how he recalled it in his diaries:

> [...] In Uman' I organise a student-political association. I write much; among others: in the genre of the Dreams of Tass [apocrypha published in Warsaw in 1820. L.Z.] – my Warsaw romances; translating from Byron: Hebrew Melodies, and others. I intend to publish two small volumes of poetry and I am helped in this by Józef Mianowski. My association is found out – by Prefect Skibowski, and through the cowardice of Mianowski. After Easter, I leave Uman'[56].

Despite this highly unpleasant situation, which could have had far worse consequences not only for Goszczyński but for Mianowski and the student members – who in the event avoided reprisals – the two stayed in touch. They would meet in Uman', or Hordaszówka, at the home of the Chaborskis or Newlińskis, and in Leszczynówka, the Krechowiecki estate, and in the Grabowskis' Aleksandrówka. Several months later all of them, bar Goszczyński, successfully completed their Uman' schooling.

> In that year of 1822 – wrote Goszczyński – my best friends left the Uman' schools: Józef Mianowski, who went to Vilnius, and Tomasz Korycki, a talented painter, also to Vilnius. I accompanied them to the home of Jan Iwański. Strange man, Tomasz Korycki. Night in Hordaszówka, his apparition, Mianowski's fright [...]. Before the departure, a sojourn in Hordaszówka. Zenon Chabrowski, who was returning to Vilnius with Mianowski and Korycki, Józef Chrząszczewski, who was travelling to Poland.[57]

---

55  [J.B. Zaleski], *Pisma Józefa Bohdana Zaleskiego*, vol. 2, Lviv 1877, p. 173. The poem's first lines are cited in: W. Nehring, *Z młodych lat*, p. 178; H. Zathey, *Młodość Bohdana Zaleskiego (1802–1830)*, Kraków 1886, p. 10.

56  S. Goszczyński, *Podróż mojego życia*, p. 38.

57  *Ibidem*, p. 39.

16                                                                CHAPTER 1

Mianowski's last meeting with Goszczyński in Poland probably took place in
1829 in the Kresowieckis' Leszczynówka[58]. In the 1830s and 1840s they mainly
saw each other in Paris.

Mianowski was shortly to meet up with many of his Uman' colleagues at
the University of Vilnius. There he broadened his circle of acquaintances.
However, his friendship with the two Seweryns – Goszczyński and Gałęzowski,
the latter becoming a closer friend in Vilnius than he had been previously –
stood the test of time. He was in contact with them almost to the last, and to
the very end he tried to give them every kind of assistance – financially, in the
case of Goszczyński, and in Gałęzowski's case by caring about the family he
had left behind in the homeland.

His final school diploma was in Latin:

*No. 37*
*Auspiciis Augustissimi*
*Et Potentissimi Imperatoris*
*Alexandri I Autocratoris*
*Omnium Rossiarum etc.etc.etc.*

*Nos Scholae Humanensis in Gymnasii loco habitae in Universitatis Litterarum*
*Caesareae tutela florentis, Praefectus et Praeceptores testamur GD Josephum*
*Mianowski Ignatii filium ex Districtu Haysynensis oriondum, aetatis suae annum*
*nunc XIX agentem, in Scholae nostrae classibus a Prima ad Sextam inclusive linguis,*
*litteris et disciplinis quae in Scholis docentur, addiscendis octennio dedisse operam,*
*deligentiaeque suae in*

*Doctrina christiana insignem,*
*Ethicae insignem,*
*Geographiae insignem,*
*Lingua Polonica magnum,*
*Latina magnum,*
*Rossica insignem,*
*Franco-Gallica magnum,*
*Germanica insignem,*
*In Phisica insignem,*
*Zoologia insignem,*
*Botanica insignem,*
*Mineralogia insignem,*
*Mathesi elementari insignem,*
*Algebra insignem,*
*Jure naturae insignem,*
*Historia Universali insignem,*
*Arte delineandi mediocrem fructum percepresse*

---

58    *Ibidem*, p. 56.

UKRAINE – THE MIANOWSKI FAMILY – UMAN'

*Ecundem pietatem et obsequium in Praeceptores sincerum, legum observantiam summam, mores integros, bonarum artium Doctoribus aeque ac condiscipulis probasse. In cuius sententae nostrae fidem, litteras has manifestas, Acholae nostrae Sigillo munitas, Ei Collegio Nostro Basiliano Human Calendis Julii M.DCCCXXII Ao Profectus Scholae & Praec. Eloquentiae P. Leontius Skibowski: Ords D.B.M.*

– Praec. Juris et Historiae Dr. Emilianus Lewinski, Ords D.B.
– Mgr. Praeceptor Phisicae et Historiae Naturalis Bartolami Litynski, Ords D.B. Magni
– Praec. Mathesos P. Nazarius Zatthier, Ords S.B.M[59].

In translation, this means as follows:

*No. 37
By the Will of His Most Distinguished Majesty
The Omnipotent Emperor
Alexander I, Sole Ruler
Of all Russias etc.etc.etc.*

*We of the Gymnasium of the Uman' School being under the mighty care of the Imperial University, Prefect and Teachers do testify that Józef Mianowski, Esq, son of Ignacy, of the county of Hajsyn, currently nineteen years of age, did in our School take instruction from the first year to the sixth, with the inclusion therein of languages, literacy and subjects taught in the School, and demonstrated a passion for learning, and diligence, and displayed progress in his education as follows:*

*in the Christian Religion considerable,
in Ethics considerable,
in Geography considerable,
in the Polish Language great,
in Latin great,
in Russian considerable,
in French-Gallic great,
in German considerable,
in Physics considerable,
in Zoology considerable,
in Botany considerable,
in Mineralogy considerable,
in elementary Mathematics considerable,
in Algebra considerable,
in Natural Law considerable,
in General History considerable,
in the Art of Drawing, he gained middling profit.*

*Meanwhile, in his religiousness and sincere dedication to the Teachers, in adhering to all laws, in the purity of his behaviour and excellent conduct he gained the respect of both*

---

59    L. M é y e t, *Przyczynki historyczno-literackie*, sheets (k.) 6–7.

*Teachers and school colleagues. On this we express our profound conviction and certify it by this document confirmed by the seal of the School in Our Basilian College of Uman' dated this the first day of July 1822.*

> *– Prefect of the School and Teacher of Elocution Fr. Leon Skibowski, of the Assembly of Saint Basil the Great.*
> *– Teacher of Law and History Dr Emilian Lewinski, Assembly of St. Basil the Great.*
> *– Master, Teacher of Physics and Natural History Bartłomiej Litynski, Assembly of St. Basil the Great.*

On completing the Uman' school Mianowski had a year's break in his education. It is likely that he spent that time on his parents' estate in the Haisyn county of the Podolia governorship. The Uman' school, meanwhile, survived till 1830. The end of its existence was thus described by Edmund Liwski:

> [...] on the 17th day of December 1830 the morning bell summoning to prayers and then to lessons was to stay silent thereafter ... since a decree came from the highest authorities, and was announced in all classes, that because of cholera, which was allegedly rampant in various counties, schools would be closed until such time as was notified by the police; neither the pupils, nor perhaps the teachers had the presentiment that it was the final hour of the existence of this school, which had been of such benefit to the country[60].

Although the school was re-opened once the cholera epidemic had passed, one year later it was finally closed. The process of dissolving the Basilian monastery lasted longer, ending in 1834.

---

60    Wołyniak, *O bazylianach w Humaniu*, p. 1147.

CHAPTER 2

# Lithuania – Vilnius – University of Vilnius – The Medical-Surgical Academy – The Konarski Affair

## Lithuania

> Land of my birth, my sacred Lithuania,
> Sifted through with slender grass and yellow sand!
> Untamed but tranquil, apparently quite modest,
> Not like Italy or Helvetia, as I understand,
> Where the fields are like an Eden, where the mountains are colossal,
> Where there are lakes and cataracts, and the forests burst with blossom.
> Italians paint these landscapes, which our folk greedily buy,
> Lithuania, you'll never reach such fame! And yet
> Look deep into your heart: you're worth,
> Much more than meets the eye ...[1]

## University Of Vilnius

> Vilna totius Lituaniae urbs celeberrima[2]

Ukraine played a special role in the creative work of Zaleski, Goszczyński and Grabowski – Mianowski's colleagues from the Uman' 'provincial school'. They became the main representatives of Ukrainian romanticism in 19th century Polish literature. Rus made its mark on everybody who was raised there. Interestingly, though it was Vilnius that exerted the most indelible influence on Mianowski, and it was with that city that he retained the greatest emotional ties, although, once again, we lack firm evidence of this in the source materials, with perhaps one exception: the speech he gave at the inauguration of Warsaw's Main School.

---

1    L. Kondratowicz, *Urodzony Jan Dęboróg*, [in:] *Złota przędza poetów i prozaików polskich*, ed. P. Chmielowski, vol. 3, Warsaw 1886, p. 510.

2    Based on a woodcut by L. Kosmulski. T. Łopalewski, *Między Niemnem a Dźwiną. Ziemia Wileńska i Nowogródzka*, London 1955, p. 146.

© BRILL SCHÖNINGH, 2024 | DOI:10.30965/9783657794720_003

As Tadeusz Bobrowski wrote:

> The people who relocated to Vilnius were predominantly young, less well-off, seeking professional higher education. They hailed from schools in Winnica, with their established reputation, though not as renowned as those of Krzemieniec – or even from the Uman' (Basilian) colleges, which in the twilight of their existence had the good fortune to count among their alumni: Grabowski Michał, Zaleski Bohdan and Goszczyński Seweryn. Despite which the former students from Krzemieniec behaved with an air of superiority – in Rzewuski's opinion, quite unjustifiably[3].

Mianowski began his studies at the Medical Department of the University of Vilnius in 1823 as a government scholar. He had taken lodgings in the city's third quarter, in the house of Mrs Radziszewska at no. 101 Łotoczek street, not far from the university. The decision to admit Mianowski to the student body was signed on 30th September 1823 by the University's rector, Józef Twardowski, and the acting dean, Wacław Pelikan[4]. Its content was as follows:

> Certificate
> Valid until the 1st day of July 1824
>
> *Mianowski Józef, son of Ignacy, 21 years of age, native of the Kiyiv governorship, Uman' county, Śmiła parish, having lodgings in the 3rd quarter on Łotoczek street in house of Radziszewska No. 101, admitted as a pupil of the University for the present academic year to the Medical Department, is to attend lessons in Human and Comparative Anatomy, Physiology, Pathology, Pharmacopoeia, Pharmacy and anatomical sessions and to carry out duties specified on the reverse page of this certificate.*
>
> *Approved at the session of the Government of the Imperial University of Vilnius, with the appropriate signature and application of the University seal. This the 30th day of the month of September 1823.*
>
> Rector Józef Twardowski
> (p.p.) Dean Deputy Professor Wacław Pelikan
> Secretary Norbert Jurgiewicz[5]

---

3  T. Bobrowski, *Pamiętnik mojego życia*, vol. 1, *O sprawach i ludziach mego czasu*, ed., introduction, notes S. Kieniewicz, Warsaw 1979, p. 470.

4  L. Méyet, *Przyczynki historyczno-literackie*, sheet (k.) 8. Abbreviated version published in *Z życia Mianowskiego. Trochę faktów i dokumentów*, 'Tygodnik Ilustrowany' 1903, no. 24, pp. 456–466.

5  L. Méyet, *Przyczynki historyczno-literackie*, sheet (k.) 8.

# LITHUANIA – VILNIUS – UNIVERSITY OF VILNIUS

Student duties were described in detail:

### Duties

To respect one's superiors at the University and elsewhere in the country obediently,

1) To live piously in accordance with the tenets of one's creed, doing no harm to anyone, and when harm is done to oneself to seek redress not personally but through legal means.

2) To attend lessons regularly and apply oneself to one's studies assiduously.

3) Not to enter any unions or associations.

4) For the whole duration of being at the University not to wear any attire other than the prescribed uniform and never to leave one's lodgings without it.

5) Not to attend any theatrical play, ball, or similar public entertainments without having obtained written permission from the Rector.

6) Not to go beyond the city precincts for walks or even botanical research without said permission.

7) Not to frequent public premises such as eateries, billiard halls etc for purposes of enjoyment or entertainment.

8) Not to read or purchase books that oppose religion or the order of the country, or are indecent, or do not belong to the programme of study.

9) Without having obtained permission, certification or patent not to stray beyond the precincts the University.

I have accepted these duties,
and confirm this with my handwritten signature,
Józef Mianowski[6]

In addition to studying hard and making notable progress, for which he received from the University authorities a written commendation and a financial prize, Mianowski began to be a guest at the home of professor of medicine August Bécu, where he would run into such invitees as Adam Mickiewicz, Antoni Gorecki, Eustachy Januszkiewicz, Antoni Odyniec, Aleksander Chodźko, Julian Korsak, Karol Sienkiewicz, Ludwik Spitznagel, and many others. He made friends with the Słowacki family: Juliusz, five years his junior, his stepsisters, Hersylia and Aleksandra and Juliusz's mother Salomea, Bécu by her second marriage. Mianowski also befriended other professorial families: the Śniadeckis, Zofia *née* Śniadecka and her husband, historian Michał Baliński, and the family of Józef Jaroszewicz[7].

---

6 *Ibidem*, sheets (k.) 8–9.

7 [T. i H. Januszewscy], *Listy Teofila i Hersylii (z domu Bécu) Januszewskich do Józefa Mianowskiego*, p. 13.

By this time Vilnius had acquired something of the local colour of a provincial Russian city. The future medical doctor Stanisław Morawski, who enrolled at the University in 1818, recalled his first impressions of a visit to the nonagenarian *stolnikowa* – keeper of the table, or the household – Mrs Brygida Janowiczowa *née* Kaszycówna:

> Madame stolnikowa lived in her own house on Zamkowa street and even in older times had known how to arrange it according to all of today's rules of comfort. In those days the lower and upper hallways and staircases were heated – in some instances. In that respect Vilnius was still, as it is now, very peasant-Russian. Much pride. Few things or true comforts. As for Kowno: eternal city. To this day there are no entrance halls! The guest has to leave his overcoat, or expensive fur coat, on the stairs, which are guarded by no one, or drag his servant after him. [...] She held an open table for relatives, acquaintances, and friends. One needed only to call at around one o'clock in the afternoon to find a place and a very tasty luncheon. Whatever was finest in Lithuania as soon as it arrived in Vilnius it found its way to her house and had to be there. [...] Which was why my father [...] ordered me to be a frequent visitor, where I constantly ran into Radziwiłłs, Tyzenhauzes, Chreptowiczes, Weysenhoffs, Platers, Jelskis, Przeździeckis, Tyszkiewiczes, Wojniłłowiczes and others[8].

As Morawski noted, in her conversations she was apt to say: *how can someone be poor?* I doubt that the young student Mianowski frequented such salons. As an impoverished government scholar, he would probably need to find other social circles, though Vilnius was not a big city and there must have been some intermingling among the various milieus.

Though even in her salon Madame *stolnikowa* played host to other, less distinguished guests:

> In Mme. stolnikowa's house I made the acquaintance of, apart from the great gentlemen, two famous medical doctors, much in demand: the Jew Leiboschütz, or Lejboszyc, as he is commonly known, blind by that time but a brilliant, truly rare man endowed with exceptional medical intuition about whom everybody said: 'Deus et Judeus'; and Barankiewicz, of usurped fame, as is often the case a medic-ignoramus, renowned for the great fortune amassed from his practice and the fact that Germans abroad called him not Barankiewicz but 'Baron von Kiewicz'[9].

As we can see, the more well-heeled burghers of Vilnius availed themselves not only – or probably in the case of some milieus, not even primarily – of

---

8 S. Morawski, *Kilka lat mojej młodości w Wilnie (1818–1825)*, ed., introduction A. Czartkowski, H. Mościcki, Warsaw 1959, pp. 60–63.

9 *Ibidem*, p. 64.

LITHUANIA – VILNIUS – UNIVERSITY OF VILNIUS

the services of university physicians, but of those in private practice with an established reputation.

Social life was flourishing. The Bécus held Vilnius soirees, designed mainly with children in mind, but also involving adults, both from the household and outside. Particularly popular at the time were living paintings. The young Juliusz Słowacki recalled an evening during which Olesia Bécu was Judith, Juliusz's governor Józef Massalski was Holofernes, while Teofil Januszewski became the donkey on whose back Mme. Salomea rode into the salon with little Fredzio – Ludwik Spitznagel's younger brother – simulating the flight into Egypt[10].

The city and the university, were abuzz with news of the investigation against pupils of the fifth year of Vilnius's gymnasium, triggered by the ill-fated appearance on their blackboard of the slogan *Long live the Constitution of the Third of May, oh such a sweet memory for our compatriots*, which was then replicated on the wall of the Dominican monastery. In October 1823 the inquiry was fully under way. On 22 October Jan Jankowski made a deposition which revealed the existence of the Society of Filarets[11]. Mianowski, at the time a newly arrived student, remained on the side-lines of these events. Nonetheless, by 1824 he would have had occasion to meet the students as they were successively released on bail.

The tragic death of August Bécu, struck by lightning on 8 September 1824 and immortalised by Adam Mickiewicz in his *Forefathers' Eve*, caused the family particular distress. Its Mickiewiczian interpretation left an especially painful imprint on the young Juliusz Słowacki. Nonetheless life went on, and Salomea Bécu's home continued to play host to its habitués – including Mickiewicz, who before his departure wrote a farewell poem in Mme. Salomea's visitors' book[12]. The persons involved in the investigation into Vilnius's Filomats and Filarets and frequenting the Bécu salon included, apart from Mickiewicz, Aleksander Chodźko, after his release from custody in 1824 and prior to his departure for Petersburg, and Antoni Edward Odyniec, a friend of the landlady and her stepdaughters. After the trial, this whole circle of friends, except for those, who were forced to leave Vilnius or chose to do so as a precautionary measure, continued to meet in the Bécu house until 1827, when Salomea and her family moved to Krzemieniec.

---

10 Słowacki's letter to his mother from Paris, 5 February 1835, [in:] J. Słowacki, *Korespondencja*, ed. E. Sawrymowicz, vol. 1, Wrocław 1962, p. 281.

11 J. Borowczyk, *Rekonstrukcja procesu filomatów i filaretów 1823–1824*, Poznań 2003, p. 227. The Filarets and Philomathes were secret organisations, mainly of students of Vilnius University.

12 J. Kleiner, *Bécu Salomea (1792–1855)*, PSB, vol. 1, Kraków–Wrocław 1935, p. 393.

24                                                                    CHAPTER 2

For Mianowski, as for the whole of the University community, these events were a profoundly distressing experience. He was, let us recall, a man of exceptional sensitivity, and openheartedness. We can suppose, however, that the trial of the filomats and filarets strengthened his conviction that for a person of his modest means, studying at the government's expense, the only route to a further career was that of continuing to study hard and gaining a degree.

Regrettably, there is no detailed information regarding Mianowski's academic progress in this period. All that is known was that even at this stage he was spotted by Śniadecki as an outstanding student.

He completed his studies in 1827, and graduated on 28th July 1828, as a Doctor of Medicine on the basis of his thesis on tetanus (*De tetano*)[13]. He began work as an assistant to Jędrzej Śniadecki in his internal medicine clinic at Vilnius University. He soon became his favourite apprentice and collaborator. His first accolade came two years later: on 28th December 1830 he received a diamond ring for impeccable service. In July 1831 at his own request, he was transferred to the Russian military infirmary in Vilnius and, as described by Stefan Kieniewicz, during the uprising in Lithuania he treated the sick and the wounded on both sides of the conflict. For this, on 2nd March 1831 he received the highest expression of gratitude from the Tsar[14].

It would appear, that Professor Jędrzej Śniadecki played a key role in Mianowski's career. First and foremost a chemist and biologist, he was also successful in Vilnius as a medical doctor and was exceptionally popular as a writer and satirist. As Stanisław Brzozowski writes, with regard to the beginnings of Śniadecki's career:

> In 1797 at the Vilnius Academy, he began lecturing in pharmacy and chemistry in the Polish language, which scandalised even such an enlightened man as Marcin Poczobut, who opined on that subject that 'it is not right to make science so common'.

> However, the academic youth and the public, attending in large numbers from the town, took a different view. The hall assigned to the young professor's lectures was full to the gills, and Śniadecki's rhetoric truly gripped and enchanted his listeners. This had an effect, on his medical practice, which very quickly began to grow[15].

---

13    M i a n o w s k i [Josephus], *Dissertatio inauguralis medico-chrurgica de tetano observationes trec cum epicrisi exhibens quam publice defendet auctor Josephus Mianowski* [...], Vilnae [1828], printed by N. Glűcksberg, ss. nlb 2, 51, nlb. 1 (Dis. Univ. Vil., Med. Ordo). Por. RGIA, f. 733, op. 147, e.hr. 752, *Formulărnyj spisok o službe*, sheets (k.) 3–23; S. K i e n i e w i c z, *Mianowski Józef*, p. 523; J. B i e l i ń s k i, *Stan nauk lekarskich*, p. 310.

14    RGIA, f. 733, op. 147. e.hr. 752, sheets (k.) 3–23.

15    S. B r z o z o w s k i, *Jędrzej Śniadecki jego życie i dzieła*, Warsaw 1903, pp. 21–22.

# LITHUANIA – VILNIUS – UNIVERSITY OF VILNIUS

At the point when Mianowski was beginning his studies, Jędrzej Śniadecki was 55 years old and his position both at the University and in Vilnius society was firmly established. From 1805 onwards he wrote regularly for the 'Vilnius Daily'; he worked on his most important thesis, *A Theory of Organic Beings*; and from 1817 the Society of Scoundrels, of which for a certain time he was president (later called Dignitary), produced every Saturday a popular gazette called 'Gutter News' which pilloried obscurantism, backwardness, and ignorance. The periodical's heyday were the years 1818–1822, after which Śniadecki went into retirement, though not, as it turned out, for long. As Brzozowski wrote:

> Śniadecki remained a pensioner, however, for all of two years: in 1824 he was called to take up the Chair of clinical medicine at Vilnius University. In that post he remained, and even when the University was closed and the Medical-Surgical Academy was created, he stayed *in situ* until his death[16].

He died on 11th May 1837.

In my opinion Mianowski's conservatism must have received 'a good schooling' from Jędrzej Śniadecki, which would have been an important spur in shaping an enlightened and open mind in the young doctor as he embarked on his further life. It also made him resilient to attitudes of ultra-conservatism. He would have learnt to distance himself from well-worn, and thus most likely conservative points of view, and must have known and appreciated the role of a good sense of humour. He would also have learnt the value of intellectual freedom in the academic world and in private life – and recognised a good joke or an acerbic, sarcastic comment. Otherwise, his old master would not have accepted manifestations of 'doltishness' or 'narrow-mindedness' on the part of his protégé. I doubt, however, that this resulted in a drastic change in Mianowski's character. He remained a polite and uncommitted gentleman, much less free-thinking than his mentor.

On returning to his university Chair Śniadecki set about finding a successor, at least in the capacity of director of the university clinic. Why the choice fell on Józef Mianowski is a moot point. It would appear, that the deciding factors, apart from his character traits of politeness, kindness, and good manners, also included – perhaps even primarily – his scientific achievements in the field of medicine and his well-entrenched position as a medical practitioner in the city, as well as his social connections, not least with various professorial families, and in particular his close relations with the family of Salomea Bécu *née* Słowacka.

---

16    *Ibidem*, pp. 34–35.

He was well acquainted with Juliusz Słowacki. They attended the same university, though when Słowacki was beginning his studies Mianowski had already completed his. They were brought closer together during encounters in the Bécu household, to which Mianowski was introduced probably through the offices of Jędrzej Śniadecki. During the Easter vacation of 1828 Słowacki and Mianowski made a joint excursion to Troki, where they visited the ruins of the, as yet unrestored castle of the Lithuanian grand dukes Kiejstut and Witold on the island of the lake of Galwe[17]. They may even have partaken of Troki's famous *kibiny karaimskie*, though no mention of this is to be found in the correspondence. Salomea wrote about their trip in a letter to Antoni Odyniec, dated 11 April:

> Julek had a fine Easter; he longs for the holidays, and it makes me happy that they will be all-the-more pleasant for him. I advised him that prior to his departure he should visit Vilnius and its environs *en amateur*, and in particular: the churches containing paintings by Smuglewicz and Czechowicz. So, he started by visiting Troki and he sent me a sketch of the view of the lake with its island built up by the castle and all of that by the light of the moon. A pleasant lad, he is beginning to pander to my fantasies and that makes me happy[18].

The two of them also frequently stayed in Jaszuny, on the estate of Jędrzej Śniadecki, 27 versts south of Vilnius on the river Mereczanka. From 1828 onwards a permanent resident there was Jędrzej's brother, Jan Śniadecki; next to the seventeenth century palace[19] he built a new manor designed by Bolesław Podczaszyński, housing an impressive library and a collection of astronomical instruments brought over from Vilnius. Management of Jaszuny was taken over by Michał Baliński after his marriage to Zofia Śniadecka, daughter of Jędrzej. Jaszuny was therefore a favourite meeting place, both in summer and winter, of the Śniadeckis and Balińskis, but also of their friends, like Mianowski or the Bécu family. It was from Jaszuny that Słowacki retained the most cherished

---

17  For the process of the castle's later restoration by Vilnius's experts in antiquity, headed by Wandalin Szukiewicz, see L. Zasztowt, *Wileńscy miłośnicy 'starożytności' w latach 1899–1914*, 'Kwartalnik Historii Nauki i Techniki' 1990, no. 2–3, pp. 259–283; S. Lorentz, *Album wileńskie*, Warsaw 1986.

18  L. Méyet, *Przyczynki historyczno-literackie*, sheet (k.) 11. Juliusz Słowacki's etching in L. Méyet, *Z nieznanych pamiątek*, 'Tygodnik Ilustrowany' 1900, no. 42. Cf. L. Méyet, *Listy Juliusza Słowackiego z autografów poety wydał* [...], vol. 1, Lwów 1899, p. 46.

19  E. Chwalewik, *Zbiory polskie. Archiwa, biblioteki, gabinety, galerie, muzea i inne zbiory pamiątek przeszłości w ojczyźnie i na obczyźnie w porządku alfabetycznym według miejscowości ułożone*, vol. 1, Warsaw–Kraków 1926, p. 135.

# LITHUANIA – VILNIUS – UNIVERSITY OF VILNIUS

memories of his Vilnius youth[20]. This was how he recalled the period in a letter sent to his mother from Paris on 8 December 1832. He was 23 years old:

> This letter will probably find Mianowski staying with you, so I commend myself to his memory; those were different times, when we would return from Jaszuny at night on our *perekladnyye* [Russian: horse-drawn carts]. We felt good then, we felt good on *kucyja* [Christmas Eve: *Kūčios* in Lithuanian] in Jaszuny. When I recall this, I have the impression that I've become an old man; the truth is, already at the time I believed myself to be a fully-fledged adult, while others considered me to be a child[21].

Słowacki's circle of acquaintances during his studies at the University of Vilnius included, apart from Mianowski, Józef Antoni Beaupré, Anicenty Regnier, Stanisław Kierbedź, Ludwik Trynkowski, Maciej Wołonczewski, Ignacy Hołowiński, Aleksander Tyszyński, Ignacy Iwanowski, Henryk Choiński, Antoni Muchliński, Felicjan Tustanowski, Konstanty Tyszkiewicz and many others. Of those who remained in the homeland after the November uprising Słowacki's closest ties were with Mianowski and Beaupré[22].

Soon the ties with the Słowacki family were to become closer still, since Olesia, Juliusz's stepsister, decided to offer herself in marriage to the young and increasingly prominent Doctor of Medicine. She related this in a letter to Odyniec dated 6th March 1829:

> I hope, Sir, I am not saying farewell to you for long. Fate decrees that we always meet each other unexpectedly: that it seems is the will of Providence, and it may be that something will bring you over to Vilnius from the second world. Do not look for me any further, I shall always remain in Vilnius, in Vilnius I shall always be happy, because in Vilnius I have found everything[23].

Olesia was the older daughter of Doctor August Bécu. She was born in 1804 and brought up in Vilnius. Entering the world of adults she shone, in Odyniec's words, with the full radiance of beauty, combining the magnificent stature of Pallas with a typical Polish demeanour: blue-eyed, cheerful, and gentle. By Her younger sister, Hersylia, was by contrast characterised by features of an Eastern

---

20  Jan Śniadecki i Michał Baliński were buried in the Jaszuny cemetery. L. Méyet, *Listy Juliusza Słowackiego*, vol. 1, p. 10.

21  *Ibidem*, pp. 157–158.

22  L. Janowski, *W promieniach Wilna i Krzemieńca*, Vilnius 1923, pp. 120–121.

23  L. Méyet, *Przyczynki historyczno-literackie*, sheets (k.) 11–12.

28 CHAPTER 2

type. As Odyniec recalled she was a brunette of Oriental complexion, along Greek or Arab lines[24].

On hearing of Olesia's engagement Słowacki wrote to her from Warsaw on 15 September of that year:

> Your letter, Olesia, brought me much joy, one can see from it that you are happy now and expect to be happier still, the only thing needed is a professorial Chair and everything will be fine. I would write separately to Dear M [Mianowski], but these days I am so busy that even to you I am not writing as extensively as I should like. So, give him greetings on my behalf, and if he has forgotten me, then remind him it is the same Julek with whom he travelled to Troki[25].

At that time Mianowski was described by Józef Bieliński on the basis of accounts by Maciej Łowicki and Michał Grabowski, as follows:

> He was a tall, dark-haired man, somewhat bald, with an expressive, drawn-out face and swarthy complexion. His demeanour was exceptionally polite, friendly, pleasant; his speech was fast and easy, and almost stuttering in its animation[26].

What guided Olesia in her decision it is difficult to say. Mianowski was only one of her many possible candidates. Józef Mikulski, later a professor in Krzemieniec, was one suitor, and there were several others. The whole situation was thus described by Słowacki in a letter of 20 June 1829:

> I am sincerely ashamed that I have not written to you for so long, my Olesia, in part my excuse could be a fever which just like last year in springtime did not fail to call on me, and not content with paying me one visit returned with a second one ten days later, probably so that I could make up for the lack of dear Mianowski, who last year was so effective in fighting it off. I have by now received two letters from you, the first demanding that I guess everything, it aroused my curiosity to a considerable degree, because I remember how in a letter to Hersylka you insisted that you were in no way inclined towards M. [Mianowski], although the re-heating of doughnuts and saving them for him caused us to believe quite the opposite; with your second letter you solved that puzzle, although admittedly my curiosity had already been sated by a letter from Hersylka and Teofil, who trusting less in my perspicacity explained the whole thing directly without beating around the bush, including an episodic depiction of the despair of the second M [Mikulski], wandering erratically above the precipices of his garden and not wanting to hurl himself into them only because it

---

24    *Listy Juliusza Słowackiego zebrane i częściowo ogłoszone przez Leopolda Méyeta*, ed. M. K r i d l, vol. 3, Warsaw 1915, p. 13.

25    L. M é y e t, *Przyczynki historyczno-literackie*, sheet (k.) 12; *Listy Juliusza Słowackiego*, vol. 2, p. 46.

26    L. M é y e t, *Przyczynki historyczno-literackie*, sheet (k.) 13.

LITHUANIA – VILNIUS – UNIVERSITY OF VILNIUS

would go against the Englishness so deeply engraved in his entire bearing, but you previously unmoved by the moans of the four Michaels; sparing a small sigh for the hat lost at one time on the castle hill, you will forget about the hapless Anglomaniac, who will similarly stifle his sorrow, talking to his favourite horse in a language of love. Not to dwell any longer on the sorry fate of jilted lovers I wish to tell you, Dear Olesia, that I am filled with joy at your happy state as you write now and the pleasant hopes you have for the future; I also think with pleasure that if I happen to be travelling through Vilnius not everything there will be foreign to me, and I will find my sister's home, friendly, congenial, in which everything will interest me and delight me ... but will we ever have a chance to meet?[27]

As early as September 1829 it became known that Mianowski would be appointed to his desired 'Chair', or more exactly that he would take up the post of *assistant* in the University clinic. Słowacki wrote about this in a letter to Olesia dated 8 September[28]. His official 'Description of service' (*Formuliarniy spisok o sluzhbie* in Russian), drawn up for the requirements of the Russian authorities, states that from 29 July 1828 he was a doctor (of medicine) and from 1 September 1828 was employed as an assistant to the chief surgeon of the University clinic. He performed well and on 28 December 1830 was awarded by His Imperial Majesty with a diamond ring. As already mentioned, in February 1831 he volunteered to work in the Vilnius infirmary, where he treated wounded soldiers and insurgents. Other sources suggest that he actually set up and managed the whole institution.

Martial law was in place in the north-western governorships (Vilnius, Grodno, Minsk and the Białystok region) from as early as 1st December 1830. In its wake, many people were arrested and exiled to Siberia. But widespread insurrectional activity did not break out until February 1831 in Żmudź (Samogitia) after an imperial *ukaz* announced the conscription of recruits. In April Russian forces carried out a brutal pacification of the Kowno region and the civilian population of the town of Oszmiana, while among the heaviest clashes one took place on 29th April of that year (the battle of Kiejdany). Among the last, unsuccessful conflicts was the battle of Połąga in May 1831.

The insurrection entered a successive phase in May, when the armies of the Polish Kingdom marched into the Grodno region under the command of General Dezydery Chłapowski. The armed struggle reached its peak on 19 June 1831 with the unsuccessful attempt to seize Vilnius by the joint forces of Chłapowski and General Antoni Giełgud, who had previously fought a

---

27  *Listy Juliusza Słowackiego*, vol. 3, pp. 30–32. More regarding Mikulski, the rival suitor turned down by Olesia, is to be found in Słowacki's letter of 8 September 1829. *Ibidem*, p. 42.

28  *Ibidem*.

victorious battle at Rajgrod. The longest lasting armed unit was that of Marcely Szymański: while conflict on a wider scale had ceased, his forces went on fighting till November 1831, in areas which included the Oszmiany region and the Nalibodzka Wilderness[29]. It might be added that this was a period which experienced a cholera epidemic, especially in the Polish Kingdom, with a death toll of almost 14,000 (out of a total 3.9 million inhabitants of the Kingdom). Brought over, it was thought, by Russian troops stifling the November Uprising, it was fortunately not so widespread in Lithuania; in Austrian Galicia, meanwhile, the number of deaths exceeded 100.000 (out of a population of over four million)[30].

On 2nd March 1831 – when the uprising was fully under way – Mianowski received a personal commendation from the Tsar for setting up and managing his military infirmary[31].

The hardships of the insurrection in Lithuania did not engender a change of plans, and even though the peak of armed conflict fell precisely on March and April 1831[32], Mianowski did not wait till May for the situation to calm down and decided to finally tie the knot with Olesia. Throughout that period, we should add, Vilnius remained in Russian hands, and the failed attempt to regain it did not take place until 19 June.

And so, on 27th April 1831 Mianowski married the stepsister of Juliusz Słowacki, Aleksandra Bécu. The wedding was a major event in Vilnius. The marriage took place in the university church of St. John, and the celebrant was the newly ordained bishop and suffragan of the Vilnius diocese, Fr Benedykt Kłągiewicz. The witness for the bridegroom was Jędrzej Śniadecki; for the bride it was Jakub Bécu, August's brother-in-law, at that time a clerk in the Liceum of Krzemieniec[33].

---

29　J. Feduszka, *Powstanie listopadowe na Litwie i Żmudzi*, 'Teka Komisji Historycznej OL PAN' 2004, vol. 1, pp. 110–160.

30　B. Dzierżawski, O. Hewelke, W. Janowski, J. Zawadzki, *Cholera, jej dawniejsze epidemje u nas, przyczyny, objawy, zapobieganie i leczenie*, Warsaw 1892 (copy from 'Kronika Lekarska'). Cited after R. Kuzak, *Epidemie cholery w XIX-wiecznej Polsce. Zapomniana choroba zabiła setki tysięcy ludzi*, 'Wielka Historia'. https://wielkahistoria.pl/epidemi e-cholery-w-xixwiecznej-polsce-zapomniana-choroba-zabila-setki-tysiecy-ludzi.

31　*Ibidem.*

32　W. Tokarz, *Wojna polsko-rosyjska 1830–1831*, vol. 1, Warsaw 1993, p. 226 & following. Cf. E. Gulczyński, *Rok 1830–1831 w Wilnie*, Vilnius 1933; S. Rabinowiczówna, *Vilnius w powstaniu roku 1830/1831*, Vilnius 1932; See also V.V. Garbačova, *Paustanne 1830–1831 gadou na Belarusi*, Minsk 2001, p. 59 & following.

33　L. Méyet, *Przyczynki historyczno-literackie*, sheet (k.) 13. Cf. J. Mianowski, 'Tygodnik Ilustrowany' 1865, no. 286, p. 97–98; D. Beauvois, *Szkolnictwo polskie na ziemiach litewsko-ruskich 1803–1832: Uniwersytet Wileński*, vol. 1, Rome–Lublin 1991, p. 221.

LITHUANIA – VILNIUS – UNIVERSITY OF VILNIUS

In the view of the bride's family the union, besides being founded in great, reciprocal love, was a good catch for Miss Bécu. That was also the view of Juliusz Słowacki. He wrote: *My best regards to the most beautiful Olesia. Oh, does she know how to live in this world! The old girl has certainly done well for herself*[34]. Juliusz was also happy to learn that Olesia was pregnant. He even had a humorous suggestion for a name for the Mianowskis' child:

> Write to Olesia and tell her I'm always thinking of her and often talk about her with people here who know her. And write to me too, tell me how they're getting on – if they have a son, they should call him Februarius; I don't know how that anecdote by Günter entered my mind[35].

Sad to say, the marriage was short-lived[36]. Ill with tuberculosis, Aleksandra died six days after giving birth, on 23rd May 1832. She spent her last days on the estate of Markucie near Vilnius. With her prematurely born son Jan she was interred in the Rossa cemetery.

A certain light on Mianowski's stance is shed by the facts of his future wife's illness. It had begun much earlier. In December 1829 Aleksandra Bécu's condition was serious, though yet no one recognised this: it was put down to normal female ailments. Mianowski blamed himself for not being able to cope with his fiancée's increasing infirmity. The whole situation was made more complicated by some social misunderstandings and, probably, by the looming deadline of the wedding. Teofil Januszewski, not fully aware of the threat, wrote to Mianowski from Krzemieniec:

> Why do you fear that we might be blaming you for Olesia's suffering; it is true that we do not know each other enough to rely on one another, and the only excuse you may have is that you consider us to be practically strangers, which is why you seek to justify your conduct before us; but how far have we parted company in our opinions! You say you are the cause of Olesia's suffering; we say, we always say that for her and because of her you are exposed to painful ordeals. Believe me, dear Brother-in-law, the vengeance of those whom you consider your enemies was always aimed at Olesia, her alone. They knew well from where to strike, and they succeeded. What can we do; let it not deter the two of you, see it through, and God will change everything. We cannot foresee when will finally arrive for you the propitious outcome; in the present complications it is impossible to discern a change for the better, but we hope that a time will come when

---

34  Letter from Słowacki in Paris to his mother, 20 October 1831, [in:] J. Słowacki, *Korespondencja*, vol. 1, p. 84.

35  Letter to mother, 24 January 1832, [in:] *ibidem*, p. 93.

36  M. Czapska, *Ludwika Śniadecka*, Warsaw 1958, p. 108.

you enjoy happiness. We need only to find the means to speed that moment up[37].

Did Mianowski already realise then that he was dealing with tuberculosis? It seems that initially he may not have spotted the symptoms, for all that he was a medical practitioner. Nonetheless we can be certain that in 1831, when they took their marriage vows, he was aware that his newly wed bride was incurably ill.

The death of his wife was for Mianowski a tragedy which he could not shake off for many long years. Unfortunately, no personal written records of his state of mind are extant. How strongly he experienced it and how long was the mourning that he imposed on himself over his wife and child we can only deduce from the letters of Juliusz Słowacki and of Hersylia and Teofil Januszewski. Słowacki learned of Olesia's death several weeks later. He wrote to his mother: *Oh Mother! Olesia! What a calamity! I thought of her for a long, long time – why will you not describe her death – her last words? I would wish to know about everything – I, who saw her all my life*[38]. He recalled Olesia many times in later letters.

Teofil Januszewski consoled Mianowski as best he could:

> You are severely hurt, dear Józef, such a short time spent with such a good person, so quickly did your happiness end – her life, which she had only just begun to make use of. Józef, I contemplate this with tears in my eyes. I share your grief even more for the fact that I was struck by it perhaps even more painfully. [...] Dear Józef, you joined our small family just as it is becoming smaller still, the ties that bound it together should be growing closer, should be tightening. Consider us to be your best friends, because we owe to you the brief but real happiness of poor Olesia – we are beholden to you for her[39].

Aleksandra Mianowska (1804–1832) was laid to rest in the Rossa cemetery in Vilnius alongside her father August Bécu (1774–1824) and her son Jan (born and died on 17th May 1832)[40]. The whole tragedy thus took place 17 days after the official closure of the University of Vilnius, on 1st May. It was – so it seemed at

---

37 Letter from Teofil Januszewski in Krzemieniec to Mianowski, 1 December 1829, [in:] [T. i H. J a n u s z e w s c y], *Listy Teofila i Hersylii (z domu Bécu) Januszewskich do Józefa Mianowskiego*, pp. 11–12.

38 Letter dated 4 July 1832, [in:] J. S ł o w a c k i, *Korespondencja*, vol. 1, p. 121.

39 T. Januszewski's letter from Krzemieniec to Mianowski, 3 June 1832, [in:] [T. i H. J a n u s z e w s c y], *Listy Teofila i Hersylii (z domu Bécu) Januszewskich do Józefa Mianowskiego*, pp. 14–15.

40 *Cmentarz na Rossie w Wilnie, historia, sztuka, przyroda*, ed. A.S. C z y ż, B. G u t o w s k i, Warsaw–Kraków 2019, pp. 513–515.

LITHUANIA – VILNIUS – UNIVERSITY OF VILNIUS 33

the time – the most tragic and saddest period in Józef Mianowski's life. Yet the future was to bring him more sad surprises.

Despite the tragic death of his wife and child Mianowski kept up relations both with Salomea and with Juliusz Słowacki; he visited the former in Krzemieniec and the latter in Paris. After the death of August Bécu, and especially following Salomea's move to Krzemieniec, Mianowski gradually took over the management of her financial affairs in Vilnius. His closest ties, however, were with Aleksandra's sister, Hersylia, married to Teofil Januszewski, until they were obliged to move to Kaługa in the wake of the Szymon Konarski affair in 1838[41]. He occasionally exchanged letters with Juliusz Słowacki and received books from him. His last meeting with Słowacki was in Paris in 1847. In December of that year, he also called on Salomea[42].

The closure of the University on 1st May 1832 and the subsequent conversion of its Medical Department into the Medical-Surgical Academy was not without serious losses. Even earlier, after the uncovering of the Vilnius conspiracy in 1824, many professors were forced to 'voluntarily' leave Vilnius or were officially instructed to do so. At the same time Józef Zawadzki and his famous bookstore lost privileged status as the University publisher, while most of the 'card dealing' was now done by the new rector, Wacław Pelikan. As Stanisław Morawski wrote: Mikołaj Nowosilcow gave the orders, Pelikan carried them out. Part of the old professorial body was criticised in the city for its subservience to the new rector, who openly used his position for material gain[43].

Mianowski found himself at the centre of these events. His protective umbrella was provided for him by Jędrzej Śniadecki, whose own position was safe. The question arises as to why Mianowski was not linked to the Filomats and Filarets. He began his studies in 1822, so it would appear he had little chance of entering the hierarchic structures of the Society of Filomats, which anyway ceased its activity a year later. This was even more the case with the Society of Filarets, whose activities were discovered by Nowosilcow. On the other hand, in 1822 the Filomats counted 172 members, thus constituting quite a substantial community[44].

---

41 L. Méyet, *Przyczynki historyczno-literackie*, sheets (k.) 14–15; *Listy Juliusza Słowackiego*, vol. 1, p. 107. Korrespodence with the Januszewskis: 'Biblioteka Wieku' 1897, vol. 43. See also G. z Günterów Puzynina, *W Wilnie i w dworach litewskich. Pamiętnik z lat 1815–1843*, Vilnius 1928, p. 128l. Cf. [T. i H. Januszewscy], *Listy Teofila i Hersylii (z domu Bécu) Januszewskich do Józefa Mianowskiego*.

42 *Listy Juliusza Słowackiego*, vol. 1, pp. 87–88, vol. 2, p. 271.

43 S. Morawski, *Kilka lat mojej młodości w Wilnie*, pp. 345–348.

44 Dr Szeliga [J. Bieliński], *Dokumenta urzędowe z 'Teki' Rektora Twardowskiego*. 'Archiwum do Dziejów Literatury i Oświaty w Polsce' 1889 (Kraków), vol. 6, pp. 170–335.

The professional and academic career of the young doctor grew promisingly. On 1st September 1831 he embarked on a course of lectures in physiology for second' and third' year students at the Medical Department, transferring when the university was closed to the newly formed Medical-Surgical Academy. As recorded in the 'Description of Service' mentioned earlier, on 13th December he was elected member of the Imperial Medical Society in Vilnius, and a year later, on 1st September 1832, he was appointed assistant to the professor at the medical clinic of the Medical-Surgical Academy[45].

Documents of Imperial Medical Society of Vilnius suggest that he had become a member of the Society much earlier, in 1829. Indeed, in that year, with Adolf Abicht as president and Feliks Rymkiewicz as vice-president, he became the Society's secretary. He continued in that post in 1830, when Jędrzej Śniadecki took over the presidency, and in 1831 when Konstanty Porcyanko acceded to the post[46].

In 1829 the Society decided to resume publication of 'The Journal of Medicine, Surgery and Pharmacy' which had been suspended one year earlier. In November professors Abicht and Rymkiewicz were tasked with drawing up a programme for the periodical. The 216th session of the Society in January 1830 voted to submit the programme to the Ministry of Public Education with a request for approval; it also appointed an editorial committee for the journal, comprising professors Śniadecki, Abicht, Porcyanko and Rymkiewicz, the apothecary Aleksander Woeleck, and Józef Mianowski. By the end of February, they had the imprimatur of the minister of education, Karl von Lieven[47].

On the dissolution of the University in May 1832, Mianowski, along with the majority of academic' employees of the Medical Department, was awarded his successive diamond ring for exemplary work[48]. Interestingly, he was not impeded in this even by the negative, scheming opinion of Rector Pelikan, in which Mianowski, as well as Fr. Michał Bobrowski, the former rector Szymon Malewski and numerous others were described as not conforming to the rules[49].

---

45  RGIA, f. 733, op. 147, e.hr. 752, Formulărnyj spisok o službe, sheets (k.) 3–23. Cf. J. Bieliński, *Stan nauk lekarskich*, pp. 576–579; J. Róziewicz, *Polsko-rosyjskie powiązania naukowe (1725–1918)*, Wrocław 1984, pp. 185–187; W. Zahorski, *Zarys dziejów Cesarskiego Towarzystwa Lekarskiego w Wilnie 1805–1897*, Warsaw 1898, pp. 70–71.

46  J. Bieliński, *Cesarskie Towarzystwo Lekarskie Wileńskie, jego prace i wydawnictwa (1805–1864)*, Warsaw 1890, pp. 20, 53. H. Ilgiewicz, *Wileńskie towarzystwa i instytucje naukowe w XIX wieku*, Toruń 2005, p. 64.

47  J. Bieliński, *Cesarskie Towarzystwo Lekarskie Wileńskie*, p. 12.

48  This took place on 23 May 1832. RGIA, f. 733, op. 147, e.hr. 752, *Formulărnyj spisok o službe*.

49  M. Czapska, *Ludwika Śniadecka*, s. 107. A "fairly positive" assessment of Pelikan was made by his protégé, Stanisław Morawski, who was nonetheless aware of the two-faced nature of his patron. See. S. Morawski, *Kilka lat mojej młodości w Wilnie*, s. 244–248, 332.

LITHUANIA – VILNIUS – UNIVERSITY OF VILNIUS

By this time Mianowski had moved to accommodation near Vilnius's Ostra Brama, in Ostrobramska street, in a house owned by a certain Żaba[50].

No records unfortunately remain of Mianowski's reading matter when a student first at the gymnasium and then the university in Vilnius. Indirectly, however, we can reconstruct his likely literary interests. He was undoubtedly a reader of the successive works of Józef Ignacy Kraszewski. Let us recall that the years 1838–1842 saw the publication of Kraszewski's only scholarly work: the four-volume *Vilnius: From its Beginnings to the Year 1750* (Vilnius 1838–1842, vol. 1–4)[51]. He was sure to have read Mickiewicz: published in the 1830s were, among others, his *Pan Tadeusz* (1834) and *Forefathers' Eve* Part III (1832). He would surely have read Juliusz Słowacki, whom he valued and knew personally. Unfortunately, we do not know which of Słowacki's émigré works, published abroad, reached Vilnius. Nonetheless the contact Mianowski had with Juliusz's mother Salomea is likely to have given him the opportunity to acquaint himself with works that Juliusz sent to his mother. Also, he will surely have read the émigré writings of his friend Seweryn Goszczyński, whose most famous novel, *Kaniów Castle*, was available in Warsaw in 1828. He must also have read Michał Grabowski – his novel *Koliszczyzna* was published in Vilnius in 1838, while the five volumes of *Stannica hulajpolska* came out in 1840–1841. He would also have known and read Antoni Malczewski's *Maria: a Ukrainian Novel* (Warsaw 1825), and was probably familiar with the works of his friend from schooldays Józef Bohdan Zaleski, bard of pan-Slavism in its Polish version, building on the ideals of the old Commonwealth with a prominent role for the Latin church. Most of Mianowski's school colleagues and friends belonged to what is known as the Ukrainian school in Polish literature of the first half of the 19th century. They were also leaders of what we might call the second file of Polish romantics, remaining in the shade of Mickiewicz and Słowacki.

It is evident for all to see that Mianowski must have been in thrall to the newly emerging and triumphant romanticism. His connections with representatives of that movement are undeniable. I suspect, however, that with the advances in his medical and academic career and the strengthening of his connections with the higher echelons of Vilnius, and later of Petersburg and Warsaw, his literary preferences would have undergone a certain evolution. Was he, in the 1830s, familiar with the oeuvre of Aleksander Fredro, whose most famous comedies were already being performed in theatres in the 1820s?

---

50   Probably Jan Marcinkiewicz-Żaba, Vilnius governorship marshal in the years 1834–1840. T. Bairašauskaitė, *O litewskich marszałkach gubernialnych i powiatowych (do 1863 r.)*, 'Przegląd Wschodni' 1997, vol. 4, no. 2 (14), p. 433. Cf. G. Puzynina, *W Wilnie i w dworach litewskich. Pamiętnik z lat 1815–1843*, Chotomów 1988, p. 284.

51   K. Sołtys, *Józef Ignacy Kraszewski jako historyk: naukowy fundament wykładu dziejów Litwy w monografii Wilna*, Warsaw 2013.

It is likely that he was, not least because of the passions and satirical interests of his learned mentor Jędrzej Śniadecki.

But he would also surely have been *au courant* with the masterpieces of contemporary French and Russian literature. He undoubtedly read Alexander Pushkin, all whose major works, including theatrical ones, saw their publication in the 1820s and 1830s. *Eugene Onegin* came out in instalments in 1825–1832, and as a single volume for the first time in 1833. Mikhail Lermontov's most important works were published in the late 1820s and the 1830s. From the end of the 18th century the king of literature for children and youth was Ivan Krylov. Mianowski is sure to have read the theatrical pieces of Nikolai Gogol: the first performances of *The Government Inspector* took place in Moscow and Petersburg in 1836; *The Marriage* first came out in 1842.

Given his increasingly established position in the salons of Vilnius, he would surely have been versed in French literature, acknowledged as the height of intellectual fashion at the time. And he had a good mastery of the language. He would have read both the poetry and prose of his near-contemporary, Victor Hugo, member of the Académie française from 1841. He probably also read the novellas of Prosper Mérimée, whose publication also coincided with the 1830s. Did his reading stretch to Honoré de Balzac? It seems likely that he would have known at least his most popular works, which first appeared in print in that period.

### The Medical-Surgical Academy of Vilnius

The Medical-Surgical Academy was in the opinion of contemporaries an institution of learning of a high standard, very much continuing the traditions of the former Medical Department of the University of Vilnius from which it originated. Józef Bieliński considered it one of the more admirable establishments of its kind in the Empire. Among the renowned figures employed there he listed the honoured professor Mikołaj Mianowski, the 'public' full professors Adolf Abicht, Jan Karol Baerkman, Józef Korzeniewski and Feliks Rymkiewicz and the associate professors Ignacy Fonberg and Iwan Leonow, as well as the adjuncts Ludwik Siewruk and Karol Edward Miriam. In this rollcall of the great and the good of the Academy he also found a place for Józef Mianowski[52].

The Academy's inauguration took place on 1st September 1832. It was described thus:

---

52    J. Bieliński, *Stan nauk lekarskich*, p. 87.

[...] what followed was the ceremonial inauguration of the Imperial medical-surgical academy before a separate commission, composed of Real Councillors of State and knights Gromov and Pelikan and the Councillor of the estate of Khoraninov. Following Holy Mass in the academic church of St John and the singing of Veni Creator, in the presence of the head of the Vilnius diocese the Bishop Suffragan and Knight J.W. Kłągiewicz, and of the clerical body of the Main Seminary, the professors, students of medicine and assembled populace – the higher officials, men of the cloth, military and civilians who had received invitations on the previous day gathered at the eleventh hour in the new, beautifully adorned debating chamber of the former University of Vilnius. On the arrival of His Highness Prince Dolgoruky, adjutant-general of His Imperial Majesty, wartime governor of the governorships of Vilnius and Grodno and of the Białystok region, when the Real Councillor of State and Knight His Highness Gromov, the most senior member of the Commission, began the session with a short introduction to this ceremonial Act, the secretary of the Commission Collegial Assessor Nestor Kukolnik read out the more important points of the Statute conferred on the Most Blessed Medical-Surgical Academy, and called on the new members of the aforementioned Academy to carry out their duties. After which the whole assembly made its way to one of the academic halls, specially prepared for this purpose, where the archimandrite of the Vilnius monastery of the Holy Ghost, the most reverend Platon, held a service, and after sending heart-felt prayers to the Host of Our Lord for the Most Precious health of the Emperor of All Russias NICOLAS I, whom we have the fortune to be ruling over us, he addressed the congregation about the need to fear God in the pursuit of scholarly excellence. The ceremony ended with a luncheon in the library hall, prepared by members of the newly formed Medical-Surgical Academy, where toasts were drunk to the health and long life of His Most Revered Majesty[53].

The creation of the Academy saved a certain part of the University's legacy, also in material terms. For example, it inherited 6,590 works in 13,240 volumes from the former Medical Department; with 3,000 books from the Medical Institute, it was able to retain in Vilnius over 16,000 titles[54]. Most of the University's other books travelled to Kyiv, to the University of St Vladimir founded towards the end of 1833.

From its inception the Academy was or considered to be one of the best scientific institutions in the Empire. One factor in this assessment were the university hospitals, known as clinics.

In 1832 the population of Vilnius was 35,922 inhabitants of both sexes. It had four hospitals: The Sisters of Mercy on Sawicz street (114 beds for 2,541 patients treated in a year), the hospital of the Sisters of Mercy at St James (225 beds and 1191 patients in a year), the hospital of the Infant Jesus on Misjonarska street, dedicated to children (229 patients per year) and the Jewish hospital

---

53     *Ibidem*, pp. 83–84.

54     M. B r e n s z t e j n , *Biblioteka uniwersytecka w Wilnie do roku 1832-go*, Vilnius 1922, p. 90.

on Nos. 546 and 548 Żmudzka street (208 beds and 2072 patients per year). In addition to these four there were three Academy clinics – medical, surgical and obstetric (30 beds each) and a small hospital of the brothers of St John of God (the only Lithuanian infirmary looking after patients with psychological disorders, with, in 1832, 12 beds serving 35 patients). Finally, there was a large military hospital on Antokol, spread out over two separate buildings, very modern in their heyday[55]. Naturally Mianowski's work was mainly concentrated on the University clinics, later re-named as Academy clinics, belonging to the Medical-Surgical Academy.

After passing an examination in particular therapy and, based on a thesis he presented on the theory of treating T.B. with the method of Réne Laënnec, in December 1834 Mianowski was appointed to the post of adjunct of the Academy. At the time he was delivering lectures in physiology, general therapy, and on zoophysiology for veterinarians. Until 1835, in this last subject he was still able to conduct the course in Polish[56].

What was a typical week of work for Mianowski? Timetables preserved from the academic year 1834–1835 allow us to reconstruct his duties.

In the first semester he taught zoophysiology for veterinarians on Tuesdays and Saturdays from 4 to 5 p.m[57]. General therapy for third-year students was delivered in Latin on Tuesdays and Saturdays from 9 till 10.30 a.m. On Mondays, Wednesdays, and Saturdays from 10.30 a.m. till noon he lectured in Latin to second-year students on the physiology of the human body. This schedule was complemented by daily sessions for the fourth and fifth year, of what was termed the therapeutic clinic, led by Jędrzej Śniadecki with the assistance of Mianowski, from 8 a.m. and from 6 p.m. The sessions were in fact linked to the daily rounds of the wards involving the head doctor of the clinic.

So, to sum up: Mianowski's weekly schedule amounted to twelve hours in the therapeutic clinic, four teaching general therapy, six hours of the physiology of the human body and two of zoophysiology. Twenty-four in total[58]; 192 per semester if one excludes the clinical ward rounds, 384 if the rounds are part

---

55    M. Baliński, *Opisanie statystyczne miasta Wilna*, Vilnius 1835, pp. 107–108, 153.

56    Mianowski's appointment as adjunct took place on 22 December 1834 (3 January 1835). S. Kieniewicz, *Mianowski Józef*, p. 523. L. Zasztowt, *Kresy*, p. 107. Cf. J. Szujski, *Józef Mianowski rektor Szkoły Głównej Warszawskiej (wspomnienie pośmiertne)*, 'Przegląd Polski' yea. 13, 1878/1879, vol. 3, pp. 456–466; M. Łowicki, *Duch Akademii Wileńskiej. Z czasów Szymona Konarskiego pamiętnik ucznia wileńskiej Akademii Medyko-Chirurgicznej*, Vilnius 1925, p. 1 & following.

57    His course was based on Michaela von Erdelyi's *Versuch einer Zoophysiologie des Pferdes und der übrigen Haussäugethiere*, Wien 1829. Cf. J. Bieliński, *Stan nauk lekarskich*, p. 414.

58    *Ibidem*, pp. 100, 103, 106.

THE MEDICAL-SURGICAL ACADEMY – THE KONARSKI AFFAIR                    39

of the equation. To cope with such a workload, one needed not only to possess exceptional knowledge – with no time left for further improvement – but also to be in good health and display physical and intellectual resilience. The challenge was perhaps alleviated to some degree by the fact that the lectures were based on textbooks approved by the Academy. Thus, they did not require too much weight to be put on one's personal writing and research. Mianowski's zoophysiology course followed a book by an Austrian professor of veterinary studies, Michael von Erdelyi, while in physiology he took his cue from Augusto Sebastiani[59].

Physiology was a subject that Mianowski lectured in till the end of his tenure at the Academy. In the last years of its activity, he also taught what was referred to at the time as general physicians' subject matter (*vrachebnoye vieshchestvosloviye* – the examination of medical substances) as well as the art of writing prescriptions. Short curricula of these subjects in the academic year 1839–1840 have been preserved, written in somewhat opaque and rather convoluted language[60].

> Physiology was a subject of lectures in the Latin language, delivered for four and a half hours every week by the full professor Józef Mianowski, based on a work by Sebastiani (*Physiologia generalis*, Groningae 1835. *Specialis*, Ibidem 1838). After presenting the differences between organic and inorganic bodies the lecture contained: an explication of the concept of the life force and its salient features, a determination of the position held by the mature, most highly developed animals in the order of organic creatures, it described the structure of their bodies in general chemical and anatomic conditions and explained the path taken by the organic beginnings of both simple and anatomically complex parts, and finally by the various systems and organs that comprise the body of an animal. Presented physiology was the precise functioning of processes of adaptation (*assimilatio*), sensitivity to stimuli and questions of propagation[61].

Mianowski taught medicine and prescription writing in Latin, basing the lectures on the German-language texts of Fleischmann[62] and Richter[63], for four and a half hours a week for each subject.

---

59    J. Bieliński, *Uniwersytet Wileński (1579–1831)*, vol. 3, Kraków 1899–1900, p. 443. A.A. Sebastiani, *Physiologia generalis*, Groningae 1835; *idem, Physiologia specialis*, Groningae 1838.

60    RGIA, f. 733, op. 95, e.hr. 401, *Otčet po Imperatorskoj Vilensoj Mediko-Chirurgičeskoj Akademej za 1840 god*, sheet (k.) 10, 13.

61    *Ibidem*, sheet (k.) 10.

62    Fleischmann, Melh form. Med. Concin. Permultis exemp. Illustr., Vind. [avae] 1832.

63    Richter, *Ausführt. Arzneumittellehre*, B. 5, Wien 1832. Possibly August Gottlob Richter (1742–1812).

Detailed accounts were given of the essence of medications, their effects, and the sub-division of physicians' remedies into classes and categories, with a description of the strength of each of them, and in relation to the dosage and modality of their application as physicians are wont to prescribe. As to the art of writing prescriptions there was an introduction to the general concepts of weights and measures, followed by a detailed presentation, with examples, of the different ways of prescribing medicines, both for external and internal use; after that, the participants engaged in practical exercises related to these skills.

The year 1835 was especially propitious in the career of the young doctor. In May he was promoted to the seventh grade in the ranking of government employees: he was a councillor to the court, backdated to September 1833, and in October he received yet another diamond ring – his third – for exemplary service[64].

By that time, he had several works in progress, including clinical observations and extracts from international medical literature, leading to a magnum opus which was to ensure him a professorial post in the Academy. It was eventually published in two volumes by the firm of Zawadzki in 1837 – a comprehensive treatise *On the Fractures of Bones*[65].

Józef Bieliński provides us with an overview of this work. The first chapters, from the first to the sixth, were devoted to the discussion of general issues concerning bone fractures. The following chapters, from the seventh to the twelfth, concerned the analysis of fractures of individual bones. The first, general part, dealt with the classification and sub-division of fractures. The causes of general fractures and the issues of diagnosis, prognosis and treatment of fractures were discussed. Mianowski also presented the theory of the formation of ossification (*callus*).

In the second part, the author presented what was known at the time about fractures of various parts of the skeleton. Fractures were discussed in the following order (Chapter 7): A. Fractures of the head bones: 1) bones of the nose, 2) zygomatic bone, 3) upper jaw, 4) lower jaw. As Bieliński noted, there was no mention of the skull bones. In the eighth chapter, the author dealt with: B. Fractures of the trunk bones, in the following order: 1) vertebral fractures, 2) sternal bone, 3) ribs, 4) pelvic bones. In the ninth chapter, C. Fractures of the upper limbs (higher members, according to Mianowski's term) are presented: 1) shoulder blades, 2) clavicle, 3) arm (the latter divided into fractures: a) neck, b) shaft and c) supracondillotic part), 4) forearm (divided into fractures:

---

64     His confirmation as court councillor was awarded retrospectively from 1 September 1833, by decree of the governing Senate dated 15 May 1835.

65     [J. Mianowski], *O złamaniach kości, przez* [...], printed by Zawadzki, vol. 1, 210 pages + III tables; vol. 2, 270 pages + X tablic, Vilnius 1837.

THE MEDICAL-SURGICAL ACADEMY – THE KONARSKI AFFAIR 41

a) both bones, b) spoked (fibula), c) ulnar bone, 5) outgrowth fractures (divided into: (a) fist bones, (b) hand bones and (c) finger bones. The tenth chapter discusses D. Fractures of the lower limbs, divided into: 1) fractures of the thigh, 2) patellae, 3) shins, 4) feet. All these types of fractures are arranged in detail, as they are in the ninth chapter (letter C)[66].

Mianowski's treatise received a positive review in volume 14 of the new edition of 'Scientific Depictions and Deliberations'[67]. He was praised for the thoroughness of his taxonomy and elaboration but criticised for the inadequacy of the Polish language employed in the terminology[68]. According to Bieliński, there was speculation among some alumni of the Academy that Seweryn Gałęzowski, an outstanding surgeon and associate professor of the Medical Faculty of Vilnius University since 1828, contributed to the creation of *On Fractures*. It was even believed that Gałęzowski, not Mianowski, was the real author of the work[69].

It seems likely that these rumours were unfounded. Mianowski and Gałęzowski had been friends since their schooling in the county of Uman', and that friendship was all the stronger after Mianowski's arrival in Vilnius. There is no doubt that Gałęzowski, who from 1824 onwards was an adjunct in the University clinic, a favourite and friend of Pelikan and his successor to the Chair of surgery, was able to help Mianowski during his studies. But in 1828 the University sent Gałęzowski on a scholarly mission abroad from which he never returned. Engaged in the struggles of the November rising he was granted an amnesty but decided to stay beyond the borders of the Empire[70]. It cannot be ruled out, however, that Mianowski cooperated with Gałęzowski over his treatise. Even before 1828 Mianowski had assisted Gałęzowski in preparing his course in surgery, picking out articles in French and German periodicals[71].

Mianowski's medical practice was also flourishing. Apart from heading the medical department in the Jewish hospital, he was gradually, as an assistant to the by now rather grey-haired Jędrzej Śniadecki, becoming one of the most sought-after doctors in Vilnius. He was on call not just as a physician but also as a friend to the aristocratic salons of the Günters, Wittgensteins, Łopacińskis and many others[72].

---

66  J. Bieliński, *Stan nauk lekarskich*, p. 310.
67  'Wizerunki i Roztrząsania Naukowe' 1837, vol. 25, pp. 103–119.
68  J. Bieliński, *Uniwersytet Wileński*, vol. 2, p. 340.
69  *Idem, Stan nauk lekarskich*, p. 310.
70  H. Więckowska, W. Szumowski, *Gałęzowski Seweryn (1801–1878)*, PSB, vol. 7, Kraków–Wrocław 1948–1958, p. 252.
71  J. Bieliński, *Stan nauk lekarskich*, pp. 576–578.
72  G. z Günterów Puzynina, *W Wilnie i w dworach litewskich*, pp. 128, 194, 290–291.

In June 1837 he was appointed honorary member of the Imperial Medical-Surgical Academy of St Petersburg, a title corresponding (more or less) to a doctorate *honoris causa* which also testified to scientific and practical achievements). In mid-August he went abroad for a year to further his studies[73].

The application to go abroad was submitted by Mianowski together with another doctor, Józef Korzeniewski, son of Jan (1806–1870). They planned the journey was for August, to be able to take part in the September congress of doctors and nature researchers in Prague, and the assistant professors justified it with the desire to 'meet many outstanding' scholars. This was an important argument from the point of view of the Academy's policy[74]. Elena A. Vishlenkova points out that both medics were alumni of the Medical Institute of Vilnius University, from which they graduated in 1822. Mianowski received the title of Doctor of Medicine in 1828, Korzeniewski a year later. Both worked in clinics of the University – from 1832, of the Academy. Korzeniewski specialized in surgery, and Mianowski in physiology. In 1834, both became adjuncts at the Medical and Surgical Academy[75].

Mianowski sent detailed reports to the Academy regarding his officially granted leave of absence; he wrote whom he had met and talked to, and which places he had visited. Having stayed in Prussia and Austria he asked for an extension of his sojourn and permission to make additional excursions to France and Britain. The Ministry demurred, arguing that physiology was not such a specialist field of study as to warrant devoting to it so much time and money, but he managed at least to reach Paris. It was probably at this point that what won the argument was that Mianowski's research stretched beyond physiology and into gynaecology and midwifery. It would thus have been seen as worthwhile for him to stay in Paris. On the other hand, it is possible that he went to Paris without informing the authorities.

He returned to Vilnius in August 1838. As mentioned earlier, in addition to Prague in Bohemia he had stayed in Berlin and Paris. This resulted in further professional successes. By December he had become a corresponding member of the Royal Berlin Medical-Surgical Society, named the Hufeland after the prominent doctor, professor of pathology and special therapy in Berlin, Christoph Wilhelm Hufeland (later the popular *Hufelandische Stiftungen*), and

---

73    Mianowski became an honorary member of the Imperial Medical-Surgical Academy in Petersburg on 23 June 1837. The only Pole to have preceded him in obtaining this title was Jędrzej Śniadecki, in 1817. Cf. J. R ó z i e w i c z, *Polsko-rosyjskie powiązania naukowe*, p. 185. Mianowski remained abroad from 15 August 1837 to 15 August 1838.

74    Lietuvos Valstybinis Istorijos Archyvas [LVIA], f. 720, op. 1, d. 4537, sheet (k.) 30.

75    E.A. V i s h l e n k o v a, book in preparation (information from the author).

THE MEDICAL-SURGICAL ACADEMY – THE KONARSKI AFFAIR 43

two years later he was made an honorary member of the Society of Physical and Chemical Sciences in Paris[76]. The latter choice was undoubtedly influenced by the work published in 1838: *Observationes exactis medici instituti a. 1834–1835 depromptae clinici*, which – as Stefan Kieniewicz writes – is the history of the Vilnius internal medicine clinic with a particular emphasis on the period when in charge of it was Jędrzej Śniadecki[77]. Incidentally, the announcement of this work was also rewarded with personal praise from the then Minister of the Interior, who was ultimately in charge of the Academy. It can also be added here that Mianowski had already published reports on the clinic's activities, among others in the 'Medical-Surgical and Pharmaceutical Journal of Vilnius'[78]. During this time, he also wrote his largest, already mentioned, two-volume work in the field of surgery *On the Fractures of Bones*.

Apparently, another task that Mianowski was commissioned to carry out during his stay abroad was to persuade the then twenty-two-year-old Berlin neurologist, Robert Remak, already known in the medical world for the discovery of non-core nerve fibres (known as the Remak fibres), to come to Vilnius and start working at the Academy. In that, however, he was unsuccessful[79].

After returning from abroad, Mianowski taught physiology at the Academy, initially as an associate professor, and from January 1840 as a full professor[80].

Mianowski's accommodation in Vilnius was probably on the premises of the Chemical College, which Jędrzej Śniadecki had instructed to be built much earlier, at the end of the 18th century, replacing a former Calvinist chapel. It was opposite the church of St Michael, at the crossroads between St Michael's Lane and Wolan Street[81].

There seemed to be no stopping Mianowski as he pursued a brilliant medical career and scaled the rungs of the tsarist Empire's administrative hierarchy. But on his return from abroad he unexpectedly found himself in a quite new and unforeseen role. Loyal as he was to the Russian state, the scholar and

---

76    He became a corresponding member in Berlin on 12 December 1837, and an honorary one in Paris on 7 April 1839.

77    *Observationes exactis medici instituti a. 1834–1835 depromptae clinici*, 'Collectanea Medico-Chirurgica Acad. Vil.' 1838, pp. 233–250. Report in 'Pamiętnik Towarzystwa Lekarskiego Warszawskiego' 1839, vol. 2, pp. 650–653. Cf. BN II, manuscript (rkps) 7861, L. J a n o w s k i, *Notatki bio-bibliograficzne dotyczące osób z kresów wschodnich dawnej Rzeczypospolitej*, vol. 6, sheet (k.) 103.

78    Zdanie sprawy z kliniki, 'Dziennik Medyczno-Chirurgiczny i Farmaceutyczny Wileński' 1830.

79    W. Z a h o r s k i, *Zarys dziejów Cesarskiego Towarzystwa Lekarskiego*, p. 70.

80    LVIA, f. 721, op. 1, d. 24, sheet (k.) 3.

81    H. Lichocka, *Chemia Jędrzeja Śniadeckiego*, 'Opuscula Musealia' 2019, no. 26, p. 25. Information on Mianowski's apartment: J. B i e l i ń s k i, *Stan nauk lekarskich*, pp. 578–579.

44                                                                                                    CHAPTER 2

scientist needed to prove, at whatever cost, that he was also a fervent Pole. The situation took him by surprise, and the position he took in circumstances which were never fully explained came perilously close to ending in tragedy.

### The Konarski Affair

Mianowski probably first met Szymon Konarski, emissary of the émigré Association of the Polish People, in Vilnius, before going abroad; but certainly, it was no earlier than the end of 1835 and no later than the first half of 1837. During his first stay in Vilnius Konarski assumed the leadership of the clandestine union of students of the Medical-Surgical Academy, whose members included the undergraduates Franciszek Sawicz and Jan Zahorski; among its sympathisers were Canon Ludwik Trynkowski, the lawyer Stanisław Kozakiewicz and, apparently, some professors.

Konarski returned to Vilnius several times. In May 1838, with police on his trail he narrowly avoided arrest in the wine bar of Nitel Rosental (aka Tryntroch) in Niemiecka street, and for a brief period went into hiding in the clinic of the Academy, feigning illness. This refuge was secured for him by the students Sawicz, Zahorski and Aleksander Hryckiewicz.

According to Władysław Zahorski, all of this took place with the consent of Józef Mianowski, and indeed it was apparently Mianowski himself, assisted by the student Aleksander Eisenbletter, who oversaw Konarski's transfer from the wine bar to his clinic. However, this did not prevent the emissary being arrested along with his travelling companion, the student Ignacy Rodziewicz, on their way to Minsk on 27 May 1838. Archbishop Zygmunt Feliński believed that not only did Mianowski come to the aid of Konarski, but he was one of the organisers of the conspiracy[82].

It cannot be ruled out that, as W. Zahorski claims, Konarski had already been a patient of the Academy's clinic at an earlier juncture, perhaps at the end of 1835 or in 1836. That may have enabled him to meet some of the academy's professors. Much less clear, however, is the putative role played by Mianowski himself in providing shelter for Konarski in May 1838, because according to administrative documents he was away from Vilnius until 15 August 1838,

---

82    W. Zahorski, *Szymon Konarski. (Życie i czyny)*, Vilnius 1907, p. 40; S. Kieniewicz, *Konarski Szymon*, PSB, vol. 13, Wrocław 1967–1968, p. 479; A. Barszczewska, *Szymon Konarski*, Warsaw 1976, p. 101 & following. Cf. J. Remy, *Higher Education and National Identity. Polish Student Activism in Russia 1832–1863*, Helsinki 2000, p. 109 & following.

# THE MEDICAL-SURGICAL ACADEMY – THE KONARSKI AFFAIR

returning over two months after the arrest[83]. However, there are materials from his stay abroad which indicate that in May 1838 Mianowski was still in Vilnius.

On the day of Konarski's execution, carried out on the morning of 27 February 1839 in Pohulanka, Mianowski is reported to have burst into tears during his lecture. He was himself arrested one and half years later, on 9 September 1840. Ten days later another professor of medicine from the academic clinic was arrested: Gustaw Belke[84].

By the first of September of the previous year Mianowski had already reached the sixth grade in the administration structure, with the position of collegial councillor, while from 24 January 1840 he was full professor of physiology at the Academy[85]. Kieniewicz writes that, at the moment of his arrest he had in his hand a letter appointing him to a chair in Petersburg, on account of the expected closure of the Vilnius academy.

The minister of public education at the time, Sergey S. Uvarov, had decided to dismiss Mianowski from office as far back as April 1841, confirming that decision in September, even though the Vilnius governor-general Fyodor J. Mirkowicz argued in his correspondence that no proof had been found against the doctor, and he himself did not confess to anything[86].

Mianowski was incarcerated from September 1840 to the autumn of 1841, a total of 14 months[87]. During that period the Medical-Surgical Academy of Moscow strove unsuccessfully to retrieve the money it had sent to cover Mianowski's transfer to Moscow, where prior to his arrest he had agreed to lecture in physiology.

His long period of interrogation in prison took a heavy toll: he came very close to taking his own life. Kieniewicz makes it clear that what saved him were his Petersburg connections with influential patients. Pressure was also brought to bear on Uvarov by members of both Polish and Russian aristocracy. We know that in Vilnius the moving force behind the campaign to free him was Princess Leonilda Wittgenstein of the Bariatyńskis[88]. We can surmise

---

83   Mianowski's personal assistance is confirmed in: Z.S. F e l i ń s k i, *Pamiętniki*, Warsaw 1986, s. 124–125; W. Z a h o r s k i, *Szymon Konarski*, s. 46.

84   Belke was arrested on 19 September 1840. S. K i e n i e w i c z, *Mianowski Józef*, p. 523; L. Z a s z t o w t, *Kresy*, pp. 113, 117; RGIA, f. 733, op. 31, d. 128, *Ob areštovanii Professorov Mianovskogo i Bel'ka. Ob. uvolnienii ih ot služby*, sheet (k.) 21 & following. Toż LVIA, f. 567, op. 2, no. 4537.

85   RGIA, f. 733, op. 147, е.нк. 752, *Formulărnyj spisok o službe*.

86   S. K i e n i e w i c z, *Mianowski Józef*, p. 523; RGIA, f. 733, op. 31, d. 128, Letter from S. Uvarov to do F. Mirkowicz, 1 April 1841; Letter from Mirkowicz to Uvarov, 5 May 1841, sheets (k.) 21–22 & following.

87   LVIA, fond 721, op. 1, d. 24, k. 8.

88   G. z Günterów P u z y n i n a, *W Wilnie i w dworach litewskich*, s. 290.

that these efforts had the desired effect on the Investigation Commission in Vilnius whose members were: Aleksandr A. Kavelin as chairman, Colonel Vladimir I. Nazimov, later to become Vilnius's governor-general, and Colonel Asinkrit I. Lomachevsky, head of the gendarmerie (and author of memoirs from that time, published in 1873[89]). All three played a crucial role in freeing Mianowski, and Kavelin was even named the professor's protector[90]. Professor Gustaw Belke was also declared innocent.

On 24 October 1841 Mianowski was released from prison, cleared of all charges[91]. He received 14 months' back pay and an ex-gratia payment, amounting to 5000 roubles in total. Furthermore, he received confirmation of his appointment in Petersburg to the chair of psychiatry[92]. We may add that for a certain time the authorities considered the possibility of transferring him to Moscow to take up the post of professor of physiology at that city's Medical-Surgical Academy, an idea which was finally abandoned[93]. The information about his arrest was removed from his personal files, and the whole case was so thoroughly covered up that even in mid-1841 (and so at a time when he was still under arrest) some influential imperial officials did not know if his arrest was in connection with the Konarski case or that of Józef Zaliwski[94].

We shall probably never find out if Mianowski was indeed involved in the hiding of Szymon Konarski. If he was, then his release must have been secured by persons at the highest level of the state, and the final decision would undoubtedly have fallen to Nicolas I himself. It would also have been the Tsar's decision to offer Mianowski an amnesty when it was proven he could not have participated directly in hiding the Polish conspirator since he was abroad at the time. The question of the dates of that stay abroad was central to proving Mianowski's innocence. And there is no doubt that setting up for him a separate Chair of psychiatry in Petersburg was a decision taken by the Tsar[95].

---

89   See A.I. Lomačevskij, *Iz vospominanij žandarma 30. i 40. godov*, S.-Peterburg 1873.

90   G. z Günterów Puzynina, *W Wilnie i w dworach litewskich*, p. 311; T. Bobrowski, *Pamiętnik mojego życia*, vol. 1, p. 450; J. Remy, *Higher Education and National Identity*, p. 136 & following.

91   LVIA, fond 720, op. 1, d. 4537, k. 30.

92   He received precisely 1428 roubles and 57 kopecks in moral damages, equivalent to a year's income. LVIA, fond 720, op. 1, d. 4537, k. 30. In total, according to other sources, his compensation amounted to 5000 roubles. *Ibidem*, k. 36.

93   RGIA, f. 733, op. 31, d. 128. Letter from the Ministry of Public Education to the rector of the Vilnius Academy, 1 August 1840, k. 7.

94   *Ibidem*, Letter from the Vilnius General-Governor to Uvarov, 5 May 1841, sheet (k.) 22. Cf. B. Limanowski, *Józef Zaliwski bohater z powstania 1830–31 r.*, [np] 1913.

95   LVIA, fond 729, op. 1, d. 4537, k. 36.

# THE MEDICAL-SURGICAL ACADEMY – THE KONARSKI AFFAIR

A rather critical opinion regarding Mianowski as a doctor during his work at the Vilnius Medical-Surgery Academy was given by Józef Bieliński, an authority on the local medical milieu. It is, however, a very unfair judgement – in my opinion – though interesting in the details it provides of the doctor's relations with colleagues and students. Bieliński writes:

> In the Academy he lectured in the Polish language on zoophysiology following the work by Erdelyi up to the year 1835, when Jakowicki, having acquired the degree of veterinary surgeon, took over the Chair; while Mianowski, promoted on 27th April of that year to the position of associate professor, began lecturing on physiology based on the manual by Sebastiani. Aside from which, he was Śniadecki's adjunct in the therapeutical clinic.

> He came from Ukraine. Born in 1804 in Uman', he studied hard at the then famous Uman' gymnasium, going on to study medicine in Vilnius and in 1827 graduating as a doctor. Staying at the University, he became an assistant at the clinic, whose head at the time was Śniadecki. He received his doctorate in 1828. Mianowski had a great friend in Seweryn Gałęzowski and took an active part in the latter's preparations for a course in surgery by selecting for him appropriate articles from French and German periodicals. It seemed likely that Mianowski would follow in the footsteps of his friend the surgeon – but his appointment to the post of Śniadecki's assistant heralded a change of direction. In the Academy he returned one more time to surgical work but was never a surgeon. In the last year of the University's existence, he was directed to deliver lectures in physiology and was entrusted with running a temporary military infirmary, for wounded patients. He was generally respected in the Academy both by colleagues and students. He travelled for two years abroad, mainly applying himself to physiology, a field which at that time was undergoing huge developments. We mentioned earlier that he was instructed to recruit Remak for the Academy, which mission he did not accomplish since Remak rejected the offer. He returned to Vilnius and spent some time in prison, from which he was released thanks to the protection of Kavelin, who arrived in Vilnius at that time and specifically for that purpose. Several months later he was awarded a full professorship. In 1840 he left Vilnius to take up the post of professor of physiology in Petersburg. [...]

> Dr Łowicki and Grabowski have sent over a description of Mianowski from his days as professor in Vilnius. We all remember him as the rector of the Main School, a serious, ageing man; let us see what he was like in his time at the Academy. Grabowski writes: 'Mianowski was tall, dark-haired, somewhat bald; a tight, expressive face, swarthy complexion; an extremely polite demeanour, friendly, pleasant; a fast, easy way of speaking, but with not much expression. With his popularity he gained the hearts of the young'. 'He was well suited', writes Dr Łowicki, 'to being a good professor, but he could be better as a rector and a doctor practising in wealthy homes, because in his youth he was a handsome, debonair man-about-town rather than a good professor – daily he wasn't too keen on being the latter. At Śniadecki's side he worked well and was in the right place, but since he failed in his aspiration to take Śniadecki's place, and

he may have considered Rymkiewicz to be less worthy than him, so he treated his work in the infirmary and his evening clinical visits as something of a chore. The same applied to physiology course, which he took over from Rymkiewicz in 1838/9. He would deliver one lecture well, to the benefit of the students, and the next two would be slapdash in the extreme. He was incredibly lively, polite in a dandyish way; in his manner of speaking, he was almost on the verge of stuttering ... he would always wear a tailcoat, or in winter a lightweight brown Spanish jacket. The students joked that his flat by the chemistry room was never heated, because his youthful blood was enough to keep him warm. I knew his students in Petersburg, and they spoke about him in almost the same way – that he had all the skills necessary to be a professor but gave more shoddy lectures than any that were useful to the students'. Later on, Dr Łowicki comments that on issues of great import one could not rely on Mianowski: being lively and scatter-brained he could not conceal what needed to be hidden, and in his forgetfulness, he left subjects of great weight to the will of God. That the consequences of this could be most dire was something personally experienced by Dr Łowicki[96].

It would appear, that these opinions contain a trace of jealousy, since none of the doctors mentioned by Bieliński had a career comparable to that of Mianowski. But the comments on the lack of concern for quality in the lectures are quite probably correct. This is confirmed in later memories of the higher education institutions of Petersburg and Warsaw. Unquestionably, he was an excellent practitioner of medicine. Teaching, on the other hand, he sometimes regarded as a necessary evil.

---

96  J. Bieliński, *Stan nauk lekarskich*, pp. 576–579.

CHAPTER 3

# Russia – Petersburg

*Before my eyes stretched a larger part*
*Of Petersburg with boulevards and chapel spires.*
*It was truly a composition by the Velvet Breughel.*
*Words cannot convey the colours of that painting. [...]*
*You need to be a Russian, an emperor even,*
*not to let Petersburg life overwhelm you now:*
*great fêtes in the evenings, such as only Russia sees, courtly praise in the morning,*
*ceremonies, receptions, public celebrations, parades on sea and land [...]*[1]

In Petersburg at the end of January 1842 Mianowski began lecturing in psychiatry at the Academy, dividing his time between that and the position of chief doctor of internal medicine in the Second Hospital of the Land Armed Forces[2]. The hospital was opened in 1840 and placed under the aegis of the Academy, which permitted a larger intake of students. It was housed in the buildings of the former naval hospital, not far from the main edifice of the Academy (to which we shall return later). In August he was also put in charge of the gynaecological and children's clinics, while retaining his post of chief doctor in the military hospital[3]. At the same time – on the academic side – he lectured in other subjects at the St Petersburg Imperial Medical-Surgical Academy where, as mentioned above, he was a professor at the women's and children's clinics and the hospital therapy clinic in the Second Land Armed Forces Hospital[4]. The Academy reported directly to the Ministry of War. He resided at No. 2 Nikolskaya street[5].

---

1 Despite his distaste for Russia and criticism of its political system, the Marquis Astolphe de Custine did in his famous pamphlet acknowledge the glamour and beauty of its northern capital. See A. de C u s t i n e, *Listy Z Rosji. Rosja w 1839 roku*, Paris 1988, pp. 81, 84.
2 From 19 January 1842. RGIA, f. 733, op. 147, e.hr. 752, *Formularniy spisok o sluzhbe*.
3 Appointed on 22 August 1842. *Ibidem*.
4 *Sankt-Peterburskij Adress Kalendar za 1850 g.*, part 1, Ch. 2, pp. 33, 34. https://www.booksite.ru/fulltext/164547/index.html.
5 [N.I. C y ł o w], *Gorodskoy ukazatel', ili adressnaya kniga prisutstviennyh miest, uchebnyh zavedienij, vrachei [...] na 1850 god*, Sankt Peterburg 1849, p. 85. Nikolskaya street, not far from the cathedral of St Nicholas, bore this name from 1769. In 1892 it was renamed Glinka Street. The present Nikolskaya street is in the Vyborg district, far from the centre of Petersburg. https://vivaldi.nlr.ru/bx000040079/view/?#page=107.

© BRILL SCHÖNINGH, 2024 | DOI:10.30965/9783657794720_004

A few words about the Academy's history. Founded on 18th December 1798 in the reign of Paul I as the Medical-Surgical Academy, by the mid-19th century it was being officially termed 'Imperial', though formally the word was only added to its name on 10th June 1881, when it adopted the new name of Imperial Warfare-Medical Academy. On its foundation it reported to the Medical College; in 1803 its oversight was transferred to the Ministry of the Interior; in 1810 it was placed under the aegis of the Ministry of Public Education, before returning to the Ministry of the Interior in 1822. From 1838 it found itself managed by the Ministry of War and its Department of Military Settlements (*voyennykh poselyeny*); then from 1857 it reported directly to the minister of war, and from 1866 to the chief warfare-medical (warfare-sanitary) inspector[6].

The Imperial Warfare-Medical Academy was an institution of higher education whose task was to train doctors for practice in the land and naval forces and to upgrade their qualifications. Its main overall aim was to develop the medical sciences in Russia. It was managed by: a meeting of professors and its chairman (1798–1808), a president (1808–1867) and – in its last period – a commander (1867–1917). Scientific issues were dealt with by a professorial conference. Between 1838 and 1854 the academy's structure also included a curator, supported by a chancellery (re-named in 1846 as a governing board). The Academy's medical department was flanked by veterinary and pharmaceutical units.

In various periods of its existence the Academy comprised institutes (Anatomical-Physiological, Chemical and Physical-Surgical) and clinics: the Second Hospital of the Land Armed Forces (a clinic, from 1869 onwards), and the Naval Hospital. It also contained a museum and botanical gardens, a library, and other units. In 1809–1844 the Academy also had a branch in Moscow[7]. Among its eminent professors were the psychiatrist and neurophysiologist Vladimir M. Bekhteriev (1857–1927), the clinician and anatomopathologist Sergey P. Botkin (1832–1889), the physiologist and Nobel laureate Ivan P. Pavlov (1849–1946), the outstanding surgeon Nikolai I. Pirogov (1810–1881) and the physiologist Ivan M. Sechenov (1829–1905). During Mianowski's period of employment at the Academy one of the students, and then from 1862 a professor of chemistry, was Aleksandr P. Borodin, an outstanding composer and member of the innovative group of composers known as the Mighty

---

6  *Imperatorskaya Voenno-Medicinskaya Akademia (1798–1918)*, [in:] *Putevoditel' po rossiyjskikh arkhivakh* f. 316, e.hr. 43567, (1800–1917), op. 1–69, 71. http://guides.rusarchives.ru/terms/17/8651/imperatorskaya-voenno-medicinskaya-akademiya.

7  *Ibidem*.

Five – the others being Miliy A. Balakirev, César A. Cui, Modest P. Mussorgsky, and Nikolai A. Rimsky-Korsakov.

When Mianowski started working in Petersburg, the highest authority among the lecturers of the Academy was Nikolai Pirogov, who took up his post at the same time. Sechenov, on the other hand, began teaching there in 1860, by which time Mianowski had already retired. By Tadeusz Bobrowski's account, two Polish professors other than Mianowski were employed at the Academy: the pharmacologist Henryk Kułakowski, who arrived in Petersburg almost at the same time as Mianowski and initially specialised in skin diseases[8], and Bujalski. Polish medical practitioners with a well-established position in the city included doctors Jerzy Kozłowski, Smuglewicz and Radziwiłłowicz[9].

Both the edifice of the Medical-Surgical Academy later re-named the Imperial Warfare-Medical Academy, and the Second Hospital of the Land Armed Forces were in a building complex on the Vyborgskaya side of Petersburg – flanked by today's Academician Lebedev Street (from the east), the Bolshoy Samsonevsky Prospekt (from the west), Botkinskaya Street (from the north) and from the south the Pirogovskaya Nabierzhnaya on the bank of the Neva. When in 1835 the naval hospital was relocated on the Fontanka bank, all its premises were taken over by the Second Infantry Hospital, which is where Mianowski started his tenure[10].

He thus had all his workplaces in one location. However, when around 1850 he resided at no.2 Nikolskaya Street (the present-day Glinka Street) in the Admiralty District (*Admiraltieysky Rayon*), the distance from his apartment to the Academy was approximately 6 km. On foot, this took some 1.5 hours; the journey by horse-drawn carriage took about half that time.

---

8    *Kulakovskiy Genrik Kazimirovich*, [in:] *Russkij biograficheskiy slovar'*, Sankt-Peterburg–Moskva 1896–1918; G.M. Grecenstein, *Kulakovskiy Genrik*, [in:] *Enciklopedicheskiy Slovar' Brokgauza i Efrona*, Sankt-Peterburg 1890–1907. See https://ru.googl-info.com/87552/1/kulakovskiy-genrikh-kazimirovich.html.

9    T. Bobrowski, *Pamiętnik mojego życia*, vol. 1, pp. 448–449.

10   *Акт по результатам государственной историко-культурной экспертизы проектной документации на проведение работ по сохранению объекта культурного наследия федерального значения «Мариинский приют для воинов-инвалидов» по адресу: г. СанктПетербург, Большой Сампсониевский пр., д. 11, литера А (Большой Сампсониевский пр., 11; Комиссара Смирнова ул., 12, лит. А), входящего в состав объекта культурного наследия федерального значения «Академия Императорская Медико-хирургическая Военно-Медицинская» » (Санкт-Петербург, Академика Лебедева ул., 2, 4, 6, 8; Боткинская ул., 8, 10, 12, 13, 17, 20, 23; Пироговская наб., 1, 3; Большой Сампсониевский пр., 1, 3, 5, 11; Комиссара Смирнова ул., 10, 12, лит. А; Лесной пр., 2; Клиническая ул., 5, 9), разработанной ООО «Квадр» в 2019 г. (шифр проекта: № 07-19-П-РРФ)*, p. 11. http://kgiop.ru/media/uploads/userfiles/2019/11/06/01-26-2321.pdf.

52                                                                                    CHAPTER 3

What impression did Petersburg make on Mianowski? It is likely that on arriving from provincial Vilnius he would have been astounded. Regrettably, we have no evidence in the sources of those first reflections on the capital. What we do know is that to his last days he always returned to the city. His feelings may have been like those that Petersburg exerted on other Polish residents. Around 1894, when Nicolas II was acceding to the throne, the then youthful prince Mieczysław Pierejesławski-Jałowiecki described the city in these words:

> Petersburg struck me as beautiful. On a frosty, sun-filled February day the snow creaks under one's feet, glitters in the sun. Sleighs glide past soundlessly. A white flurry of snow bilges from the horses' hooves and settles in a silvery frost on the beaver collars, the beards of the sleigh-drivers, wrapped Russian-style in navy blue quilted coats, secured by a silk, generally red belt. Snow caps have settled on the trees in the parks and squares. A thick coat of snow has covered the streets, roofs and cornices of houses. On such days I walked unhurriedly on the bank of the Neva, unable to take my eyes of those teams of horses for which Petersburg was renowned. On one side I had the Winter Palace, a massive edifice in the style of late Baroque. On the other, beyond the low granite wall, the frozen, white glistening Neva stretched far into the distance, while across on the opposite bank from a bluish haze emerged the contours of the Pietropavlovsk Fortress and the shores of the Vassilevskaya Island[11].

Mianowski's later attachment to Petersburg seems to mirror the feelings of Adam Mickiewicz, who could not resist visiting the city three times between 1824 and 1827. It later transpired that those were the happiest years in the Bard's life.

In October Mianowski was confirmed as an honorary member of the St Petersburg Orphanage Society; two years later, in September 1844, he became director of the Alexandrian-Marian Institute[12].

In the mid-1840s Mianowski, similarly to what had taken place in Vilnius, gradually devoted himself to medical practice as a gynaecologist and obstetrician in the higher echelons of the capital's society[13]. In that period, he received official recognition for 15 years of irreproachable work and became a knight of the order of St. Stanislas, second class. In November 1845 he was dispatched by the minister of war to inspect military hospitals in Dyneburg and Vilnius[14].

In June 1847 he went abroad, including to Paris, with official instructions to familiarise himself with the organisation and practical side of clinics there

---

11   M. Jałowiecki, *Na skraju imperium i inne wspomnienia*, Warsaw 2014, p. 52.
12   Appointed honorary member on 24 October 1842; director, on 2 September 1844. From 1 September 1843 he was already a councillor of state (Fifth Grade).
13   E. Ziółkowska, *Petersburg po polsku*, Warsaw 2011, pp. 268–269.
14   Commendation for irreproachable service, 22 August 1844; order of St Stanislas, second class, 14 April 1845. See RGIA, f. 733, op. 147, e.hr. 752, *Formularniy spisok o sluzhbe.*

RUSSIA – PETERSBURG

and with the latest trends in medicine. In the event, Mianowski concentrated on studying the latest achievements in obstetrics and gynaecology, counting on having a broader client base for his practice on his return. In that period, he also called on friends in Paris; these included Juliusz Słowacki, whom he met up with for the last time. The authorities agreed to extend his sojourn abroad, originally planned for five months, by a further six weeks. He returned to Petersburg in mid-December 1847[15].

On his way back he stopped over for some time in Warsaw. There he was asked to attend to the dying Prince Ksawery Drucki-Lubecki, suffering from gout. Roger Łubieński recorded that on 17th May 1846, after the doctors had left, stating that nothing more could be done and even reported Lubecki's death to the Tsar, there appeared:

> [...] five minutes after their departure a certain Dr Mianowski, a Pole from the Vilnius Academy who has now made a reputation for himself in Petersburg. He ordered that the half-deceased Lubecki be placed in a cold bath with ice and constantly applied ice to his head, saying that this could just help to bring him round a little; and indeed, he slowly began to come to, and now almost cured he leaves his bed and walks around the room.

As Jerzy Szczepański noted, the draconian method employed by the renowned doctor prolonged Łubieński's life by a couple of days (he died on 23rd May 1846)[16].

In Petersburg, too, among Mianowski's female patients were representatives of the highest nobility, including the families of ministers – such as the wife of Sergey Uvarov, Catherine *née* Razumovska – whose husband had quite recently treated the doctor so harshly. Mianowski was soon also to attend to his daughter, Princess Aleksandra Urusova[17].

His achievements in medical practice, along with his social abilities, paved Mianowski's way to the highest position. In 1848 he became court doctor to the daughter of Nicolas I, Princess Maria Nikolaevna Leuchtenberg (1819–1876) and later also to her husband, Prince Maximilian Leuchtenberg (1817–1852). It was an informal position (I found no trace of an official appointment), but it secured access to the imperial family.

---

15     Permission to travel abroad, 27 April 1847. He departed on 11 June 1847. Agreement to extend his stay, 3 October 1847; returned on 13 December 1847.

16     J. Szczepański, *Książę Ksawery Drucki-Lubecki 1778–1846*, Warsaw 2008, pp. 81–82; R. Łubieński, *Generał Tomasz Pomian hrabia Łubieński*, vol. 2, Warsaw 1899, pp. 451–452. Cited in J. Szczepański.

17     Cf. *Uvarov Sergei Semenovich*, [in:] D.N. Shilov, *Gosudarstvennye deateli Rossiyskoy Imperii 1802–1917. Biobibliograficheskiyj spravochnik*, St. Petersburg 2002, pp. 762–763.

The position and influence Mianowski gained at the imperial court enabled him – one of the few Petersburg Poles who had such possibilities – to assist compatriots in need. We know he helped many, among them Tadeusz Bobrowski (1829–1894), who recalled in his journal:

> The most noble-minded Mianowski dedicated half of his day to his patients, but the other half, if not indeed the greater part, to intervening on behalf of his fellow countrymen in all sorts of areas and on all manner of issues. For himself, he never requested anything – for his people, he made requests constantly and for all [...], for any compatriot who turned to him he offered advice, protection, sometimes money, and always willingly and sincerely [...][18].

This was Bobrowski's account of an intervention by Mianowski:

> I found out, I no longer remember by what means, that Dr Mianowski is the physician of the minister of education, Count Uvarov. Introduced to the noble doctor by Niedzielski, I received a promise that the doctor would arrange for Princess Urusova, Count Uvarov's daughter, to write a note of recommendation to Prince Shyryński. I do not think I could have even dreamt of a more effective form of support[19].

By that time Mianowski had joined Petersburg's influential conservative coterie, close to Archbishop Ignacy Hołowiński, with whom he had anyway long been on friendly terms through the Słowacki family. Members of this circle included ultra-conservatives such as the author of *Soplica's Mementos* and *November*, Henryk Rzewuski, and the editor of the 'Petersburg Weekly', Jan Emanuel Przecławski[20]. Mianowski had similarly close relations with the later archbishop of Vilnius, Wacław Żyliński. As Mikołaj Tarkowski writes:

> [...] receiving the pallium by Father Wacław Żyliński in St. Catherine's Church in St. Petersburg on 21st December 1856, was preceded by the following events: 'Bishop Żyliński was good friends with the prior of the Dominican fathers in Petersburg and the professor of the Clerical Academy prelate Jakubielski. These two placed before the dying metropolitan Ignacy Hołowiński a letter for his signature, written by Dr Józef Mianowski and addressed to the Holy Father, requesting that Bishop Wacław Żyliński be appointed Archbishop of Mohylev'[21].

---

18  T. Bobrowski, *Pamiętnik mojego życia*, vol. 1, pp. 439, 451. Cf. A. Kijas, *Mianowski Józef*.

19  T. Bobrowski, *Pamiętnik mojego życia*, vol. 1, p. 439.

20  *Ibidem*. Cf. L. Bazylow, *Polacy w Petersburgu*, Wrocław 1984, pp. 203–205; J. Tazbir, *Wstęp*, [in:] H. Rzewuski, *Listopad*, Kraków 2000.

21  M. Tarkowski, *Polacy na Litwie i Białorusi pod rządami Aleksandra II (1855–1881). Studium historyczno-prawne*, Gdańsk 2018, p. 119. Cited in I. Wodzianowska, *Rzymskokatolicka Akademia Duchowna w Petersburgu*, Lublin 2007, pp. 5–25.

Zygmunt Szczęsny Feliński, later to become Archbishop of Warsaw, took a very critical view of this situation. He wrote:

> The dying man [Ignacy Hołowiński] had not even yet closed his eyes when ambitious intrigues broke out at his bedside by those who were hoping for his clerical bequest. No sooner had Dr Mianowski told those close to Hołowiński that he was on the point of dying than the prelates, who coveted his offices, went to the dying man's friends, imploring them for the good of the Church that they persuade him to petition the emperor and request that the persons by them indicated be appointed metropolitan and rector of the Academy[22].

As we can see, Mianowski – often called out to attend to the ailing – had many opportunities to influence not only Russian aristocrats from the imperial elite but also the princes of the Roman Catholic Church.

What made Mianowski stand out among the many Poles living in Petersburg? In the words of Bobrowski:

> The simplest issue which had even a hint of nationalism about it appeared to the Polish denizens of the capital at the time to be so embarrassing that they refused to pursue it not only in deed and word, but even in thought. The exceptions were very few. The most outstanding was Dr Mianowski, whose extensive connections in all the capital's affairs – and he had them everywhere – he drew on to aid and assist his countrymen. For himself, he did not ask anybody for anything. For his kinsmen, he asked everybody without respite. He was too busy and distracted to concentrate and organise, but [...], for any compatriot who turned to him he offered advice, protection, sometimes money, and always willingly and sincerely, to the point of exhaustion, even though he was often quite crudely taken advantage of, because often even lawyers exploited him for their own affairs[23].

Of other positive examples he mentioned only Ignacy Iwanowski of Petersburg University (died in 1836) and the general and engineer Stanisław Kierbiedź. For the most other Polish officials in the city the one redeeming feature was their general aversion to corruption and bribery and thriftiness when it came to public money. That clearly set them apart from the customary way of doing things.

Successive years brought further accolades. In April 1848 Mianowski was appointed Knight of the Order of St. Anne, second class, and in December received the highest commendation from the emperor. Half a year later, at the official behest of Princess Maria Nikolaevna, he accompanied her on a two-month tour abroad. He must have carried out his duties well, since as a

---

22    Z.S. Feliński, *Pamiętniki*, p. 439.
23    T. Bobrowski, *Pamiętnik mojego życia*, vol. 1, pp. 450–451.

56 CHAPTER 3

reward he was promoted to the Fourth Grade: an actual councillor of state, corresponding to the rank of rear admiral in the navy and major general in the army[24].

In the 1850s, Mianowski continued to be a professor at the Academy and chief doctor at the Second Hospital of Land Armed Forces in Petersburg. At the same time, he carried on practising medicine, remaining as court physician to Grand Princess Maria, whom he accompanied on foreign journeys, including in 1856 and 1858[25]. Not unsurprisingly, in recognition of his medical care over the emperor's sister (her brother, Alexander II, acceded to the throne after the death of their father, Nicolas I, in 1855) he received further tributes. If a doctor could earn the appreciation of 'Europe's chief policeman', as Nicolas I was referred to, it was even more natural that he would merit the respect of Nicolas's liberal successor.

There is no doubt however that it was not so much the positions he held and the medals that ensured his status in Petersburg: it was first and foremost his access to the imperial family. As far back as 1852 Nicolas I had awarded Mianowski a commendation for 20 years of unimpeachable service. Three years later for his service of over 25 years in academic positions he was awarded a salary of 1428 roubles and 50 kopecks per annum, while retaining all his earlier emoluments. At the end of the Crimean War, he received an Order of St. Anne, second class with an imperial crown and dark bronze medal for his services in that war in 1853–1856; two years later he was honoured for a quarter of a century of irreproachable service[26].

In 1855 Mianowski belonged to a group of people who welcomed a proposal to find a Medical-Surgical Academy in Warsaw[27]. He probably did not foresee at the time that he would soon find himself in the capital of the vassal Polish Kingdom, and not just as a full professor but as rector of the revived Polish university, though one not bearing that name.

In 1860 he decided to go into retirement. What the reasons were for that decision one can only speculate. He was 56 years old and was in effect at the

---

24    Order of St. Anne, 11 April 1848; Tsar's commendation, 6 December 1848; on 9 June 1849, detailed to accompany the Grand Princess; returned to service at the Ministry of War on 15 August 1849. Appointed actual councillor of state, 23 April 1850. Cf. J. S z u j s k i , *Józef Mianowski, rektor Szkoły Głównej*, p. 466.

25    He accompanied the Princess on her foreign travels from 25 August to 15 December 1856. Detailed to supervise her return, 29 July 1858.

26    25 years of service – commendation on 22 August 1858; dark bronze medal awarded on 26 August 1856; order of St. Anne with imperial crown, 15 April 1856; salary from 5 January 1856.

27    S. K i e n i e w i c z , *Józef Mianowski*, p. 524.

peak of his creative powers. It may be that a key factor was the marriage that he entered, probably at around that time, with a young Russian of German descent, Nadezhda, daughter of Adolf Ferdinand von Haller, councillor of state and Anna Katharina Paucker (1813–1890). We are told by Artur Kijas that Nadezhda was a Catholic. Her father was, like her newly wedded husband, a medical practitioner, and came from Estonia. One might presume, however, that in view of the German origins of the Haller family they would have been Lutherans or Orthodox. Mianowski's 'Description of Service' from the year 1868 confirms that his wife's faith is in fact Orthodox. But we cannot rule out the possibility that she converted to Catholicism in Italy: on Mianowski's grave, founded by his wife, she inscribed her name as Maria – Hope.

Adolf Ferdinand von Haller (1808–1855) was from 1848 a senior doctor at the Nikolaev Engineering School[28]. But Mianowski's young Russian wife became for him a cause for many concerns. Perhaps the lack of progeny caused her to lapse with time into excessive pietism, marring the last years of his life – though on the other hand after his death she built him an impressive memorial[29]. Shortly before he died Mianowski adopted his niece, Lidia Protopopow, who took his family name[30].

Most of the Polish men living in Petersburg, as Tadeusz Borowski caustically observed, were bachelors, because – apparently – of a shortage of 'suitable women' in the capital. Hence the tendency for them to marry late in life. In Borowski's words:

> Turkułł, Mianowski and almost all the younger and more eligible officials were single, Kierbedź was a widower ... Przecławski with a Russified French woman, Hube with a former coffee server, Professor Iwanowski with a non-entity. Later Mianowski married Miss Haller, who having sunk into devotionalism, poisoned the last days of his life[31].

Mianowski's desire to take retirement was accepted by the authorities, even more so because he had the required seniority: 30 years of employment in

---

28 A. Kijas, *Mianowski Józef*.
29 T. Bobrowski, *Pamiętnik mojego życia*, vol. 1, pp. 451–452; L. Bazylow, *Polacy w Petersburgu*, p. 204; S. Kieniewicz, *Mianowski Józef*, p. 524. The vault was destroyed in the armed conflict of 1944, and then restored with the resources of the Second Polish Corps in Italy. It is now being maintained by the municipal authorities of Senigallia, which consider it to be an important historical monument. The municipality is also in contact with the present-day Mianowski Fund.
30 A. Kijas, *Mianowski Józef*.
31 T. Bobrowski, *Pamiętnik mojego życia*, vol. 1, pp. 451, 452. Cited in L. Bazylow, *Polacy w Petersburgu*, p. 204.

higher education and 28 years in hospital work reporting to the Ministry of the Interior and the Ministry of War. In acknowledgement of his many years of work he received a golden snuff box with an engraved monogram of the name of his Imperial Excellency, the title of meritorious professor and a pension of 1861 roubles per annum. In March 1861 he was also elected a second time as honorary member of the Petersburg Medical-Surgical Academy[32].

Józef Bieliński summed up Mianowski's Petersburg years thus:

> In 1840 he left Vilnius and moved to Petersburg to take up the post of professor of physiology. Furthermore, he was chief doctor at the Land Armed Forces Hospital no. 2, in the department of internal medicine. In that post he had great achievements to his credit, because after the Academy was closed many Polish young people began studying medicine in Petersburg, and Mianowski was their chief mentor and advisor. Several fortunate cases in obstetric practice brought him to the attention of the highest echelons; and he was thus appointed physician to the Imperial Court. He retired in 1860 and moved to Italy[33].

Having gone into retirement Mianowski initially settled down in Albano, near Rome, renowned for its picturesque views. The decision to leave Petersburg stemmed from strictly private family matters, probably connected with the state of health of his wife[34].

When in June 1862 he appeared in Warsaw, work on the Main School was already well under way. The month before had seen the promulgation of three imperial decrees, drawn up by Margrave Aleksander Wielopolski, head of the civil government in the Kingdom. The third of these concerned the reform of public education in a national spirit and the restoration of the Polish University in Warsaw, after it had been closed in the wake of the November uprising[35].

Wielopolski consulted Mianowski on the organisational framework of the planned Main School, and even asked him to try to persuade Antoni Małecki, professor at the University of Lwów, to take up the Chair of Polish literature in

---

32  The golden snuff box was presented on 3 December 1860; the retirement pension commenced on 25 December 1860; the honorary membership of the Academy was granted on 21 March 1861.

33  J. Bieliński, *Stan nauk lekarskich*, pp. 577–578.

34  A. Białecki, *Rektor Józef Mianowski w Warszawie od 1862 do 1869 r.*, 'Niwa' 1879, no. 99, p. 160; J. Szujski, *Józef Mianowski, rektor Szkoły Głównej*, p. 466.

35  K. Poznański, *Reforma szkolna w Królestwie Polskim w 1862 roku*, Wrocław 1968; idem, *Geneza Szkoły Głównej Warszawskiej*, 'Przegląd Historyczno-Oświatowy' 1963, no. 3, p. 271–302; idem, *Reforma szkolna w 1862 r.*, [in:] idem, *Oświata i szkolnictwo w Królestwie Polskim 1831–1869. Lata zmagań i nadziei*, vol. 2 *Szkoły rzemieślniczo-niedzielne*, Warsaw 2001, p. 138 & following.

RUSSIA – PETERSBURG

Warsaw. Mianowski met with Wielopolski probably in June 1862[36]. Travelling to Lwów, he knew already that his candidature for the future rector of the Main School stood a considerable chance of success.

Despite the failure of the mission in Lwów things were quickly gathering momentum.

On 24th September in Albano Mianowski received a telegram from Kazimierz Krzywicki, acting director of the Government Commission for Religious Faiths and Public Education, informing him of his appointment to the post of full professor and rector of the Warsaw Main School. Mianowski was fully aware of the support he enjoyed on the part of Krzywicki, who was a good friend of Archbishop Zygmunt Szczęsny Feliński from Dorpat. When Aleksander Wielopolski was sidelined in the spring of 1863, it was Krzywicki who took over the role of principal custodian of the school, at the personal request, as it happens, of Grand Duke Constantin. Mianowski's bond with Krzywicki stemmed not only from a common political outlook but also from many years of friendship. As he wrote to Krzywicki three years later – on 12th December 1865 – in a letter cited by Grzegorz Bąbiak:

> In general, Sir, you can ponder with pride what you have achieved for our school, our country, for it is to you above all that we owe the opening of our Main School. And if you had not managed to accomplish with unbelievable haste everything that was necessary for it to come into being, the misfortunes which would have befallen our country would later have been an obstacle to it. And the Lord only knows what course all this would then have taken – we have saved ourselves *par la force du fait accompli*[37].

In a letter he sent to Alesander Wielopolski three days after Krzywicki's telegram, he expressed his consent to undertaking such a momentous mission, advising also that on 5th October he would be leaving for Warsaw via Civita Vecchia, Marseille, and Petersburg.

One might want to comment on this curious and circuitous itinerary. It is likely that Mianowski wanted – at least as far as Petersburg was concerned – to sound out more information on the prospects and future of the institution about to be created in Warsaw. The letter was worded as follows:

---

36  A. Kij a s, *Mianowski Józef.*

37  *Szkoła rozumu i charakteru. Szkoła Główna Warszawska (1862–1869). Materiały do dziejów,* p. 46.

60 CHAPTER 3

Excellence!

J'étais bien loin de m'attendre à l'importante nouvelle, que Votre dépêche télé-graphique du 24 de ce mois m'a apportée à Albano – je Vous ai répondu sans hésiter car une fois que je peux d'une manière honorable être utile à mon pays, aucune considération ne pourrait m'arrêter. Vous me trouvez apte à la grande mission à laquelle Vous me destinez – je ne sais pas jusqu'à quel point je pour-rais répondre à cette haute confiance, mais soyez persuadé que je tiendrai à l'honneur de la mener et que j'employerai tous mes moyens à servir la cause publique dans la voie d'ordre et de dévouement à mes dévoirs. Je m'embarquerai demain en huit c'est-à-dire le 10 octobre à Civita Veccia pour Marseille et j'irai directement à Petersbourg – c'est à que j'attendrai Vos addresses – je ne pouvais pas partir plus tôt car il n'y a qu'une fois par semaine que le bateau part directe-ment pour Marseille. Si dans les avancements et reformes que vous me proposez d'introduire dans le ministère de l'Instruction publique il y a des questions qui concernent la faculté de médcine, ne croyez. Vous pas pouvoir attendre mon arrivée à Varsovie? En homme du métier je pourrai peut être Vous être utile. Je suis avec respect de Votre Excellence le très humble et devoué seviteur.

J. Mianowski

In translation, it reads as follows:

Excellency,

I had not been expecting the important news that your telegraphic message of 24th of this month brought to me in Albano – I replied immediately, for if I may have the honour to serve my country, no considerations will stand in my way. You believe that I am suited to the great mission that you are summoning me to – I do not know the degree to which I will be able to accomplish it, but be assured that I shall take it as a point of honour to lead this mission and will employ every means to serve the public cause in the way of order and fulfilment of my duties. I shall leave tomorrow, i.e., 10th October, from Civita Vecchia for Marseille, and will travel directly to Petersburg – where I shall await your addresses – I was not able to depart earlier, because the direct ship to Marseille sails only once a week. If in your proposed process of perfecting and reforming the Ministry Public Enlightenment there should arise issues concerning the Medical Department, perhaps you could wait till I arrive in Warsaw? Being a specialist, I might be of assistance to you.

I remain with respect for Your Excellency as a humble and devoted servant.

J. Mianowski[38]

Rome, 27th September old calendar / 9th October 1862

---

38  J. Szujski, *Józef Mianowski, rektor Szkoły Głównej*, p. 467; A. Białecki, *Rektor Józef Mianowski*, p. 160; S. Kieniewicz, *Mianowski Józef*, p. 524. Mianowski's retirement lasted less than two years: from 25 December 1860 to 8 November 1862.

CHAPTER 4

# Polish Kingdom – Warsaw

*How beautiful is this city of Warsaw! and still it grows and prettifies itself like a coquette; although there's no denying that it is old, maybe very old. – But what's the harm in that? – a city is not a woman, with her steady decline, ending her days jaundiced, sick and wrinkled[1].*

*Riding around the city should be at a moderate trot, keeping to the right-hand side of the street. If it is necessary to overtake the carriage in front, it is permissible to pass it on the left. Galloping and racing are forbidden. [...] It is forbidden to ride your horse on the sidewalks and paths laid out in Ujazdowskie Avenue and Łazienkowski Park for those proceeding on foot[2].*

In Warsaw, Mianowski earned plaudits with the speech he gave on 25 November 1862, the day of the Main School's inauguration. According to some sources it was delivered in an auditorium hastily adapted for the purpose from a room housing sculptures and plaster-casts (and currently the seat of the Historical Department, formerly the Historical Institute of the University of Warsaw). Others report that the opening ceremony took place in the Kazimierzowski Palace, a claim which is probably incorrect[3]. In his address he referred to the traditions of the University of Vilnius, speaking as one of its alumni; to the secret Filaret student organisation; to the long-standing links of Poland with Western culture and to the Polish national, moral and civic spirit. He said: *today, as a new fountainhead of national learning springs up in the very capital of our Kingdom, who cannot help but see in this the harbinger of a new era, foreshadowing a happy future?* He went on to say: *learning does not merely enlighten and give credit to nations; it also lifts them up after their downfall[4].*

---

1  J.S. Bogucki, *Wizerunki społeczeństwa warszawskiego. Szkice obyczajowe*, Warsaw 1844, p. 11.
2  *Treściwy zbiór przepisów policyjnych, administracyjnych i sądowych dla właścicieli domów i mieszkańców m. Warszawy*, Warsaw 1883, pp. 117, 118.
3  A. Szwarc, *Akademia Medyko-Chirurgiczna i Szkoła Główna, 1857–1869*, [in:] *Dzieje Uniwersytetu Warszawskiego 1816–1915*, ed. T. Kizwalter, Warsaw 2016, p. 448; *Szkoła rozumu i charakteru. Szkoła Główna Warszawska (1862–1869). Materiały do dziejów*, p. 49.
4  *Mowa miana przy otwarciu Szkoły Głównej warszawskiej 25 listopada 1862 r.*, [in:] A. Kraushar, *Siedmiolecie Szkoły Głównej warszawskiej 1862–1869. Wydział Prawa i Administracji. Notatki do historii szkół w Polsce*, Warsaw 1883, pp. 148–153; A. Białecki, *Rektor Józef Mianowski*, pp. 162–163; S. Kieniewicz, *Akademia Medyko-Chirurgiczna i Szkoła Główna*, p. 322. Reprints: *Księga pamiątkowa zjazdu byłych wychowańców Szkoły Głównej Warszawskiej w 50-tą rocznicę jej założenia*, Warsaw 1914; *Szkoła rozumu i charakteru. Szkoła Główna Warszawska (1862–1869). Materiały do dziejów*.

© BRILL SCHÖNINGH, 2024  |  DOI:10.30965/9783657794720_005

It needs to be said that from today's perspective this speech, despite the most obsequious expressions of gratitude to His Most Eminent Excellency Emperor Alexander II Romanov, to his viceroy in the Polish Kingdom Grand Duke Konstantin and to others, touched the most sensitive strings in the minds of the Varsovian and Polish public of the time. The praise lavished on the achievements of Poland and the Commonwealth not only in the academic but also in the political sphere, and the examples cited of Poland's best universities, their professors and alumni, ran very close to risking a harsh intervention by the Russian authorities and censors. As it happened, however, censorship had just undergone a considerable easing. I suspect that Mianowski was fully aware of what was possible and what was not within the political constraints of the time. The thaw that followed the Crimean War and the liberalisation of the political system at this early stage of the new emperor's rule seemed not to pose yet any grave threat, though the inhabitants of the Empire were quite soon to realise that liberalisation had its severe restrictions. And the covert, unofficial modus operandi of the Russian authorities had one priority above all: to take aim at all clandestine and conspiratorial organisations.

Mianowski took a gamble nonetheless – and delivered an address which even today can be read as a paean not only to Poland and Polishness, but also to fundamental values, that of freedom and its significant role in Polish civilisation. It is worth citing his speech in full:

Gentlemen!

Here we are at the first public sitting of our Main School, and I, speaking for the first time from this rostrum to the people assembled here, believe I shall be expressing a sentiment common to all of us when I commence my speech with a tribute of thanks to the our merciful Monarch, to whose diligence and beneficence we owe this new institution of learning, a stake in a new life for our nation. And we extend this feeling also to the distinguished person of his Imperial-Royal Highness the Duke Viceroy [Konstantin Mikolayevich Romanov (1827–1892) – L.Z.], under whose caring supervision our School will be seeing its growth. And what better occasion than today is it to pay due homage and express our gratitude to this excellent statesman who for so long has shown himself to be solicitous of our national learning, and now holds the reins of the civil government of this country? It is to him, gentlemen, that our school owes its organisation, indeed owes its existence.

This is a newly opened addition to that learning which for so long illuminated Poland, which made of our nation a power and enabled it to contribute so much to the Christian world; a new addition to that great Western civilisation which once with great glory we cultivated here at home and with such distinction fostered in countries and peoples further afield; through this learning we joined the ranks of European nations and endowed Europe with so many foreign lands, because as one of the great minds of this century correctly said: where Latin ends, there ends Europe, and by the term Latin we all understand the great legacy of the ancient world, which, enlivened by the Christian spirit, has become the highest moral and intellectual treasure of the West; we understand above all those fields of learning which the wisdom of centuries has for so long and so accurately termed the humanities, because only they in the Christian community ensure the full development of the person and the citizen.

Learning does not merely enlighten and give credit to nations, it also lifts them up after their downfall; and where shall we find better examples and reminders of this great truth than right here, in our own history? In the frequent succession of our nation's downfalls and resurgences, revival of life has always gone hand in hand with a revival of learning, and the development of the Main School preceded, and sometimes laid the ground for, the development of the state. When in the 14th century Poland began to regain her strength after centuries of dissolution and enfeeblement, a wise and virtuous king [Casimir the Great (1310–1370) – L.Z.] deemed this Cracovian Alma Mater to be one of the main factors in the national restoration, and its final establishment by the great Jadwiga [Jadwiga of Anjou (1373–1399) – L.Z.] ensured that her memory would remain permanently entrenched in the gratitude of the nation; and if in the two successive centuries, the 15th and 16th, this country of ours stood so high in glory and esteem and rose to the highest ranks in Europe, this magnificent achievement was in no small measure due to the role of the University of Cracow; from it came men who not only disseminated education in the homeland itself, but even contributed to some enormous stepping stones in the progress of general scholarship, making our name known throughout the civilised world. Grzegorz of Sanok [c. 1407–1477 – L.Z.], Piotr of Bnin [c.1430–1494 – L.Z.] and so many others breathed fresh life into classical antiquity, into history; and the first of the abovementioned, the said Grzegorz of Sanok, by declaring war on scholasticism, so rightly described by him as a daydream, became a herald of a modern, empirically based philosophy, a forerunner, one might say, of Bacon [Francis Bacon (1561–1626) – L.Z.]. In the holy science of our faith, suffice it to say that alumni of the Cracow Main School, Mikołaj Trąba [c. 1358–1422 – L.Z.], Jan Elgot [c. 1398–1452 – L.Z.] etc., left their mark, indeed played a major role in the councils of all Christianity in Constance and Basel; and it is a pleasure and honour for a 19th century alumnus, a Pole, who holds dear the hard-fought principle of freedom of conscience, to recall that in the 15th century at one such council it was only the Polish theologians who defended the holy right to tolerance and had no hand in the burning at the stake of the Czech Huss [Jan Hus (1370–1415) – L.Z.]. In the natural sciences mention needs to be made of Załuziański [Adam Załuziański, (1558–1613 – L.Z.), botanist, sometimes known as the 'Polish Linnaeus'], in whose extant works later scholars find to their astonishment germs of the discipline that was subsequently immortalised by Linnaeus [1707–1778 – L.Z.]. As for Brudzewski [Wojciech Brudzewski (1445–1495) – L.Z.], his light will shine long by dint of the one who eclipsed it, keeping his name for grateful posterity; it needs only be said that he tutored a pupil who rose above him, that he was the master of our very own Copernicus, who rose above him, who in the real sense of the word: Levered the world's mass onto new tracks ...

[...] *Coelique meatus*
*Descripsit radio, surgentia sidera dixit*

(Of the paths of the heavens
He described the trajectory, and marked the rising stars)

But beyond nurturing these scholarly geniuses, the Jagiellonian school had to its credit an even more formidable achievement for the country: it produced citizens of great stature, seasoned in public and political life, statesmen who carried on their shoulders the burden of governments and courts of justice of a more powerful state: such as Zbigniew Oleśnicki [Poland's first cardinal (1389–1455) – L.Z.], who was the monarch's right hand in all issues of the nation; or Jan Długosz [chronicler (1415–1480)], who could accomplish the most difficult and complicated missions, benefitting his king and country, with no detriment to his conscience as a Christian and chaplain, and whose historical and political creations, so highly prized, were for so long preserved even in concealment as arcana imperii [secrets of authority]; or Tomicki [Piotr Tomicki, royal secretary (1464–1535) – L.Z.], to whose indefatigable efforts we owe the preservation of archives, acts and treaties of the earlier state; all those students, teachers and rectors of the Jagiellonian University were the fathers of an abundant generation of our great statesmen of the 15th and 16th centuries, whom their Alma Mater prepared for public office. The combination of a humanitarian education gained at the great Jagiellonian school on the one hand, with political skills, acquired in royal and national councils, on battlefields and in diplomatic negotiations on the other, was precisely the characteristic feature of the sons of Poland in those outstanding times, and at their head everyone pictures in his mind the figure of the great chancellor and hetman, attired with equal dignity in a doctoral toga and a senator's coat; from the field camp, in charge of the army, he sent letters to the great humanists of his time; in his earlier days he was rector of the Paduan academy, and when approaching old age he was the great vanquisher of the German archduke [Jan Zamoyski (1542–1605) – L.Z.].

Later times saw the darkening of the horizons of learning; the Main School became mired in stagnation and fog, and with it the nation, ever more stagnant, headed towards downfall, until the moment came when it was completely excised from the map of Europe! But when later, thanks to the mercy of the Lord, and thanks also to the magnanimous Monarch, the name of Poland was once again restored to life, the first sign of this blissful change, the harbinger of a happy future, was the kindling of two new flames of education: that school of Krzemieniec and the school of Wilno, which handed down from the generation of the time the light of life, the lampas vitae. Handed right down, one could say, to this very generation which painstakingly grew among us. Those schools resuscitated life in our homeland, its intellectual, moral and literary life, and if our poetry has shone with such bright and sunlit radiance, if it still commands such unextinguished enthusiasm at home and increasing respect and admiration abroad, to whom do we owe this if not to the school of Wilno, if not to its magnificent pupil, Mickiewicz, whose name has become the glory not just of one nation but of a whole family of peoples, the pride of Poland and the Slavonic world.

POLISH KINGDOM – WARSAW

Today, when a new flame of national learning is lit in the very capital of our Kingdom, who can fail to see the portent of a new era, the making of a propitious future? Each one of us understands that, because it fulfils the most ardent wishes that each of us has long harboured in his heart of hearts. But may we also understand the duties that are demanded of us by the fortunate acquisition of this fount of knowledge and life. May we understand that we have been given a foundation stone on which the edifice of the future can safely and successfully be constructed, and without which any construction must collapse to the ignominy of the present generations and the destruction of future ones! The young, upright and noble, so passionately enamoured of their country and so eagerly anticipating their accession to the temple of learning opened here, will appreciate the apprehensive love contained in my words, and I have no doubt will take to heart the reminder of an old pupil of the Wilno school that if that particular seat of learning turned out to be of such benefit to the country, of such glory to the nation, the merit lies not with its teachers, but to a far greater extent with its pupils, with the national, moral and civic spirit which those young people were able to nurture among themselves and with their own resources.

Sirs, in our hands is only the governance of this newly founded school; in the hands of the noble youth is its destiny[5].

The course of the entire opening ceremony of the Main School was described in detail by Józef Ignacy Kraszewski. Apart from Mianowski, other university professors made speeches: the historian Józef Plebański, the dean of the Faculty of Law Jan Wołowski, the Metropolitan Archbishop of Warsaw Zygmunt Szczęsny Feliński; while the first lectures were given by the lawyer Józef Kasznica in the field of encyclopedia of law, the chemist Józef Natanson (the history of chemistry in the context of natural history research) and the lawyer Władysław Holewiński (the role of historical studies in legal sciences)[6].

The rector immediately threw himself into creating the school from the ground up: he hired academics, organised lectures, adapted available spaces. The school also gained support from Warsaw's citizens by offering, on Mianowski's initiative, lectures open to the public[7].

He moved into lodgings not far from the Main School – now the University – on Świętokrzyska street (then spelt Święto Krzyzka), listed as no. 1334 a. His

---

5   *Księga pamiątkowa zjazdu byłych wychowańców Szkoły Głównej Warszawskiej w 50-tą rocznicę jej założenia*, Warsaw 1914, pp. 33–37. See also *Szkoła rozumu i charakteru. Szkoła Główna Warszawska (1862–1869). Materiały do dziejów*, pp. 150–153, which also gives more information about the reaction to Mianowski's speech in the press.

6   J.I. K r a s z e w s k i, *Otwarcie Szkoły Głównej w Warszawie*. Cited in *Szkoła rozumu i charakteru. Szkoła Główna Warszawska (1862–1869). Materiały do dziejów*, pp. 159–161.

7   L. Z a s z t o w t, *Popularyzacja nauki w Królestwie Polskim 1864–1905*, Wrocław 1989, pp. 215–216. A. S z w a r c, *Akademia Medyko-Chirurgiczna i Szkoła Główna*, pp. 442–444.

66 CHAPTER 4

address was to be found among those of Warsaw's other medical practitioners, for instance in the 'Warsaw Guide' of 1869[8].

At that time Mianowski's remuneration amounted to a professor's salary of 1500 roubles (rs.) per annum, an additional 600 rs. for his duties as rector and 1500 rs. to cover the cost of accommodation. He was also appointed member of the Council of the Governmental Commission for Religious Faiths and Public Education and elected honorary member of the Warsaw Medical Society[9].

The nascent Main School was formed based on the Imperial-Royal Warsaw Medical-Surgical Academy, which following the transformation became the school's first department – the Medical Department. The Academy was founded in 1857 on the strength of the 'Highest' (i.e., imperial) decree of 4th June of that year[10]. Mianowski played a personal role in its foundation, since – as mentioned earlier – he was a member of a Petersburg group arguing for the desirability of opening the Warsaw school. A motion passed by a committee convened by the Viceroy of the Kingdom postulated the creation of a medical school; it was addressed to the Council of State in Petersburg, which, according to Polikarp Girsztowt, changed its name from Medical School to Academy. Meanwhile the Department for the Affairs of the Polish Kingdom sought the advice of doctors: Wacław Pelikan, Otzolig (?), Professor Mianowski and Markus (Stanisław Markusfeld?). It was decided to afford the Medical-Surgical Academy in Warsaw a status on a par with that of its Petersburg namesake[11].

The Academy's Governing Committee was composed of doctors who were soon to become the bedrock of the Main School's Medical Department. There were nine of them, including six who lectured at the school: Teofil Lesiński, Master of Pharmacy Ferdynand Werner, Master of Pharmacy, Ludwik Neugebauer, Doctor of Medicine, Dr Ludwik Zeiszner, Titular Professor of Physical and Mathematical Sciences Stanisław Przystański and Titular Professor of Natural Sciences Jerzy Aleksandrowicz (Alexandrowicz), as well as doctors Andrzej Janikowski, Bącewicz and Andrzej Boholubow. The Committee was chaired by the Chief Health Inspector of the Kingdom, Dr

---

8    Directory of addresses of Warsaw doctors: *Józef Mianowski*, [...] *S-to Krzyzka 1334a*, 'Przewodnik Warszawski informacyjno-adresowy na rok 1869 z dołączeniem kalendarza i taryfy domów' 1869, p. 294.

9    Delegated to the Polish Kingdom and appointed Council member on 8 November 1862; elected honorary member of the Warsaw Medical Society on 1 January 1863.

10   P. Girsztowt, *Rys historyczno-statystyczny Cesarsko-Królewskiej Warszawskiej Medyko-Chirurgicznej Akademii od jej zawiązku w dniu 4 czerwca 1857 r. aż do wcielenia do Szkoły Głównej dnia 1 października 1862 r.*, [in:] *Wykaz Szkoły Głównej Warszawskiej w letnim półroczu roku naukowego 1864/5*, Warsaw 1865, pp. 7, 9.

11   *Ibidem*, p. 10.

POLISH KINGDOM – WARSAW

Wiktor Kochański (soon to be replaced by Dr Jankowski as acting chairman). Kochański was further appointed president of the Academy.

In the five years of its existence the Academy changed its premises three times. It was first located at no. 73 Jezuicka Street, originally the seat of Jesuit schools and subsequently of the Medical Department of the Royal University of Warsaw and the Pharmaceutical School. It then moved to the Casimir Palace in the old University. Finally, in 1857, it was housed in the Staszic Palace, which before the uprising was the seat of the Warsaw Society of Friends of the Sciences[12].

From the moment the Main School was founded Mianowski counted on its being transformed into a fully-fledged university. He probably did not realise, however, that from the very outset the Russian plan was to make Warsaw's new university a purely Russian institution. All this coincided with the first attempts to create a Russian university. On 30th August / 11th September a Highest rescript was addressed to the Viceroy of the Kingdom, Fyodor Berg, concerning the reorganisation of the educational system in the post-uprising Kingdom. On the strength of this rescript the head of the Governmental Committee for Public Education, Fyodor Witte, instructed the rector of the Main School to prepare for the transformation of the school into a university by convening a commission under his chairmanship to oversee the plans and statute of the future university. Mianowski invited several full professors to be members: Jerzy Aleksandrowicz, Antoni Białecki, Tytus Chałubiński, Polikarp Girsztowt, Władysław Holewiński, Józef Kasznica, Józef Kowalewski, Jan Papłoński, Jan Wolfram and the lawyer Otto Fiszer. Kazimierz Kaszewski, head of the Main School's chancellery, became the commission's secretary. Later – Polikarp Girsztowt records – the committee was whittled down to Białecki, Kasznica, Fiszer and Kaszewski. The statute of the Imperial-Royal University of Warsaw, running to 164 articles, was duly drawn up and submitted to the Governmental Commission for Public Education on 5th/17th January 1865[13]. It was, however, rejected, and played no role in successive discussions on the shape of the future Imperial University of Warsaw.

In organising the Main School Mianowski, apart from seeking the assistance of the Margrave Aleksander Wielopolski himself and the most senior officials of the Governmental Commission, relied primarily on professors of law and, to

---

12  *Ibidem*, pp. 31–32.

13  *Ibidem*, pp. 120–121; J. Schiller, *Powstanie Cesarskiego Uniwersytetu Warszawskiego w świetle badań archiwalnych*, 'Rozprawy z Dziejów Oświaty' 2002, vol. 41, pp. 99–102; J. Schiller-Walicka, *Cesarski Uniwersytet Warszawski: między edukacją a polityką 1869–1917*, [in:] *Dzieje Uniwersytetu Warszawskiego 1816–1915*, p. 570 & following.

68                                                                                                          CHAPTER 4

a lesser extent, on former professors of the Medical-Surgical Academy and the emerging Medical Department.

The Main School had its seat in the grounds of the old University of Warsaw from the period of 1816–1831; its central premises were in a separate building, standing to this day, to the right of the campus as seen from the main gate and now housing Archaeology. The ceremony of its opening, after renovation, took place on 16 (28) November 1865 at 11 a.m. It was conducted by Fyodor Witte, director of the Commission of Public Education, dedicating the building to the school in the presence of Rector Mianowski and two deans: the Doctor of Medicine Aleksander Le Brun and the astronomer Jan Baranowski. Part of its space was occupied by a chemical workshop[14].

The school was composed of four departments: Medical, Law and Administration, Mathematical-Physical and Philological-Historical. Their deans were, respectively, Aleksander Le Brun, Walenty Dutkiewicz, Jan Baranowski and Józef Kowalewski.

The teaching staff was not large in number. As Andrzej Szwarc has noted it was initially to comprise 35 full professors, 15 associate ones, 11 assistant professors and four lectors – 65 in total. In practice the numbers grew. In 1863 the headcount was 61 persons, including 19 full and five associate professors, 17 assistant professors, four lectors, two readers, two dissectors, two embalmers, three clinical and dissecting room assistants and two cabinet custodians. As Szwarc pointed out, later staff numbers increased, primarily through the addition of unpaid readers and salaried assistant professors. In its last year of existence, the Main School employed 91 professional staff[15].

From its inception, many young people found the new institution inspiring. Edmund Jankowski recalled:

> At the lectures the crowds were teeming like a hive of bees, very many keen students had to stand for lack of room, resting their notes for hours [...] on windowsills, or against the wall, sometimes on the backs of their colleagues.

But in the most recent study of the Main School's history Andrzej Szwarc has cast doubt on the verisimilitude of this description[16].

It is interesting to see those of Warsaw's medical practitioners who were connected to the Academy and the School from the point of view of where they

---

14    J.L. S z p e r l, *Pracownia chemiczna*, [in:] *Szkoła rozumu i charakteru. Szkoła Główna Warszawska (1862–1869). Materiały do dziejów*, p. 209.

15    A. S z w a r c, *Akademia Medyko-Chirurgiczna i Szkoła Główna*, pp. 443–445.

16    E. J a n k o w s k i, *Szkoła Główna Warszawska*, 'Tygodnik Ilustrowany' 1903, no. 23. Cited in *ibidem*, p. 553.

POLISH KINGDOM – WARSAW

lived. As mentioned earlier, Mianowski resided in Świętokrzyska Street. Tytus Chałubiński, the capital's most popular doctor, lived at no. 411 on Krakowskie Przedmieście, Polikarp Girsztowt in Jasna Street, no. 1364a, Ludwik Hirszfeld at no. 471g Rymarska Street, Henryk Hoyer at 544n Długa Street, Wiktor Kochański, now long forgotten but then the chief physician of the Kingdom, lived at Złota Street, no. 1518/9, Ludwik Natanson at no. 1369 Szkolna Street, Ludwik Neugebauer at no. 794c Elektoralna Street, Wiktor Szokalski was on the Marszałkowska (no. 1492b) and Emil Wolfram at 1726d Wiejska. All those abodes were located within what is today the city centre and their distance from the Main School was no more than about 3 km (a 45-minute walk)[17].

During the January uprising Mianowski tried on the one hand to restrain the young people from participating in it, or even from showing any public signs of support. On the other hand, he aided and offered refuge to those who joined the insurrection. As it happens, this involved not just students at the school but also several persons from outside, including members of the uprising's clandestine leadership[18]. It is known that there was a series of cases where the students' participation was concealed, their names fictitiously and retrospectively entered in the records so that they could avoid reprisals. The result of these efforts was a success: most of the students remained in the institution; their studies uninterrupted. Rumours were also spread, both in Petersburg and in Paris, that the students had severed relations with the Central Committee of the National Government, which was the insurrection's high command[19]. This helped Mianowski to use his influence in Petersburg and protect the school, save it from closure and allow it to function normally. Other universities, as had more than once occurred in similar circumstances in the past, were closed. It is worth reminding we once again that as early as in September 1864 a plan was in place to convert the School into a Russian university. This was put on hold[20]. The event finally happened five years later.

Police records from the last phase of the 1863 uprising contained the information that in that period 15 students were arrested, a search was on for a further 20, and 40 were under investigation. As was observed by Grzegorz Bąbiak,

---

17  'Przewodnik Warszawski informacyjno-adresowy na rok 1869 z dołączeniem kalendarza i taryfy domów' Warsaw 1869, pp. 293–295.

18  For instance, the son of Dr. Seweryn Gałęzowski. See the Warsaw University Library, Reference no. 361, *Pamiętnik Natalii z Bispingów Kickiej.* Autograph, manuscript, sheet (k.) 241.

19  A. K r a u s h a r, *Kartki z pamiętnika Alkara*, Pt. 2, Kraków 1913, p. 37; *Pamiętniki Ignacego Baranowskiego*, Poznań 1923, p. 447 & following; S. Kieniewicz, *Powstanie styczniowe*, Warszawa 1983, p. 322; *idem, Mianowski Józef*, p. 524.

20  *Szkoła Główna Warszawska (1862–1868)*, vol. 1, Kraków 1900, p. 54.

70                                                                                    CHAPTER 4

these numbers were quite low, given that over 1,400 students were enrolled in
Years I and 2. But it was surely the case that many more had their role in the
insurrection concealed[21].

Despite the conciliatory stance of the students the Kingdom's new viceroy,
General Fyodor Berg, considered closing the school down. Reports from the
national police of the Central Committee of the National Government, which
led the insurrection, indicate that it was precisely the unbending stance of
Rector Mianowski that prevented this from happening. In issue no. 6 of the
'Directives and News from the National Police, 22nd December 1863, we read:

> The thought [that the Main School is continuing its activity] has led Berg to his
> hundredth successive act of madness, it has given him several sleepless nights,
> so the other day he summed the rector Mianowski and despotically ordered him
> to close the Main School. Mianowski replied that the Main School had been
> opened by order of the Tsar, so by his order it can be closed, which convinced
> Berg; he therefore telegraphed Petersburg to obtain a final decision on the sub-
> ject. We do not wish to guess what in respect of the continuing existence of
> the Main School such a sincere friend of progress as is the Tsar will be gracious
> enough to decide – but we will allow ourselves the expectation that it will be
> in favour if not of total abolition then at least closure pending a new directive,
> which we can predict will not be forthcoming, since that was also the fate of the
> once thriving University of Warsaw[22].

However – as we know – the school was not closed.

To this day it is unclear what part Mianowski had in 1863 in confidential
negotiations involving Aleksander Wielopolski, the Grand Duke Constantin
and, on the other side, the right wing of the 'white' camp: Karol Majewski,
Edmund Taczanowski and Zygmunt Chmieleński. As Stefan Kieniewicz has
written, these negotiations allegedly took place in June and July and may have
been influential in Majewski's taking the reins of the National Government[23].

Mianowski himself was not only well informed about the activities of the
'white camp' but took part in talks aimed at passing the National Government
from the 'reds' or 'anarchists' and placing it in the hands of the 'whites' – the
conservatives. This is how Stefan Kieniewicz describes the situation, probably
drawing on Walery Przyborowski's History of Two Years:

---

21   *Szkoła rozumu i charakteru. Szkoła Główna Warszawska (1862–1869). Materiały do dziejów*,
     pp. 50–51.

22   *Ibidem*, p. 54–55. Also contains a fuller picture of the circumstances of the reprisals
     against the Main School.

23   S. Kieniewicz, *Powstanie styczniowe*, pp. 523, 630; I. Koberdowa, *Warszawska Rada
     Miejska 1861–1863*, 'Rocznik Warszawski' 1962, vol. 3, p. 130 & following.

POLISH KINGDOM – WARSAW

[...] 'a certain faction of the nobility-white party' saw the need to bring new people into the government, in anticipation of intervention by the powers. Thus, a discussion took place with the participation Kronenberg, Kurtz, Rector Mianowski, Ruprecht et al, where a proposal was made to Majewski that he forms a new government, for the time being a secret one. In case Poland were deemed to be a belligerent party there was talk of creating a public government, where alongside J.T. Lubomirski, one of the Zamojskis, Kurtz and Kronenberg there would also be a place for Majewski.

Kieniewicz adds: *We have no way of verifying this information, but if such a discussion did take place it would of course have been after 23rd May* [1863][24].

It is worth pointing out that for the conservatives of that period the issue of *to fight or not to fight?* was of key importance. On the one hand, should they renounce the fight, they might be facing a charge of national apostasy; on the other, they were aware that joining the struggle could lead to even greater civilisational losses. For many conservatives, such as Aleksander Wielopolski, Włodzimierz Spasowicz, Kazimierz Krzywicki, but also Mianowski and other professors at the Main School who well versed in the realities of Russian politics, these decisions had broader implications. This is because a place needed to be found in the complicated political jigsaw of the Tsarist empire. The conservatives wished to modernise the state, even such a state as the Polish Kingdom. They wanted to do this in a series of small steps, accruing modest liberties and broadening internal autonomy. But the times were particularly unfavourable, since for many of the young and the more radical the struggle was being fought not for minor concessions but for everything[25]. Let us bear in mind too that the conservatives tended to be deeply religious, although – in my opinion – they were not at one with those Catholic fanatics who 'hated all that was foreign'.

An ironic comment of sorts on the role performed at the time by Mianowski was the dark bronze medal he received as a memento of the suppression of the Polish 'revolt' in 1865[26].

Would the Main School have persisted for eight years had it not had Rector Józef Mianowski as its principal? This remains an open question. In my opinion the rector's life story, his links with the aristocratic elite of the Russian Empire, close relations with the Tsar's family and numerous contacts with leading lights of the imperial bureaucracy of the time, first and foremost in Petersburg and to a lesser degree in Warsaw – these were the only reason why

---

24    S. Kieniewicz, *Powstanie styczniowe*, p. 523.
25    This was pointed out by Grzegorz Bąbiak. See *Szkoła rozumu i charakteru. Szkoła Główna Warszawska (1862–1869). Materiały do dziejów*, p. 71.
26    The medal was awarded on 20 May 1865.

the Russian authorities not only did not close the School down but allowed it to continue through to the end of the 1860s[27]. None of the Warsaw officials, including Margrave Wielopolski, Krzywicki and the School's other professors had such a gamut of connections and possibilities. Not even the orientalist Józef Kowalewski (1801–1878), three years older than Mianowski, a filomat and rector of the University of Kazan, on and off, in 1854–1860 (often, incidentally, mistaken for Mianowski because of their similar appearance) was so close to the Petersburg establishment. Perhaps the one Pole who had connections at a similar level in Petersburg was Stanisław Kierbiedź, a close friend of Mianowski's. But he was fulfilling his life mission as a lecturer and, above all, engineer, being sent out from the capital to all corners of the Empire to build rails and bridges.

In short, at that moment in history Mianowski was – in my view – indispensable particularly to the Russians, but also to the Poles. But it needs to be said that when it came to so-called big politics, when for example the future of the university in Petersburg was being settled, Mianowski's influence was rather limited and by the same token he certainly did not have much say in the eventual fate of the Warsaw school. According to Joanna Schiller-Walicka, Mianowski played a negligible role in any high-level decisions regarding the Main School and then the Imperial University of Warsaw. If proof of that were needed, we need only recall what happened in 1864–1865 to the plan's university drawn up by the group of Main School professors under Mianowski's chairmanship.

If he had really been of critical importance, particularly so for the Russians, why was he not offered the post of rector of the Imperial University? There is not even a trace of his candidature in any document.

There are however different opinions as to why the Main School managed to last out for 8 years. According to Joanna Schiller-Walicka, all actions taken regarding the Main School in the years 1864–1869 were first and foremost part of a specific political project to create a Russian university in the Polish Kingdom, driven primarily by a mistrust and fear of Poles at Russian universities, generally viewed as a subversive element. For Poles, we need to remember, a *numerus clausus* – maximum number admitted – had been introduced in Russian higher education in 1862. Furthermore, the Russian authorities took certain steps in the cultural area. Among various initiatives this involved the dissemination of Russian language, culture, and scholarship in tandem with the burgeoning political project of pan-Slavism and nationalisation of the

---

27    *Szkoła rozumu i charakteru. Szkoła Główna Warszawska (1862–1869). Materiały do dziejów*, p. 81 & following.

POLISH KINGDOM – WARSAW

Empire, i.e., of cultural Russification. In this situation Mianowski was merely a pawn, albeit one treated with kid gloves (hence those medals and emoluments), but he personally played no part in the grand scheme of things, which was much more far-reaching and high-ranking. All the documents we know – Polish or Russian, official or private – make no mention of any role he may have played in maintaining the school, and then in its transformation into the Imperial University of Warsaw[28].

One fact we can agree on: up to the moment when the final decisions were taken on converting the School into the Imperial University and erecting the framework based on which the latter would operate, political expediency dictated that as rector of the Main School Mianowski was convenient both for the Russians and the Poles.

The 1860s in Warsaw were for Mianowski a period of intensive work. Interestingly, general opinion about his activities was extremely favourable, except in the circles of the Medical Department where he was judged rather critically. One reason for this may have been the fact that he carried out no teaching, as had been the case earlier in Petersburg where his lectures were delivered by assistances. There were also reservations by the school's medical staff concerning the rector's administrative skills, and it was observed that in his scientific work he was resting on his laurels[29].

Invariably, however, he enjoyed the goodwill of students and the Warsaw intelligentsia, including professors outside the Medical Department. His kindness and benevolence became almost proverbial[30]. He helped not only old friends, such as Seweryn Goszczyński to whom he sent money in Paris[31], but also young scholars newly arrived in Warsaw, such as Stefan Pawlicki, and students. He also helped old fellow countrymen, among them probably Apollo Korzeniowski[32]. He even mediated in seemingly minor affairs, e.g.

---

28   From Joanna S c h i l l e r-Wa l i c k a's publishing review.

29   Cf. *J. Mianowski. Listy do Kazimierza Krzywickiego (1865–1878)*, ed., introduction A. Wrzosek, 'Archiwum Historii i Filozofii Medycyny' 1927, vol. 7, pp. 126–127; *Szkoła Główna Warszawska (1862–1869)*, vol. 2, Kraków 1901; S. Konopka, *Wydział Lekarski Szkoły Głównej (1862–1869)*, 'Roczniki Uniwersytetu Warszawskiego' 1963, vol. 4, pp. 14–22; H. Nusbaum, *Udział Wydziału Lekarskiego Szkoły Głównej Warszawskiej w ogólnej twórczości naukowej*, 'Archiwum Historii i Filozofii Medycyny' 1927, vol. 6, no. 2, pp. 126–139.

30   M. Brykalska, *Aleksander Świetochowski*, vol. 1, pp. 21–23.

31   National Library manuscript 2956, *List J. Mianowskiego do S. Goszczyńskiego z dn. 12 sierpnia 1867 r*, sheet (k.) 23.

32   *Ibidem*, manuscript 2674, *List S. Pawlickiego do J. Mianowskiego z dn. 5 czerwca 1866 r.*, sheet (k.) 252; Z. Najder, *Życie Conrada Korzeniowskiego*, vol. 1, Warsaw 1996, p. 41.

74 CHAPTER 4

asking Cracow's Rector Józef Majer to assist Julia Selinger in opening a boarding house for women in Galicia[33].

Tales circulated about his kind-heartedness, how he helped a poor clerk find work in the school, how he intervened to prevent the expulsion of a student although it was fully deserved. There was a well-known case when on his way to an exquisite dinner Mianowski came across two children near his hosts' home who were suffering in the cold weather. Without giving the matter much thought he took the children into his friends' house, asked that they be fed and then took them to his own home and to arrange for further assistance[34]. He showed similar generosity with respect to students at the Main School.

After 1863, Main School students had to be in possession of a certificate, signed by the rector in person, permitting them to reside in Warsaw. An official declaration stated the following:

> These certificates are issued to those not permanently domiciled in Warsaw, who are exempt from ticket fees, permitting them to reside freely in this city, on the strength of an **Instruction** approved by the Administrative Council of the Kingdom on the day of 15th (27th) November 1863 concerning the issue of these tickets, namely: clerks and officials on active service, their wives and families, students and pupils of governmental educational institutions and apprentices, probationers and pupils of all trades and arts. These certificates compliant with the rules stated in the abovementioned **Instruction** are to be renewed annually.
>
> Signed: Warsaw Police Chief of the court of His Highness Major General Baron [Platon] Frederiks[35].

As Andrzej Szwarc writes, many Main School students were not well-off and needed financial support. As rector, Mianowski did all he could to provide them with assistance. In November 1866 he wrote to the deans: *The number of impecunious students is so large that the majority are constantly requesting scholarships, or support, or payment of their enrolment fee.* But his endeavours met with scant results. There was still little money for scholarships[36].

Mianowski is also credited with the introduction of the custom and duty of students wearing uniform. Uniforms were brought in towards the final phase of the January uprising, at the start of 1864, with the support of General Fyodor Berg, the Kingdom's Viceroy at the time. This narrative was obviously untrue,

---

33 Archive of PAN i PAU in Kraków, Reference no. 2020, *List J. Mianowskiego do J. Majera z dn. 30 lipca 1863 r.*, sheet (k.) 245.

34 A. B i a ł e c k i, *Rektor Józef Mianowski*, p. 168; F. S z [y m a ń s k i], *Z minionych dni*, 'Kurier Poranny' 1929, no. 217. Cf. M. B r y k a l s k a, *Aleksander Świętochowski*, vol. 1, 22–23.

35 *Szkoła rozumu i charakteru. Szkoła Główna Warszawska (1862–1869). Materiały do dziejów*, p. 202.

36 A. S z w a r c, *Akademia Medyko-Chirurgiczna i Szkoła Główna*, p. 526.

POLISH KINGDOM – WARSAW

since in the Empire the obligation for students to wear uniform was always in the personal gift of the Tsar, who also gave his approval to the design the uniforms, caps, and student insignia. Nonetheless the very fact that the Warsaw public deemed it to be the rector's decision was of itself significant.

There was a boycott of the imposed dress code and several dozen students who refused to comply were arrested, but the conflict was resolved – apparently due in no small measure to Mianowski's intervention, who requested a solution 'in a sincere and heartfelt, fatherly tone'. After the uniforms were introduced, students emphasised their independence by a scruffy appearance, unbuttoned jackets and caps which did not quite conform to regulations[37]. Apparently, the sentence uttered by Mianowski – it was recorded by Aleksander Świętochowski – was: *My dear ones, I beg you, put on your uniforms*[38]. It was generally believed that the rector frequently intervened if students committed some kind of misdemeanour. There was no possibility of defence, however, if a case involved participation in a national conspiracy and insurrectional activity[39]. But Mianowski's pleadings for mitigation did mean that efforts were made not to expel students even if they had committed some more serious offences. On the other hand, the rector could be resolute and strict. Without recourse to any regulations, formal charges, or procedures Mianowski removed a student accused of being a member of 'a gang which maintained a bawdy house'[40].

An interesting light on Mianowski's attitude to students is cast by the case of Stanisław Kwapiński (born c. 1859–?). He was accused by a professor at the school, philologist and expert on religion Antoni Mierzyński (1829–1907) of indecent behaviour. The investigation also revealed the involvement of Kwapiński's co-tenant, one Bronisław Krzywoszewski (1850–?). It ascertained that:

> 1. Kwapiński leads a dissolute life and brings to his abode public women, in contravention of the provisions of § 17 letter a.

> 2. that through indulging in noisy games in his abode, banging on the kitchen door of his neighbour Professor Mierzyński, demoralising the professor's maid, he committed a disturbance of the household peace of another (§ 19 letter g), which he should respect even more for being a student and his neighbour being a professor.

---

37   *Ibidem*, p. 525.
38   M. Brykalska, *Aleksander Świętochowski*, vol. 1, p. 23. Cited in *ibidem*, p. 525, 554.
39   *Ibidem*, p. 520.
40   A. Świętochowski, *Wspomnienia*, ed., introduction S. Sandler, Wrocław 1966, p. 127. Cited in *ibidem*, pp. 520, 553.

3. that in his entire conduct he serves as a bad example to others, younger than himself, and that by making public his case of syphilitic illness, even to the police authorities, he is an affront to the honour of the students at the Main School.

5. For the above reasons I have the honour to submit that Your Excellency the Rector avail himself of the right vested in him on the strength of § 34 Regulations on Order in the Main School, and in consideration of the fact that the participation of the student Kwapiński Stanisław is deleterious to order and custom, that eschewing referral to the General Council he dispenses *consilium abenndi* for a period of 2 years.

Acting judge of the Main School A[ntoni] Białecki[41].

How did Mianowski react? Well, the initial sentence of suspension of the immoral student for 2 years was commuted to one year; and 2 weeks later, on 11th May, it was modified to 'three weeks of detention conditioned on a solemn pledge of reform'. The end text was: *With this declaration of content [...] I do most solemnly promise I shall henceforth reform my life. On this day of 3rd (15th) May 1869. Stanisław Kwapiński signed in the presence of the judge*[42].

Was Mianowski's decision motivated by the promise of reform on the part of the student, or did his undoubted tolerance and liberalism stem from the fact that many such cases occurred quite frequently in the student community? Or was it that once again the kindness and compassion that was ascribed to him had the upper hand? Unfortunately, we do not know the answer to these questions.

Socially, Mianowski was valued for his courtesy, hospitality, and exquisite manners. In the early period of his stay in Warsaw, when restrictions on organising private meetings had yet to be imposed, Antoni Białecki recalled that every Saturday there was a social event in Mianowski's apartment on Świętokrzyska Street dedicated to public affairs, learning and literature. It was the professor's habit to address even his elders with the familiar second person *Ty* – You, and this was accepted by all without reservations. If he switched to the formal *Pan* – Sir – or worse still to *Pan Dobrodziej* – My very good sir – it meant he was in a bad mood. But it passed quickly[43].

In Warsaw, as in Petersburg, people made use of Mianowski's political influence and his good connections with Russians who were leading representatives of the Empire's bureaucratic elite. One person who requested Mianowski's assistance in securing a favour from Viceroy Berg was Apollo Korzeniowski,

---

41 *Szkoła rozumu i charakteru. Szkoła Główna Warszawska (1862–1869). Materiały do dziejów,* p. 427–428.

42 *Ibidem,* p. 428.

43 A. B i a ł e c k i, *Rektor Józef Mianowski,* p. 167.

POLISH KINGDOM – WARSAW                                                                 77

who wanted permission for his wife Ewa (*née* Bobrowska: they were the parents of the writer Joseph Conrad) to travel from Chernihiv, their Ukrainian domicile, for medical reasons. His intervention failed[44]. We may assume that there were others of a similar nature, especially regarding Mianowski's closer circle of friends, but, like this one, were not always successful.

Perfect testimony to Mianowski's character is to be found in a letter written to him by Stefan Pawlicki, who went on to be a resurrectionist priest (CR) and professor of philosophy and history of philosophy at the Accademia di Religione Cattolica in Rome and the Jagiellonian University in Cracow. At the time of the letter Pawlicki was appointed lecturer at Warsaw's Main School, which for him was a dream come true. Dated 5/6 September 1866, the contents of the letter were as follows:

> Your Excellency the Rector!
>
> Allow me, Sir, to begin my letter by conveying the sincerest thanks. I have been apprised by milady the countess Plater of the kindness with which you are dealing with my case, though hitherto I have done nothing to merit Your Excellency's goodwill. I can perhaps hazard the hope that the future will show I was not wholly unworthy of it. Meanwhile as regards the nearest future, I intend to pass the summer months in the country to prepare thoroughly for the new occupation while awaiting my appointment which by the grace of Your Excellency will be granted to me.
>
> In those circumstances I would not arrive in Warsaw until the autumn, at the start of the academic year, and would devote all the free time remaining to me to preparing my lectures and completing a few literary works. Nonetheless this is only an intention, which I most humbly dare to present to You; should Your Excellency deem it impractical and consider my immediate arrival in Warsaw to be indispensable, I shall wholly adapt to Your will.
>
> If I were able at the start of the academic year to begin my course of lectures, I undertake to read for five hours every week, of which three I would dedicate to the history of philosophy and two to the philosophy of law: I believe that number of hours will suffice for both subjects to be duly developed over the year and carried to their conclusion. These are merely expressions of intention, whose implementation is in the hands of Your Excellency's benevolent decision; awaiting which I declare myself to be Your Excellency's humble servant.
>
> Stefan Pawlicki
> Rogalin pod Kórnikiem
> 13th April 1866[45]

---

44   Z. N a j d e r, *Życie Conrada Korzeniowskiego*, vol. 1, p. 41.
45   National Library, manuscript 2674, *Listy literatów i uczonych polskich, głównie XIX w.*, sheet (k.) 252 (both sides). Cf. Jagiellonian Library *Inwentarz rękopisów* 8001–9000, part 2,

# CHAPTER 4

On his travels abroad Mianowski continued to stay in touch with old friends. A letter has been preserved addressed to Seweryn Goszczyński, dated 12 August 1867:

> My Worthy and Dear Friend!
>
> I was very briefly in Paris, Mr Seweryn [Gałęzowski] was unable to give me your address, and in addition I was and still am ill; I can walk only with difficulty, great difficulty, for I have an abscess in an inconvenient place, which smites me and hurts me terribly [...]. Maybe you will find a use for this small sum of money that I'm sending you, I am sorry that I cannot send you a little more [...]. I embrace you like a brother, my heart filled with extraordinary feelings.
>
> Dr Mian [Józef Mianowski Dr – Goszczyński's annotation][46].

Mianowski also participated in unofficial contacts between Russian aristocratic circles and Polish conservatives, on issues including pan-Slavic projects. The pan-Slavists were a very heterogeneous group, ranging from ministers, such as Dimitry Tolstoy and journalists, like Mikhael Katkov, to university professors and ordinary people; they established various societies such as the Russian People's Association. There were also different shades of pan-Slavism – some cultural, others political of different degrees of intensity right up to extremely reactionary. It is thus not possible today to ascertain the precise nature of these contacts. All we do know is that Mianowski liaised on the one hand with Margrave Aleksander Wielopolski and on the other with his old school friend Michał Grabowski; and that he handed the margrave missives on the topic of pan-Slavic concepts from Countess Antonina D. Bludova, whom he probably knew personally from his Petersburg days[47].

The security of Mianowski's position was confirmed by his twice being re-elected to the post of rector at the end of 1864 and in 1867[48]. The authorities' appreciation of his activities in Warsaw found its expression in 1865, when he became a knight of the order of St. Stanislaus, First Class, and in 1867, when he received the order of St. Anne, First Class[49].

---

no. 8501–9000, S. Pawlicki, *Listy moje i dzieje myśli mej od 20 października r. 1862*, sheet (k.) 259.

46  National Library, manuscript 2956, *Korespondencja Seweryna Goszczyńskiego z lat 1833–1857*, sheet (k.) 23.

47  H. Głębocki, *Kresy Imperium. Szkice i materiały do dziejów polityki Rosji wobec jej peryferii (XVIII–XXI) wiek*, Kraków 2006, pp. 480–481.

48  In both cases, he was elected by the Senate by majority vote. His second three-year term was confirmed on 16 November 1865.

49  Order St. Stanislaus awarded 26 August 1865 roku; order of St. Anne, 10 June 1867.

POLISH KINGDOM – WARSAW

He also ventured into broader areas of social work. Despite a three-month illness in 1867 and a short sojourn in Paris he agreed to become a vice-president of the Association for the Encouragement of Fine Arts[50], set up in 1860, while in the 1870s he was the first president of the Association of Agricultural Settlements and Tradesmen's Alms Houses. Thanks to Mianowski's support this Association gathered funds by organising the first series of public talks in Warsaw with the participation of numerous academics, former professors, and alumni of the Main School[51].

Meanwhile the position he held in the Association for the Encouragement of Fine Arts was that of second vice-president, alongside Justyn (Justynian) Karnicki (1806–1876), who was one of the co-founders of the Association, the first honorary director of Warsaw's Museum of Fine Arts (1862–1876), historian and archaeologist and a graduate of the University of Vilnius where the two may have got to know each other. The first seat of the Association, which was housed in the Hotel Europejski on the Krakowskie Przedmieście, was a meeting place for eminent patrons of the arts such as Baron Edward Rastawiecki, Count Aleksander Przezdziecki, Count Stanisław Zamoyski and Józef Ignacy Kraszewski, and of artists: these included Wojciech Gerson, soon to found Warsaw's only private School of Fine Arts, known as the drawing class, and also Józef Simmler, January Suchodoski and Juliusz Kossak[52]. The first painting to be purchased for the collection of the Association was Józef Simmler's *Death of Barbara Radziwiłłówna* (1860), a work characteristic of the academic style of that time and in keeping with the public's expectations of historicism in art[53]. It remains to this day one of the most important works in the canon of 19th century Polish painting.

But inexorably, changes loomed. 1867 saw the abolition of the Government Commission for Religious Faiths and Public Enlightenment, while the Warsaw Educational Region was restored to its previous administrative function. As a result, oversight of education in the Kingdom was once again integrated with the rest of the lands of the Empire. The closing down of the Government Commission meant that Mianowski ceased to be member there. On the other hand, he was appointed permanent member of the superintendent's council of the Warsaw Educational District[54].

---

50 Confirmed as vice-president 9 June 1867. He writes of his illness in the letter to S. Goszczyński cited above.

51 L. Zasztowt, *Popularyzacja nauki*, p. 221 & following.

52 Fuller information on this subject: J. Wiercińska, *Towarzystwo Zachęty Sztuk Pięknych w Warszawie: zarys działalności*, Wrocław 1968.

53 Cf. M. Poprzęcka, *Akademizm*, ed. 1, Warsaw 1977, ed. 2, Warszawa 1989.

54 Dismissal and appointment dated 1 July 1867.

80 CHAPTER 4

He was not fully aware of Petersburg's intentions concerning not only the Main School but also the future of the whole educational system in the Kingdom. This could have been a symptom of the benevolence and naivety which was sometimes ascribed to him. On the other hand, he may have had reason to hope that this time too – as at the time of the uprising – his influence at the emperor's court would enable him to guide matters along according to his wishes. Such illusions were not shared by the school's other lecturers, such as Karol Estreicher, who had already had the dubious pleasure of personally hearing the opinion of Superintendent Fyodor Witte[55].

In 1868, still entertaining illusory hopes, Mianowski continued his efforts in Petersburg to convert the Main School into a university. In this, he had some encouraging signals from the Empire's capital: confirmation of his election as vice-president of the Association for the Encouragement of Fine Arts; his appointment as consulting member of the Medical Council of the Kingdom; and above all the confirmation of his election to a third term as rector[56]. This time, too, it seems that Mianowski counted on a positive outcome and the creation of a Polish university in Warsaw – even though for a whole year Superintendent Witte had been issuing clear warnings that the school would have a 'purely Russian' character[57]. Indeed, the idea of transforming the Main School into a Russian university had been mooted as far back as August-September 1864. The Jugenheim edicts of that time were clear pointers to the way the situation would evolve. Working out the details of this operation took five years. Was it possible that Mianowski was not aware of it? It seems highly unlikely.

Admittedly, the appointment of Mianowski to his third term in office suggested that he was in a strong position. But we know that even in the elections to the second term he had a rival for the post, supported by Fyodor Witte – this was the historian and Polish philologist Jan Papłoński, at that time director of the Warsaw's Institute for the Deaf, Dumb and Blind. There were rumours that in the wake of Mianowski's expected departure the new rector of the Imperial

---

55   S. Estreicher, *Z ostatnich chwil Szkoły Głównej*, Kraków 1916, p. 6. Cf. M. Brykalska, *Aleksander Świętochowski*, vol. 1, p. 29 & following.

56   RGIA, f. 733, op. 147, e.hr. 752, Confirmation of election as vice-president, 24 April 1868; appointment as consulting member, 30 May 1868. Confirmation as rector (third term) up to 16 November 1871, *ibidem*. sheet (k.) 24.

57   *Dzieje Uniwersytetu Warszawskiego 1807–1915*, p. 370. Cf. J. Schiller, *Powstanie Cesarskiego Uniwersytetu Warszawskiego*.

POLISH KINGDOM – WARSAW

University would be Pavel Leontiev[58], professor of classics and antiquity, or von Hübbenet of Kyiv (probably Kristian Jakovlevich Gubenet, 1822–1873)[59].

In 1869 came the decision by Alexander II to transform the Main School into the Imperial University of Warsaw, which unfortunately also entailed making it fully Russian. The specific restructuring measures had been worked on from 1866, the year Dimitry A. Tolstoy became minister of public education. As Stefan Kieniewicz reported, Mianowski was initially under the illusion that the new reform would not go too far. From as far back as the end of 1863 he was president of the trustees of Warsaw's Hospital of the Infant Jesus. In 1869 he strove to set up an infirmary for the poor under the auspices of the hospital. In other words, he planned to remain in Warsaw[60].

His social world and the respect afforded him in Warsaw were undoubtedly key elements connecting him with the city. They were not limited to the Warsaw elite, extending to broader social relations. There remains in the archives a letter dated 24th May 1869, written by Mianowski to an unknown female, a visit to whose home left him stunned. He wrote:

> I returned home earlier than I had expected, still moved by the deep emotion that I experienced on leaving your home – how brief are those moments in human life and how long their memories prevail in a grateful heart! I had a great desire to go back to you, so as tell you this on that same day, but then I thought it would be better to leave it till later – so to one of the coming days.
>
> Dr Mianowski
> 24th May 1869[61]

Eventually, however, while torn by inner doubts, he took the decision to move to Italy. He left Warsaw in July, never permanently to return[62].

He had undoubtedly been under the misapprehension that he could have remained as rector of the new Imperial University. We know today that this would not have been possible: the post was to be reserved for a Russian, though admittedly this condition was not explicitly stipulated in the University Statute. Even if he could have filled the new position, this would have cancelled his

---

58  J. S c h i l l e r, *Universitas rossica. Koncepcja rosyjskiego uniwersytetu 1863–1917*, Warsaw 2008, p. 178.

59  I. B a r a n o w s k i, *Ostatnie dni Szkoły Głównej*, [in:] *Szkoła rozumu i charakteru. Szkoła Główna Warszawska (1862–1869). Materiały do dziejów*, p. 446.

60  S. K i e n i e w i c z, *Mianowski Józef*, p. 524. He was appointed president of the hospital council on 29 November 1863.

61  National Library, manuscipt 2674, *Listy literatów i uczonych polskich*, sheet (k.) 87–88.

62  A. B i a ł e c k i, *Rektor Józef Mianowski*, p. 169.

82 CHAPTER 4

whole legacy at the school up to that moment. He probably imagined, rightly, that he would have to dismiss lecturers whom he had personally taken on, since many were obliged to leave through their inability to comply with the requirement of teaching in Russian. They were given two years' grace to prepare to change their language of instruction. He would have become a puppet in the hands of Russian professors, nationalist and hostile to the Poles, their main goal being the furtherance not so much of learning as of uncompromising Russification. Although – as we know today – not all the Russian professors at the Imperial University of Warsaw were blind executors of the anti-Polish campaign imposed by the authorities, the reality was that the only almost openly pro-Polish lecturer there was Nikolai I. Karieyev, professor of general history in the years 1879–1885[63]. That at least is how he was remembered by his contemporaries. We may remind ourselves too that the Imperial University hosted a migration of 37 lecturers from the Main School for 46 Chairs. In successive years, however, and especially after that two-year period of grace, the number of Poles among the professors began to shrink systematically.

How grim was the atmosphere in the transition from the abolition of the school to the opening of the Russian Imperial University can be seen from this fragment of a letter sent from Vienna by Tytus Chałubiński to Ignacy Baranowski on 5th August 1869:

> There is not much I can tell you despite my long conversation with W[itte] about the future restructuring. The only certainty is that you will still be able to lecture in Polish for the next two years – as will I (apparently, I might then have the possibility to lecture in Latin). Over this period, however, we will be, like others in the same situation, 'on half rations', presumably because *plenus venter non studet libenter*. There are no other details; it seems they might emerge upon the arrival of the new rector. (Our previous one [Józef Mianowski] has meanwhile gone to Italy.) They say that the opening of the new university will take place on 1/13 September.

In the end, as Joanna Schiller-Walicka writes, it took place on 12th October 1869[64]. Later, just after Mianowski's death, Edmund Jankowski recalled his tenure as rector in these words:

---

63 He left a memoir, partly published in Polish translation. N.I. K a r e e e v: *Prozhitoye i perezhitoye*, Leningrad 1990.

64 Cited in J. S c h i l l e r-W a l i c k a, *Cesarski Uniwersytet Warszawski: między edukacją a polityką*, p. 586.

POLISH KINGDOM – WARSAW

Which of us, students at the time, did not bow his head in respect when from a distance he saw this universally liked and esteemed man, who already in Krakowskie Przedmieście had placed his hat in his hand as he walked to the university buildings, greeted by a deep lowering of the head on the part of every young person?

He was suited to the office he held in a way that could not be matched. A skilled diplomat, a statesman seasoned by life, fervently loving both the young and the land whose son he was, like a hen protects her chicks, so the rector of the Main School shielded both his institution and the whole community working within it from external gales, storms and dangers. How many hazards he reversed, and how many he forestalled, that we do not need to go into here; suffice it to say that he fully deserved his memorial stone, and it is only our regret that carved on it is the inscription that it was laid by just one department. All departments loved the rector in equal measure; they have all preserved the same grateful memory[65].

---

65    E. Jankowski, *Szkoła Główna Warszawska*, pp. 443–444. The reference is to the bust mentioned earlier, mounted by the Law Department in the church of the Jesuit fathers on Świętojańska street in the Old Town. It is now in the Warsaw University Museum.

CHAPTER 5

# Italy – Senigallia

Mianowski left Warsaw and settled in Senigallia (formerly Sinigalia or Sena Gallica), located on the Adriatic coast between Pesaro and Ancona, not far from San Marino. He had an imposing villa built for himself, while nearby he purchased a property for the engineer Stanisław Kierbiedź, whom he had first met as a student in Vilnius and with whom he developed greater ties of friendship in Petersburg[1].

Senigallia was already at that time something of an attractive health resort, a forerunner of Italian balneology. Its future as a tourist centre was just beginning to blossom. The town had an interesting history, harking back to antiquity. It was apparently first settled by the Gauls in the 4th century B.C. and was one of their prime seats of government on the Appenine Peninsula. This explains the second part of the municipality's name. In Roman times, too, it was a holiday destination. It formally became a Roman colony in 284 B.C., the first on the Adriatic coast, and was named Sena Gallica. But its greatest splendour came in the 15th century, when it came into the possession of Giovanni della Rovere – though it was for a certain period owned by Cesare Borgia. It was those years that gave rise to the splendid fortress of Rocca Roveresca – a stronghold that reflects the complex history of the town: originally a Roman citadel, it was reconstructed and enlarged by the della Rovere family; subsequently, incorporated into the Papal States, it served as a prison, hospital and eventually an orphanage[2].

Even in Mianowski's time the city was resplendent in its monuments. In the Piazza del Duca, you would find the Fontanna delle Anatre – Fountain of Ducks – in its north-western corner. There was another fountain in the main square of the old town, the Piazza Roma: the Fountain of Neptune. To the north of that location was the round marketplace of Foro Annoario, encircled by columns in the Doric style, with numerous stalls laden with victuals, cheeses, fish,

---

1    S. Kieniewicz, *Mianowski Józef*, p. 524. Cf. M.N. Voronin, M.M. Voronina, *Stanislav Valerianovich Kierbedz*, Leningrad 1982. Biographical notes in: PSB (S. Brzozowski), *Polski wkład w przyrodoznawstwo i technikę. Słownik polskich i związanych z Polską odkrywców, wynalazców oraz pionierów nauk matematyczno-przyrodniczych i techniki* (B. Orłowski), *Słownik Polskich Pionierów Techniki* (B. Orłowski), *Słownik Biograficzny Techników Polskich* (B. Chwaściński).

2    G. Santoni, P. Formiconi, *Senigallia, il Borgo della Posta*, Senigallia 2019, http://www.comune.senigallia.an.it/pdf/Senigallia_il_Borgo_della_Posta.pdf.

*frutti di mare*, vegetables, and fruit. And interesting too was the waterfront of the Misa River, where to this day one can admire 126 arcades hewn from Istrian stone, known collectively as the Portici Ercolani. In Mianowski's time, access from the sea to Senigallia's tiny port was through the estuary of the Misa, while on land you would enter it from the river's western, left bank, on the right-hand side going towards the river's meeting-point with the Adriatic[3].

Senigallia – and its old town located within the arc of the Misa on her right bank – was a dream place for retirement; and it had not yet become a crowded seaside resort. It guaranteed peace and quiet. This is how the small town was described in 1503 by Niccolò Machiavelli:

> The town of Sinigalia is distinct from those located at the foothills of the mountains by not much more than the sketch of an arc. And it is distant from the marina by less than a mile. Alongside the town flows a small river, which washes those of its walls which touch on Fano. A long stretch of road reaches and runs along the mountains to Sinigalia, and when you come to the river that flows through Sinigalia, you move to the left-hand side upwards along its bank; so much so that entering the area of the arc you reach the bridge which cuts across the river and almost crowns the entry to Sinigalia, not directly but transversally. Before that entrance there stands a hamlet of houses around a square; the riverbank has been channelled along one border of that square[4].

As far as we know today, nothing remains of Mianowski's villa in the suburbs of Senigallia. What has remained, and can be admired despite its somewhat dilapidated state, is the villa of Stanisław Kierbedź, known to Italians as the Villa Gherbetz. It lies to the west of the town, some 3 km (30–45 minutes' walk) from the railway station which is in the old town on the seacoast. Its address is Strada del Camposanto Vecchio 49. One can only surmise that Mianowski's home was not dissimilar.

In the 1870s Mianowski did a lot of travelling, to Paris, Dresden, and Switzerland. He always paid frequent visits to Petersburg, where he continued to look after the grand duchess Maria. In winter he often went to Rome, where he was friendly with the local Polish diaspora, revolving round the Vatican. Among his hosts were Katarzyna and Hieronim Kieniewicz[5]. He rarely stayed in Warsaw; rather, it was a point of transit on his journeys to and from

---

3 *Opis lokalizacji: Senigallia*, 'Tawerna Skipperów. Portal Żeglarzy i Marynarzy'. http://www. tawernaskipperów.pl/lokalizacja/senigallia/3315.

4 *Descrizione del modo tenuto dal Duca Valentino nello ammazzare Vitelozzo Vitelli, Oliverotto da Ferma, il Signor Pagolo e il duca di Gravina Orsini è una breve opera storica di Niccolò Machiavelli, scritta nel 1503.* https://it.wikipedia.org/wiki/Senigallia.

5 S. Kieniewicz, *Dereszewicze 1863*, Wrocław 1986, p. 182.

# ITALY – SENIGALLIA

Petersburg. As one diarist observed, his temperament underwent a notable change. Albeit still warm-hearted and polite, he was no longer as lively and smiling as in the past. An inner dejection and tranquil sadness were clearly noticeable[6].

He carried on a prolific correspondence, especially with his Polish friends from Petersburg and former Warsaw professors and literary figures, including Kazimierz Krzywicki, Kazimierz Kraszewski and Józef Ignacy Kraszewski[7]. In September 1877 he received from Kraszewski 12 volumes of the author's collected works, and, as he wrote in a letter, intended to begin reading them starting with 'Stara Baśń' – An Ancient Tale[8].

During his frequent sojourns in Petersburg, he still conducted an extensive medical practice. Apart from the grand duchess he was doctor to other princely families: the Bariatynski, Bobrynski, Naryszkin, Shuvalov, and Orlov-Davidov. Many of these Russian aristocrats had Polish family connections, including the Potocki, Łubieński and Radziwiłł clans[9].

Early in the 1870s Mianowski was awarded a Grade III rank in the civil service – that of confidential councillor, corresponding to the rank of vice-admiral in the navy and lieutenant-general in the land forces. It was quite a breach of standard regulations, since even the most distinguished servants of the Empire, if they did not belong to the aristocracy, generally did not get promoted beyond Grade IV[10].

But being in favour with the emperor's family and the Petersburg elite was not always a guarantee of easy success. In 1876 Mianowski was awarded the order of St Vladimir Class II and a bursary, but the minister of education Dmitry A. Tolstoy managed to withhold the actual granting of these honours for two years.

As far back as the end of April 1874 Pyotr A. Valuyev, at the time minister for state assets (and until 1868 minister of the interior), acting at the behest of Prince Aleksandr Bariatynski, had approached the minister of education requesting that Mianowski be granted a bursary of 3000 roubles per annum for

---

6     A. Białecki, *Rektor Józef Mianowski* p. 170; J. Szujski, *Józef Mianowski, rektor Szkoły Głównej*, p. 472.

7     *Listy do K. Krzywickiego (1865–1878)*, ed. A. Wrzosek, Poznań 1930, reprint from 'Archiwum Historii i Filozofii Medycyny' vol. 7 & following; *Listy do K. Kaszewskiego*, ed. A. Wrzosek, Poznań 1929, reprint from 'Archiwum Historii i Filozofii Medycyny' vol. 3, no. 2.

8     Jagiellonian Library, manuscript 6528 IV, *List J. Mianowskiego do J.I. Kraszewskiego z dn. 6 września 1877 r.*, sheet (k.) 2.

9     Cf. Z.S. Feliński, *Pamiętniki, passim*; M. Czapska, *Europa w rodzinie*, Warsaw 1989.

10    RGIA, f. 733, op. 121, e.hr. 101, *Delo o pozhalovanii arendy byvshemu rektoru Varshavskoy Glavnoy Shkoly taynomu sovetniku Mianovskomu*.

six years because lacked the means to support himself[11]. Earlier still a similar request had been made by Pavel J. Kotzebue, the newly appointed governor-general of Warsaw who replaced the deceased Fyodor F. Berg[12]. The issue went on for two years, with the minister refusing to give way. As late as April 1876 D.A. Tolstoy argued with Valuyev that the Main School did not conform to the authorities' expectations, and that its rector did not have any achievements to his name[13]. Eventually, however, a bursary was granted in May – lowered to 2500 roubles per annum but extended to 12 years. Thus from 1876 onwards Mianowski was receiving 5500 roubles per year, making him a man of considerable wealth[14].

It seems reasonable to ask: do not these solicitations for Petersburg funding conflict with the image of a fervent Polish patriot?

He was 70 years old at the time. He had spent his whole life in the service of the Tsar. But he never – or at least there is no evidence for it in the source materials – demeaned himself before the authorities, which was not infrequently the case with some other Poles, for example Samuel Bogumił Linde or Wacław Aleksander Maciejowski[15]. It is perhaps worth noting, though, that neither of those two scholars was popular in Warsaw society, despite their significant academic achievements – and that after the November uprising Linde behaved as Mianowski did, protecting teachers and pupils accused of participating in the insurrection. On the other hand, Linde and Maciejowski were active in an earlier period, much more liberal than the 1860s.

Mianowski's state of mind was further exacerbated by poor health. And for years now he was vexed by a fanatically religious wife.

It would be hard to expect an elderly, sick man to exercise restraint in his financial affairs – possibly the only source of satisfaction he had left. The dissolution of the Main School was a great blow to him; it seems that with some difficulty he tried to get over it, but perhaps he never fully recovered from the shock. Maybe he saw his financial success as some kind of compensation for previous losses?

---

11    *Ibidem*, Letter of P. Valuyev to D. Tolstoy, 24 April 1847, k. 1.

12    *Ibidem*, Letter of P. Kotzebue to P. Valuyev, 12 April 1874, k. 2. Cf. Ł. Chimiak, *Gubernatorzy rosyjscy w Królestwie Polskim 1863–1915*, Wrocław 1999, p. 318.

13    RGIA, f. 733, op. 121, e.hr. 101, Letter of D. Tolstoy to P. Vauyev, 4 May 1876, k. 6–7.

14    The salary of a confidential councillor was 3000 roubles per annum, on top which was the bursary of 2500 roubles; the total was thus 5500 roubles.

15    Cf. A. K u l e c k a, *Między słowianofilstwem a słowianoznawstwem. Idee słowiańskie w życiu intelektualnym Warszawy lat 1832–1856*, Warsaw 1997.

# Epilogue

Józef Mianowski died on 6 January 1879 in Senigallia. He was interred in an impressive neo-Gothic vault, put in place by his wife in the Cimitero delle Grazie – the cemetery that adjoins the church of Santa Maria delle Grazie in Senigallia[1]. At the back of the vault is a plaque with an inscription in Latin:

HEIC SITVS EST
**IOSEPHUS MIANOWSKI**
NATIONE POLONVS VIR AVITAE NOBILITATIS
MEDICVS CLINICVS CLARI NOMINIS
LYCAEI MAGNI VARSAVIAE MODERATOR SANCTIORI CONSILIO
IMPERATORIS ADSCITVS
MAIORIBUS AMPLISSIMORVM ORDINVM INSIGNIBVS
EXORNATVS
IN MVNERIBVS OBEVNDIS REi CATHOLICAE ADPRIME STVOVIT VITAMQVE
TOTAM BENEFACTIS HONESTAVIT
SYMMOS ET IMOS AEQVE SOLICITVS INVIVIT
STVDIOSISSIMUS AMICORVM
ACADEMICAE IVVENTVTIS PATRIS INSTAR
OBIIT SENOGALLIAE VI IDUS IANVAR MDCCCLXXIX
MARIA SPES MIANOWSKA [...]
SACELLUM HOC EXCITAVIT [...][2]

Which translates as:

HERE RESTS
**JÓZEF MIANOWSKI**
POLISH NATIONAL
A MAN OF VIRTUE
CLINICAL MEDICAL DOCTOR OF WELL-DESERVED FAME
RECTOR OF THE MAIN SCHOOL OF WARSAW
MEMBER OF THE IMPERIAL MEDICAL COUNCIL
AWARDED THE MOST DISTINGUISHED MEDAL

---

1   In 1902 the 'Kurier Warszawski' initiated a fund-raising campaign for a tombstone monument to Mianowski. It seems unlikely that it was not known in Warsaw that such a monument had already been erected in Senigallia by the professor's widow. *Grób Mianowskiego*, 'Kurier Warszawski' 1902, no. 104, 16 April, evening edition, p. 3. Cited in Z. Anculewicz, *Świat i ziemie polskie w oczach redaktorów i współpracowników "Kuriera Warszawskiego" w latach 1868–1915*, Warsaw 2002, p. 144, 159. Mianowski's mausoleum in an impressive neo-Gothic vault is located on the left of the main entrance to the cemetery. http://italjarek.pl/po-polskic h-sciezkach-marche-jozef/mianowski/.

2   Inscription transcribed from photograph by http://italjarek.pl/po-polskich-sciezkach-marche-jozef/mianowski/.

© BRILL SCHÖNINGH, 2024 | DOI:10.30965/9783657794720_007

IN THE PERFORMANCE OF HIS DUTIES
A GREAT SUPPORTER OF CATHOLICISM
AS HIS WHOLE LIFE WELL CONFIRMED
AND EPITOMISED
WHILE LEAVING BEHIND ALL THE SORROWFUL LIVING
DEVOTED TO HIS FRIENDS
FATHER TO ACADEMIC YOUTH A MAN OF GREAT MERIT
PASSED AWAY IN SENOGALLIA ON THE SIXTH DAY OF JANUARY 1879
MARIA NADZIEJA [HOPE – L.Z.] MIANOWSKA [...]
DID CREATE THIS SHRINE [...]

News of his death set off an avalanche of articles and recollections. Obituaries appeared in all the major newspapers and weeklies, starting with the 'Kurier Warszawski'[3]. Everyone, it transpired, remembered the achievements of Warsaw University's only rector. The Main School generation decided to commemorate him with a memorial – the memorial being the Mianowski Fund, established in 1881[4]. The project was approved on 12 July 1881, with 45 signatures, including those of Karol Benni, Tytus Chałubiński, Aleksander Głowacki, Mścisław Godlewski, Władysław Holewiński, Aleksander Kraushar, Leopold and Stanisław Kronenberg, Jakób Natanson, Stanisław Przystański, Henryk Sienkiewicz, August Wrześniowski, Kazimierz Zaleski and many others[5].

On 14 May 1903 in the church of the Jesuit Fathers in Warsaw, a bust was placed of Józef Mianowski, funded by the finances and efforts of alumni from the Department of Law and Administration. At its base an engraved inscription read:

TO JÓZEF MIANOWSKI
BORN 1804 DIED 1879
OUR BELOVED RECTOR
FROM THE GRATEFUL GRADUATES
OF THE LAW DEPARTMENT
OF THE MAIN SCHOOL
IN WARSAW[6].

---

3 *Józef Mianowski (1804–1879)*, 'Kurier Warszawski' 1879 no. 7, 10 January, p. 2; Dr Ł., *Jeszcze o ś.p. Józefie Mianowskim*, 'Kurier Warszawski' 1879, no. 8, 11 January, p. 2. Cited in Z. A n c u l e w i c z, *Świat i ziemie polskie*, pp. 940, 970.

4 S. F i t a, *Pokolenie Szkoły Głównej, passim.*

5 *Przegląd materiałów do historii Kasy*, 'Nauka Polska' 1923, vol. 4, p. 367.

6 S. B o r o w s k i, *Zakończenie*, [in:] *Szkoła rozumu i charakteru. Szkoła Główna Warszawska (1862–1869). Materiały do dziejów*, pp. 552–553.

EPILOGUE

It was later thought that the bust, along with the whole interior of the Jesuit church in Świętojańska street in the Old Town, had been destroyed during the Warsaw Uprising of 1944. However, it was found in the ruins of the church and is now part of the collection of the Warsaw University Museum[7].

Returning to the subject of the Mianowski Fund: the professors and alumni of the Main School were unanimously agreed that it was only thanks to Mianowski that the institution was able to achieve such a high standard and to survive the January Uprising. On that, no one had any doubts.

• •<br>•

Mianowski was a patriot and one of the best of Poles. We may add that he was also one of the few who managed to be favourably remembered by both Poles and Russians.

In his own way Mianowski was at odds with the Polish model of patriotism. 'He loved the fatherland to the point of madness' but was not a 'crazy patriot' or a madman – that is how his stance was defined by his close friend from their schooldays, Seweryn Goszczyński[8].

Thanks to his character traits, but also to a degree of sentimental rationalism and conservatism, he managed to avoid the darker side of Polish patriotism, though sometimes he was compelled to make an unequivocal choice. Perhaps it was easier for him than for others. He was a Doctor of Medicine, not a poet. And then one of his more important characteristics was his caution. He came from an impoverished family of gentry folk. Almost everything he achieved was the result of personal effort. He was aware that he might easily lose the position he had attained through hard work if he became involved in anti-government activity. But in hard moments of political turmoil, he was capable of remarkably courageous conduct; a critical comment made by a school colleague about his naivety, underpinned by fears or even cowardice, seems to be unfair. It is also worth bearing in mind that the academic world was, and is, not only conservative, but also wary of ostentatious behaviour, of engagement in overt political activity, especially if it involves irredentism and any sort of social movements. In this respect Mianowski was a typical representative of his milieu. One cannot expect to hear support for revolution voiced in the conventional world of academia. There, sympathies, and antipathies tend to be expressed between the lines.

---

7  *Szkoła rozumu i charakteru. Szkoła Główna Warszawska (1862–1869). Materiały do dziejów,* photograph p. 562.

8  M. J a n i o n, *Wobec zła,* Chotomów 1989, p. 9 & following.

If one were tempted to look for an ideal embodiment of Polish conservatism in its 19th-century, moderate form, then in my opinion a perfect example – not just in territories occupied by Russia, but across the whole former Commonwealth – could be provided precisely by Józef Mianowski. A conservative capable of adapting his modus operandi to the prevailing political conditions. A realist in his contacts with Russian aristocratic elites, and able with equal deftness to find his way around the Russian imperial bureaucracy. While, on the other hand, he was a person honestly striving to help his fellow countrymen, he also endeavoured to mitigate the extreme political behaviours and hot-headed temperaments of the more radical among them. In his conservatism he was thus a particularly 'romantic' Positivist. The generation that followed would be considerably more progressive and more radical in its aspirations: restoring Poland's independence would increasingly be foremost on its agenda. But the real breakthrough would come only with the people born in the 1860s. All of them would in some ways have been affected by the experience of the January Uprising of 1863. They did not of course participate in it – they had barely been born into the world – but the legend of that uprising allowed them to construct their own narrative and come up with new political projects. In this way Polish moderate conservatism, Warsaw-based Positivism, and the legend of insurrectional armed struggle became lodestars which guided such people as Józef Piłsudski, Roman Dmowski, Ignacy Jan Paderewski, Stanisław Wojciechowski and Ignacy Daszyński, as well as many others, in formulating new political ideas. In the life stories of each of those figures we can find traces of the thinking of the Positivists and the Warsaw Main School. Including the legend, now forgotten, of Józef Mianowski.

# Bibliography

Roman Aftanazy, *Dzieje rezydencji na dawnych kresach Rzeczypospolitej*, vol. 1–10, Wrocław 1986, 1991–1993.

A.K., *Odnowione groby, odnowiona pamięć*, 'Tygodnik Wileńszczyzny' http://www.tygodnik.lt/200645/wiesci6.html.

Alkar [Aleksander Kraushar], *Czasy szkolne za Apuchtina (1879–1897)*, Warsaw 1915.

Zbigniew Anculewicz, *świat i ziemie polskie w oczach redaktorów i współpracowników 'Kuriera Warszawskiego' w latach 1868–1915*, Warsaw 2002.

Stanisław Arct, *Okruchy wspomnień*, Warsaw 1962.

Tamara Bairašauskaitė, *O litewskich marszałkach gubernialnych i powiatowych (do 1863 r.)*, 'Przegląd Wschodni' 1997, vol. 4, no. 2 (14).

Michał Baliński, *Dawna Akademia Wileńska: próba jej historyi: od założenia w roku 1579 do ostatecznego jej przekształcenia w roku 1803*, St. Petersburg 1862.

Michał Baliński, *Opisanie statystyczne miasta Wilna*, Vilnius 1835.

Ignacy Baranowski, *Ostatnie dni Szkoły Głównej*, [in:] *Szkoła rozumu i charakteru. Szkoła Główna Warszawska (1862–1869). Materiały do dziejów*, introduction, selection and development Grzegorz P. Bąbiak, Warsaw 2019, pp. 446–454.

Ignacy Baranowski, *Pamiętniki (1840–1862)*, Poznań 1923.

Alina Barszczewska-Krupa, *Szymon Konarski*, Warsaw 1976.

Ludwik Bazylow, *Polacy w Petersburgu*, Wrocław 1984.

Daniel Beauvois, *Szkolnictwo polskie na ziemiach litewsko-ruskich 1803–1832: Uniwersytet Wileński*, vol. 1–2, Rome–Lublin 1991.

Daniel Beauvois, *Trójkąt ukraiński. Szlachta, carat i lud na Wołyniu, Podolu i Kijowszczyźnie 1793–1914*, Lublin 2005.

Daniel Beauvois, *Wilno – polska stolica kulturalna zaboru rosyjskiego 1803–1832*, Wrocław 2010.

Antoni Białecki, *Rektor Józef Mianowski w Warszawie od 1862 do 1869 r.*, 'Niwa' 1879, no. 99, p. 160.

[Józef Bieliński] Dr Szeliga, *Dokumenta urzedowe z 'Teki' Rektora Twardowskiego* 'Archiwum do Dziejów Literatury i Oświaty w Polsce' 1889 (Kraków), vol. 6, pp. 170–335.

Józef Bieliński, *Cesarskie Towarzystwo Lekarskie Wileńskie jego prace i wydawnictwa (1805–1864)*, Warsaw 1890.

Józef Bieliński, *Stan nauk lekarskich za czasów Akademii Medyko-Chirurgicznej Wileńskiej bibliograficznie przedstawiony. Przyczynek do dziejów medycyny*, Warsaw 1889.

Józef Bieliński, *Uniwersytet Wileński (1579–1831)*, vol. 3, Kraków 1899–1900.

Tadeusz Bobrowski, *Pamiętnik mojego życia*, vol. 1–2, Warsaw 1979.

Józef Symeon B o g u c k i, *Wizerunki społeczeństwa warszawskiego. Szkice obyczajowe*, Warsaw 1844.

Grażyna B o r k o w s k a, *Konstelacja Szkoły Głównej – Józef Mianowski*, [in:] *Szkoła Główna: kręgi wpływów*, Warsaw 2017, pp. 247–264.

Jerzy B o r o w c z y k, *Rekonstrukcja procesu filomatów i filaretów 1823–1824*, Poznań 2003.

Michał B r e n s z t e j n, *Biblioteka Uniwersytecka w Wilnie do roku 1832-go*, Vilnius 1922.

Maria B r y k a l s k a, *Aleksander Świętochowski. Biografia*, vol. 1–2, Warsaw 1981–1987.

Gabriel B r z ę k, *Józef Nusbaum-Hilarowicz. Życie, praca, dzieło*, Lublin 1984.

Karol B r z o z o w s k i, *Listy ostatniego romantyka* [...] *do Alkara (1895–1898). Kartka z pamiętnika*, Warsaw 1912.

Stanisław B r z o z o w s k i, *Jędrzej Śniadecki, jego życie i dzieła*, Warsaw 1903.

Stanisław B r z o z o w s k i, *Listy*, vol. 1–2, Kraków 1970.

Ksawery B u d y t a, *Mowa żałobna Ksawerego Budyty, kandydata teologii, wygłoszona w czasie nabożeństwa za duszę ś.p. Józefa Mianowskiego, b. rektora b. Szkoły Głównej w Warszawie, odbytego przez Jego Excellencyę JWks. Biskupa Gintowta, administratora dyecezyi płockiej w kosciel katerdralnym płockim dnia 8 lutego 1879 r. za staraniem wychowańców tej szkoły*, Warsaw 1879.

Tytus C h a ł u b i ń s k i, *Listy 1840–1889*, Wrocław 1970.

Zygmunt C h e ł m i c k i, *Mowa ks. Zygmunta Chełmickiego wypowiedziana na nabożeństwie żałobnym za duszę ś.p. dra med. Józefa Mianowskiego b. Rektora b. Szkoły Głównej, które odbyło się w Warszawie dnia 16 stycznia 1879 r. w Kościele św. Krzyża, staraniem b. wychowańców i profesorów tejże szkoły*, Warsaw 1879.

Łukasz C h i m i a k, *Gubernatorzy rosyjscy w Królestwie Polskim 1863–1915*, Wrocław 1999.

Bronisław C h l e b o w s k i, *Znaczenie Szkoły Głównej Warszawskiej w dziejach umysłowości i nauki polskiej*, [in:] *Księga pamiątkowa zjazdu byłych wychowańców Szkoły Głównej Warszawskiej w 50-tą rocznicę jej założenia*, ed. Edmund J a n k o w s k i, Warsaw 1914. *Ibidem* [in:] *Szkoła rozumu i charakteru. Szkoła Główna Warszawska (1862–1869). Materiały do dziejów*, introduction, selection and development Grzegorz P. B ą b i a k, Warsaw 2019, pp. 512–526.

Artur C h o j e c k i, *Kasa im. Mianowskiego i 'Nauka Polska'*, 'Tygodnik Powszechny' 1948, no. 25.

Lucjan C h r z ę ś c i e w s k i, *Jędrzej Śniadecki. Życie i dzieło*, Kraków 1978.

Edward C h w a l e w i k, *Zbiory polskie. Archiwa, biblioteki, gabinety, galerie, muzea i inne zbiory pamiątek przeszłości w ojczyźnie i na obczyźnie w porządku alfabetycznym według miejscowości ułożone*, vol. 1–2, Warsaw–Kraków 1926–1927.

*Cmentarz na Rossie w Wilnie, historia, sztuka, przyroda*, ed. Anna Sylwia C z y ż, Bartłomiej G u t o w s k i, Warsaw–Kraków 2019.

Bohdan C y w i ń s k i, *Rodowody niepokornych*, Paris 1985.

Maria C z a p s k a, *Europa w rodzinie*, Warsaw 1989.

Maria C z a p s k a, *Ludwika Śniadecka*, Warsaw 1958.

# BIBLIOGRAPHY

Adam Jerzy Czartoryski, *Pamiętniki i memoriały polityczne 1776–1809*, selection, development, introduction Jerzy Skowronek, Warsaw 1989.

Ryszarda Czepulis-Rastenis, *Klassa umysłowa. Inteligencja Królestwa Polskiego 1832–1861*, Warsaw 1973.

Helena Datner, *Ta i tamta strona. Żydowska inteligencja Warszawy drugiej połowy XIX wieku*, Warsaw 2007.

Михаил Долбилов, *Русский край, чужая вера: этноконфессиональная политика империи в Литвие и Белоруссии при Александрие II*, Москва 2010.

Николай Дубровский, *Официальная наука в Царствие Польском*, Санкт Петербург 1908.

Helena Duninówna, *Ci, których znałam*, Warsaw 1957.

Adolf Dygasiński, *Listy*, Wrocław 1972.

*Dzieje inteligencji polskiej do roku 1918*, ed. Jerzy Jedlicki, vol. 2–3, Warsaw 2008.

*Dzieje Uniwersytetu Warszawskiego 1807–1915*, ed. Stefan Kieniewicz, Warsaw 1981.

*Dzieje Uniwersytetu Warszawskiego 1816–1916*, ed. Tomasz Kizwalter, Warsaw 2016.

Bolesław Dzierżawski, Otton Hewelke, Władysław Janowski, Józef Zawadzki, *Cholera, jej dawniejsze epidemje u nas, przyczyny, objawy, zapobieganie i leczenie*, Warsaw 1892 (print form 'Kronika Lekarska').

*Encyklopedia Ziemi Wileńskiej. Wileński słownik biograficzny*, ed. Henryk Dubowik, Leszek Jan Malinowski, vol. 1, Bydgoszcz 2002.

Tadeusz Epsztajn, *Edukacja dzieci i młodzieży w polskich rodzinach ziemiańskich na Wołyniu, Podolu i Ukrainie w II połowie XIX wieku*, Warsaw 1998.

Stanisław Estreicher, *Z ostatnich chwil Szkoły Głównej*, Kraków 1916.

[J. Falkowski], *Wspomnienia z roku 1848–1849 przez autora 'Obrazów z życia kilku ostatnich pokoleń w Polsce'*, Poznań 1879.

Jacek Feduszka, *Powstanie listopadowe na Litwie i Żmudzi*, 'Teka Komisji Historycznej OL PAN' 2004, vol. 1, pp. 110–160.

Zygmunt Szczęsny Feliński, *Pamiętniki*, development, introduction Eligiusz Kozłowski, Warsaw 1986.

*Filozofia i myśl społeczna w latach 1831–1864*, ed. Andrzej Walicki, Warsaw 1977.

Ludwik Finkel, *Pawia – Wilno (z końcem XVIII i w początkach XIX wieku)*, Vilnius 1929.

Stanisław Fita, *Pokolenie Szkoły Głównej w życiu społecznym i kulturze polskiej*, Warsaw 1980.

Ludwik Fiszer, *Wspomnienia starego księgarza*, Warsaw 1959.

*Fundusz Kultury Narodowej (1928–1937). Zarys działalności*, Warsaw 1937.

David Frick, *Kin, Kids and Neighbors: Communities and Confession in Seventeenth-Century Wilno*, Ithacoa, Cornell University Press 2013.

David Frick (development and editing), *Wilnianie. Żywoty siedemnastowieczne*, Warsaw 2008.

Polikarp G i r s z t o w t, *Rys historyczno-statystyczny Cesarsko-Królewskiej Warszawskiej Medyko-Chirurgicznej Akademii od jej zawiązku w dniu 4 czerwca 1857 r. aż do wcielenia do Szkoły Głównej dnia 1 października 1862 r.*, [in:] *Wykaz Szkoły Głównej Warszawskiej w letnim półroczu roku naukowego 1864/5*, Warsaw 1865.

Henryk G ł ę b o c k i, *Kresy imperium. Szkice i materiały do dziejów polityki Rosji wobec jej peryferii (XVIII–XXI) wiek*, Kraków 2006.

Józef G o ł ą b e k, *Bractwo św. Cyryla i Metodego w Kijowie*, Warsaw 1935.

Seweryn G o s z c z y ń s k i, *Podróż mojego życia. Urywki wspomnień i zapiski do pamiętnika 1801–1842*, development S. P i g o ń, Vilnius 1924.

Леонид Е. Г о р и з о н т о в, *Парадоксы имперской политики. Поляки в России и руские в Польше*, Москва 1999.

Konrad G ó r s k i, *Stanisław Krzemiński. Człowiek i pisarz*, Warsaw 1985.

Wojciech G ó r s k i, *Wspomnienia*, Warsaw 1937.

J. G r a b i e c [Józef D ą b r o w s k i], *Czerwona Warszawa przed ćwierć wiekiem*, Poznań 1925.

Benedykt H e r t z, *Na taśmie 70-lecia*, Warsaw 1966.

*Historia nauki polskiej*, ed. Bogdan S u c h o d o l s k i, vol. 4: part 1–3 *1863–1918*, Wrocław 1987; vol. 5, part 1 *1918–1952*, Wrocław 1992.

*Historia nauki polskiej*, vol. 3, *1795–1862*, ed. Jerzy M i c h a l s k i, Wrocław 1977.

Piotr H ü b n e r, Jan P i s k u r e w i c z, Jacek S o s z y ń s k i, Leszek Z a s z t o w t, *A History of the Józef Mianowski Fund*, transl., ed. Jacek S o s z y ń s k i, Warsaw 2013.

Piotr H ü b n e r, Jan P i s k u r e w i c z, Leszek Z a s z t o w t, *Kasa im. Józefa Mianowskiego – Fundacja Popierania Nauki 1881–1991*, Warsaw 1992.

Irenusz I h n a t o w i c z, *Uniwersytet Warszawski w latach 1869–1899*, [in:] *Dzieje Uniwersytetu Warszawskiego 1807–1915*, Warsaw 1981.

Ireneusz I h n a t o w i c z, *Utworzenie Cesarskiego Uniwersytetu Warszawskiego w roku 1869*, 'Roczniki Uniwersytetu Warszawskiego' 1972, vol. 12, pp. 55–70.

Henryka I l g i e w i c z, *Wileńskie towarzystwa i instytucje naukowe w XIX wieku*, Toruń 2005.

*Imperium inter pares. Роль трасферов в истории Российской империи (1700–1917)*, ред. Е. Анисимов и др., Москва 2010.

*Inteligencja polska pod zaborami. Studia*, ed. Ryszarda C z e p u l i s - R a s t e n i s, Warsaw 1978.

*Inteligencja polska w XIX iXX wieku. Studia*, ed. Ryszarda C z e p u l i s - R a s t e n i s, Warsaw 1981–1985, 1987, 1991.

August I w a ń s k i (senior and junior), *Pamiętniki 1832–1876; Wspomnienia 1881–1939*, Warsaw 1968.

Bohdan J a c z e w s k i, *Organizacja i finansowanie nauki polskiej w okresie międzywojennym*, Wrocław 1971.

# BIBLIOGRAPHY

Bohdan Jaczewski, *Polityka naukowa państwa polskiego w latach 1918–1939*, Wrocław 1978.

Bohdan Jaczewski, *Życie naukowe w Polsce odrodzonej*, [in:] *Życie naukowe w Polsce w drugiej połowie XIX i w XX wieku. Organizacje i instytucje*, ed. Bohdan Jaczewski, Warsaw 1987.

Mieczysław Jałowiecki, *Na skraju imperium i inne wspomnienia*, Warsaw 2014.

Maria Janion, *Wobec zła*, Chotomów 1989.

Edmund Jankowski, *Wspomnienia ogrodnika*, Warsaw 1972.

Edmund Jankowski, *Szkoła Główna Warszawska*, 'Tygodnik Ilustrowany' 1903, no.24.

Ludwik Janowski, *W promieniach Wilna i Krzemieńca*, Vilnius 1923.

Maciej Janowski, *Narodziny inteligencji 1750–1831. Dzieje inteligencji polskiej do roku 1918*, ed. Jerzy Jedlicki, vol. 1, Warsaw 2008.

Jerzy Jedlicki, *Błędne koło 1832–1864. Dzieje inteligencji polskiej do roku 1918*, ed. Jerzy Jedlicki, vol. 2, Warsaw 2008.

Ludwik Jenike, *Ze wspomnień*, vol. 1–2, Warsaw 1909–1910.

*Józef Mianowski. Listy do Kazimierza Krzywickiego (1865–1878)*, wydał i introductionem opatrzył Adam Wrzosek, 'Archiwum Historii i Filozofii Medycyny' 1927, vol. 7, pp. 126–127.

Николай И. Кареев, *Прожытое и пиережытое*, Ленинград 1990.

*Kasa im. Mianowskiego, Instytut Popierania Nauki. Dzieje, zadania, organizacja*, Warsaw 1929.

*Kasa Mianowskiego 1881–2011*, ed. Leszek Zasztowt, Warsaw 2011.

*Katalog dzieł wydanych z zapomogi Kasy im. Mianowskiego w latach 1881–1929*, Warsaw 1929.

*Katalog wydawnictw Kasy im. Mianowskiego Instytutu Popierania Nauki oraz wydawnictw będących w zawiadywaniu Kasy*, Warsaw 1939.

Kazimierz Kelles-Krauz, *Listy*, vol. 1–2, Wrocław 1984.

Stefan Kieniewicz, *Akademia Medyko-Chirurgiczna i Szkoła Główna (1857–1869)*, [in:] *Dzieje Uniwersytetu Warszawskiego 1807–1915*, Warsaw 1982, pp. 242–377.

Stefan Kieniewicz, *Józef Mianowski (1804–1879)*, Polski Słownik Biograficzny vol. 19, pp. 523–525.

Stefan Kieniewicz, *Powstanie styczniowe*, Warsaw 1983.

Stefan Kieniewicz, *Trzy etapy rozwoju nauki w Warszawie w XIX w.*, [in:] *Historyk a świadomość narodowa*, Warsaw 1982, pp. 143–161.

Halina Kiepurska, *Inteligencja zawodowa Warszawy 1905–1917*, Warsaw 1967.

Artur Kijas, *Mianowski Józef – МЯНОВСКИЙ ОСИП ИГНАТЬЕВИЧ*, strona 'Polski Petersburg': http://www.polskipetersburg.pl/hasla/mianowski-jozef.

Jadwiga Klemensiewiczowa, *Przebojem ku wiedzy*, Wrocław 1961.

Stanisław Konopka, *Wydział Lekarski Szkoły Głównej (1862–1869)*, 'Roczniki Uniwersytetu Warszawskiego' 1963, vol. 4, pp. 14–22.

98 BIBLIOGRAPHY

Stanisław K o s z u t s k i, *Walka młodzieży polskiej o wielkie ideały*, Warsaw 1928.

Tadeusz K o r z o n, *Mój pamiętnik przedhistoryczny*, Kraków 1912.

Stefan K o z a k, *Ukraińscy spiskowcy i mesjaniści: Bractwo Cyryla i Metodego*, Warsaw 1990.

Józef Ignacy K r a s z e w s k i, *Korespondencja Józefa Ignacego Kraszewskiego*. Seria III: *Listy z lat 1863–1887*, vol. 60: M (Mianowski – Mieczyński), manuscript Biblioteka Jagiellońska.

Józef Ignacy K r a s z e w s k i, *Otwarcie Szkoły Głownej w Warszawie*, [in:] *Szkoła rozumu i charakteru. Szkoła Główna Warszawska (1862–1869). Materiały do dziejów*, introduction, selection and development Grzegorz P. B ą b i a k, Warsaw 2019, pp. 158–170.

Józef Ignacy K r a s z e w s k i, *Wilno: od początków jego do roku 1750*, vol. 1–4, Vilnius 1838–1842.

Aleksander K r a u s h a r, *Siedmiolecie Szkoły Głównej Warszawskiej 1862–1869. Wydział Prawa i Administracji. Notatki do historii szkół w Polsce*, Warsaw 1883.

[Stanisław K r z e m i ń s k i], *Dwadzieścia pięć lat Rosji w Polsce (1863–1888)*, Lviv 1892.

Ludwik K r z y w i c k i, *Wspomnienia*, vol. 1–3, Warsaw 1957–1958.

*Księga pamiątkowa zjazdu byłych wychowańców byłej Szkoły Głównej Warszawskiej w 50-tą rocznicę jej założenia*, ed. Edmund J a n k o w s k i, Warsaw 1914.

Alicja K u l e c k a, *Między słowianofilstwem a słowianoznawstwem. Idee słowiańskie w życiu intelektualnym Warszawy lat 1832–1856*, Warsaw 1997.

Rafał K u z a k, *Epidemie cholery w XIX-wiecznej Polsce. Zapomniana choroba zabiła setki tysięcy ludzi*, 'Wielka Historia'. https://wielkahistoria.pl/epidemie-cholery-w-xix-wiecznej-polsce-zapomniana-choroba-zabila-setki-tysiecy-ludzi/.

Janina L e s k i e w i c z o w a, *Warsaw XIX wieku: 1795–1918*, Warsaw 1970 (and next editions).

Janina L e s k i e w i c z o w a, *Warsaw i jej inteligencja po powstaniu styczniowym 1864–1870*, Warsaw 1961.

Bolesław L i m a n o w s k i, *Józef Zaliwski bohater z powstania 1830–31 r.*, b.m. 1913.

Bolesław L i m a n o w s k i, *Pamiętniki (1837–1870)*, Warsaw 1937; idem, *Pamiętniki (1870–1907)*, Warsaw 1958; idem, *Pamiętniki (1907–1919)*, Warsaw 1961; idem, *Pamiętniki (1919–1928)*, Warsaw 1973.

*Listy Teofila i Hersylii (z domu Bécu) Januszewskich do Józefa Mianowskiego (1829–1837)*, letters edited with an introduction and comments by Leopold M é y e t, Warsaw 1897.

Stanisław L o r e n t z, *Album wileńskie*, Warsaw 1986.

Wincenty L u t o s ł a w s k i, *Jeden łatwy żywot*, Warsaw 1933.

Tadeusz Ł o p a l e w s k i, *Między Niemnem a Dźwiną. Ziemia Wileńska i Nowogródzka*, London 1955.

Maciej Ł o w i c k i, *Duch Akademii Wileńskiej. Z czasów Szymona Konarskiego pamiętnik ucznia wileńskiej Akademii Medyko-Chirurgicznej*, Vilnius 1925.

Roger Ł u b i e ń s k i, *Generał Tomasz Pomian hrabia Łubieński*, vol. 2, Warsaw 1899.

# BIBLIOGRAPHY

Czesław Malewski, *Rodziny szlacheckie na Litwie w XIX wieku*, Warsaw 2016.

Tadeusz Manteuffel, *Uniwersytet Warszawski w latach 1915/16–1934/35. Kronika*, Warsaw 1936.

Henryk Markiewicz, *Pozytywizm*, Warsaw 1978 (and next editions).

Leopold Méyet, *Listy do Władysława Bełzy*, Warsaw 1983.

Leopold Méyet, *Z życia Mianowskiego. Trochę faktów i dokumentów*, 'Tygodnik Ilustrowany' 1903, no. 24, pp. 465–466.

*Józef Mianowski* (curriculum vitae), 'Tygodnik Ilustrowany' 1903, no. 23, pp. 457.

*Józef Mianowski*, 'Tygodnik Ilustrowany' 1865, no. 286, pp. 97–98.

Stanisław Mianowski, *Świat, który odszedł: wspomnienia Wilnianina 1895–1945*, Warsaw 1997.

Józef Miąso, *Ludwik Krzywicki (działalność i ideologia oświatowa)*, Warsaw 1964.

Magdalena Micińska, *Inteligencja na rozdrożach 1864–1918. Dzieje inteligencji polskiej do roku 1918*, ed. Jerzy Jedlicki, vol. 3, Warsaw 2008.

Aleksiej Miller, *Imperia Romanovych i nacjonalizm*, Moskwa 2006.

Stanisław Morawski, *Kilka lat mojej młodości w Wilnie (1818–1825)*, development, introduction Adam Czartkowski, Henryk Mościcki, Warsaw 1959,

Zdzisław Najder, *Życie Conrada-Korzeniowskiego*, vol. 1–2, Warsaw 1998.

Zofia Nałkowska, *Mój ojciec*, Warsaw 1953.

'Nauka Polska. Jej Potrzeby, Organizacja i Rozwój' vol. 1–25, 1918–1947; vol. 1 (26)–19 (44), 1992–2010.

Andrzej Nowak, *Od imperium do imperium. Spojrzenie na historię Europy Wschodniej*, Kraków 2004.

Henryk Nusbaum, *Udział Wydziału Lekarskiego Szkoły Głównej Warszawskiej w ogólnej twórczości naukowej*, 'Archiwum Historii i Filozofii Medycyny' 1927, vol. 6, no. 2, 126–139.

Józef Nusbaum-Hilarowicz, *Pamiętniki przyrodnika*, Lviv [1925].

Stefan Pawlicki, *Listy moje i dzieje myśli mej od 20 października r. 1862, Inwentarz rękopisów BJ*, 8001–9000, part 2, no. 8501–9000, sheet (k.) 259.

*Pierwsze sprawozdanie Funduszu Kultury Narodowej*, Warsaw 1931.

*Drugie sprawozdanie Funduszu Kultury Narodowej*, Warsaw 1934.

*Trzecie sprawozdanie Funduszu Kultury Narodowej*, Warsaw 1937.

Jan Piskurewicz, *O naukowych kontaktach warszawskich instytucji popierających rozwój nauki na przełomie XIX i XX wieku*, 'Kwartalnik Historii Nauki i Techniki' 1983, no. 2, pp. 371–386.

Jan Piskurewicz, *Sto lat związków TNW z Kasą Mianowskiego*, [in:] *Towarzystwo Naukowe Warszawskie. Sto lat działalności*, ed. Ewa Wolnicz-Pawłowska, Włodzimierz Zych, Warsaw 2009, pp. 63–70.

Jan Piskurewicz, *W służbie nauki i oświaty. Stanisław Michalski i Fundusz Kultury Narodowej*, 'Tygodnik Powszechny' 1990, no. 5.

Jan Piskurewicz, *Warszawskie instytucje społecznego mecenatu nauki w latach 1869–1906. Muzeum Przemysłu i Rolnictwa i Kasa imienia Mianowskiego*, Wrocław 1990.

Jan Piskurewicz, *W służbie nauki i oświaty. Stanisław Michalski (1865–1949)*, Warsaw 1993.

*Portrety petersburskich Polaków – Портреты петербурских Поляков, опрац. Анатолий П. Нечай*, Петербург 2001.

Karol Poznański, *Geneza Szkoły Głównej Warszawskiej*, 'Przegląd Historyczno-Oświatowy' yea. 6: 1963, no. 3, pp. 271–302.

Karol Poznański, *Oświata i szkolnictwo w Królestwie Polskim 1831–1869. Lata zmagań i nadziei*, vol. 2 *Szkoły rzemieślniczo-niedzielne*, Warsaw 2001.

Karol Poznański, *Reforma szkolna w Królestwie Polskim w 1862 roku*, Wrocław 1968.

*Przegląd materiałów do historii Kasy*, 'Nauka Polska' 1923, vol. 4.

'Przewodnik Warszawski informacyjno-adresowy na rok 1869 z dołączeniem kalendarza i taryfy domów ', Warsaw 1869.

Gabriela z Günterów Puzynina, *W Wilnie i w dworach litewskich. Pamiętnik z lat 1815–1843*, Vilnius 1928, wyd. 2 Chotomów 1988.

Helena Radlińska, *Z dziejów pracy społecznej i oświatowej*, Wrocław 1964.

Ignacy Radliński, *Mój żywot*, Łuck 1938.

Ryszard Radzik, *Między zbiorowością etniczną a wspólnotą narodową. Białorusini na tle przemian narodowych w Europie Środkowo-Wschodniej XIX stulecia*, Lublin 2000.

Johannes Remy, *Brothers or Enemies: the Ukrainian National Movement and Russia, 1840s to the 1870*, Toronto 2016.

Johannes Remy, *Higher Education and National Identity. Polish Student Activism in Russia 1832–1863*, Helsinki 2000.

Waldemar Rolbiecki, *Geneza Polskiej Akademii Nauk (1930–1952)*, Warsaw 1990.

Jerzy Róziewicz, *Polsko-rosyjskie powiązania naukowe (1725–1918)*, Wrocław 1984.

*Russia's Great Reforms 1855–1881*, ed. by Ben Ekloff, John Bushnell, Larissa Zakharova, Indiana University Press 1994.

Giuseppe Santoni, Paolo Formiconi, *Senigallia, il Borego della Posta*, Senigallia 2019. http://www.comune.senigallia.an.it/pdf/Senigallia_il_Borgo_della_Posta.pdf.

Joanna Schiller, *Materiały do dziejów Cesarskiego Uniwersytetu Warszawskiego w Rostowie nad Donem*, 'Nauka Polska. Jej Potrzeby, Organizacja i Rozwój' 2005, vol. 14 (39), pp. 237–245.

Joanna Schiller, *Portret zbiorowy nauczycieli warszawskich publicznych szkół średnich 1795–1862*, Warsaw 1998.

Joanna Schiller, *Powstanie Cesarskiego Uniwersytetu Warszawskiego w świetle badań archiwalnych*, 'Rozprawy z Dziejów Oswiaty' 2002, vol. 41, pp. 93–127.

Joanna Schiller, *Universitas rossica. Koncepcja rosyjskiego uniwersytetu 1863–1917*, Warsaw 2008.

BIBLIOGRAPHY

Joanna Schiller-Walicka, *Cesarski Uniwersytet Warszawski 1869–1917: między edukacją a polityką*, [in:] *Dzieje Uniwersytetu Warszawskiego 1816–1916*, ed. Tomasz Kizwalter, Warsaw 2016, pp. 557–704.

Apolonia z Dalewskich Sierakowska, *Wspomnienia*, development Jolanta Sikorska-Kulesza, Tamara Bairašauskaitė, Warsaw 2010.

Ignacy Z. Siemion, *Wilno chemiczne do połowy XIX stulecia*, Warsaw 2010.

Janusz Skarbek, *Koncepcja nauki w pozytywizmie polskim*, Wrocław 1968.

Janusz Skarbek, *Pozytywistyczna teoria wiedzy*, Warsaw 1995.

Zofia Skubała-Tokarska, *Społeczna rola Wolnej Wszechnicy Polskiej*, Wrocław 1967.

Juliusz Słowacki, *Korespondencja*, development E. Sawrymowicz, vol. 1, Wrocław 1962.

Władysław Smoleński, *Warunki pracy naukowej w b. Królestwie Polskim w okresie odwetu rosyjskiego za powstanie styczniowe*, 'Nauka Polska' 1923, vol. 4, pp. 354–360.

*Sprawozdanie* [...] *z czynności Komitetu Zarządzającego Kasą Pomocy dla Osób Pracujących na Polu Naukowym imienia Dr-a Med. Józefa Mianowskiego za czas* [...], Warsaw vol. 1, 1883 – vol. 21, 1903.

*Sprawozdanie* [...] *z czynności Komitetu Zarządzającego Kasą Pomocy dla Osób Pracujacych na Polu Naukowym imienia Dr-a Med. Józefa Mianowskiego za rok* [...], Warsaw vol. 22, 1904 – vol. 41, 1922.

*Stanisława Michalskiego autobiografia i działalność oświatowa*, development Helena Radlińska, Irena Lepalczyk, introduction Tadeusz Kotarbiński, Wrocław 1967.

Karolina Sołtys, *Józef Ignacy Kraszewski jako historyk: naukowy fundament wykładu dziejów Litwy w monografii Wilna*, Warsaw 2013.

Stanisław Stempowski, *Pamiętniki*, Wrocław 1953.

Filip Sulimierski, *Józef Mianowski. Wspomnienie pośmiertne*, [in:] *Szkoła rozumu i charakteru. Szkoła Główna Warszawska (1862–1869). Materiały do dziejów*, introduction, selection and development Grzegorz P. Bąbiak, Warsaw 2019, pp. 467–471.

Jerzy Szczepański, *Książę Ksawery Drucki-Lubecki 1778–1846*, Warsaw 2008.

Stanisław Szenic, *Cmentarz Powązkowski 1790–1850. Zmarli i ich rodziny*, Warsaw 1979.

Stanisław Szenic, *Cmentarz Powązkowski 1851–1890. Zmarli i ich rodziny*, Warsaw 1982.

Stanisław Szenic, *Cmentarz Powązkowski 1891–1918. Zmarli i ich rodziny*, Warsaw 1983.

Денис Н. Шилов, *Государствиенные деятиели Российской Империи 1802–1917. Биобиблиографической справочник*, Ст. Петербург 2002.

Денис Н. Шилов, Й.А. Кузмин, *Члены Государствиенного Совета Российской Империи 1801–1906. Биобиблиографический справочник*, Ст. Петербург 2007.

J. Szujski, *Józef Mianowski rektor Szkoły Głównej Warszawskiej (wspomnienie pośmiertne)*, 'Przegląd Polski' yea. 13, 1878/79, vol. 3, pp. 456–466.

Józef Ludwik S z p e r l, *Pracownia chemiczna*, [in:] *Szkoła rozumu i charakteru. Szkoła Główna Warszawska (1862–1869). Materiały do dziejów*, introduction, selection and development Grzegorz P. B ą b i a k, Warsaw 2019, pp. 209–210.

*Szkoła Główna Warszawska (1862–1868)*, vol. 1–2, Kraków 1900–1901.

*Szkoła rozumu i charakteru. Szkoła Główna Warszawska (1862–1869). Materiały do dziejów*, introduction, selection and development Grzegorz P. B ą b i a k, Warsaw 2019.

Andrzej S z w a r c, *Akademia Medyko-Chirurgiczna j Szkoła Główna 1857–1869*, [in:] *Dzieje Uniwersytetu Warszawskiego 1816–1916*, ed. Tomasz K i z w a l t e r, Warsaw 2016, pp. 415–556.

Zygmunt S z w e y k o w s k i, *Zarys historii Kasy im. Mianowskiego*, 'Nauka Polska' 1932, vol. XV, 1932, no.15, pp. 1–202.

Jędrzej Ś n i a d e c k i, *Dzieła Jędrzeja Śniadeckiego*, published by Michał B a l i ń s k i, vol. 1, Warsaw 1840.

Wiesław T h e i s s, *Radlińska*, Warsaw 1984.

Mikołaj T a r k o w s k i, *Polacy na Litwie i Białorusi pod rządami Aleksandra II (1855–1881). Studium historyczno-prawne*, Gdańsk 2018.

Сергией Т а т и щ е в, *Император Александр II. Эго жызнь и царствование*, Москва 2006.

*Treściwy zbiór przepisów policyjnych, administracyjnych i sądowych dla właścicieli domów i mieszkańców m. Warszawy*, Warsaw 1883.

Stanisław T r e m b e c k i, *Sofiówka i wybór poezji*, development Władysław J a n k o w s k i, Kraków 1925.

Agata T u s z y ń s k a, *Rosjanie w Warszawie*, Paris 1990.

Умань, *Електронная Еврейская н Эициклопедия* [онлине:] 1996, http://jewishencyclopedia.ru/?mode=article&id=14213. Cyt. za https://sztetl.org.pl/pl/miejscowosci/h/1833-human/99-historia-spolecznosci/139509-historia-spolecznosci.

Mirosław U s t r z y c k i, *Ziemianie polscy na kresach 1864–1914. Świat wartości i postaw*, Kraków 2006.

Andrzej W a l i c k i, *Filozofia a mesjanizm: studia z dziejów filozofii i myśli społeczno-religijnej romantyzmu polskiego*, Warsaw 1970.

Andrzej W a l i c k i, *Legal Philosophies of Russian Liberalism*, Notre Dame–London 1992.

Andrzej W a l i c k i, *Rosja, katolicyzm i sprawa polska*, Warsaw 2003.

Andrzej W a l i c k i, *Rosyjska filozofia i myśl społeczna od oświecenia do marksizmu*, Warsaw 1973. Extended revised edition: idem, *Zarys myśli rosyjskiej od oświecenia do renesansu religijno-filozoficznego*, Kraków 2005.

Andrzej W a l i c k i, *Trzy patriotyzmy: trzy tradycje polskiego patriotyzmu i ich znaczenie współczesne*, Warsaw 1991.

# BIBLIOGRAPHY

Andrzej Walicki, *W kręgu konserwatywnej utopii. Struktura i przemiany rosyjskiego słowianofilstwa*, Warsaw 2021.

Zygmunt Wasilewski, *Z życia poety romantycznego. Seweryn Goszczyński w Galicji: nieznane pamietniku, utwory i listy 1832–1842*, Lviv 1910

Theodore R. Weeks, *Vilnius Between Nations, 1795–2000*, DeKalb, Northern Illinois University Press 2015.

Janina Wiercińska, *Towarzystwo Zachęty Sztuk Pięknych w Warszawie: zarys działalności*, Wrocław 1968.

*Wileński słownik biograficzny*, ed. Henryk Dubowik, Leszek Jan Malinowski, Bydgoszcz 2002.

Irena Wodzianowska, *Rzymskokatolicka Akademia Duchowna w Petersburgu*, Lublin 2007.

Adam Wrzosek, *Pochwała Józefa Mianowskiego – w 50 rocznicę Jego śmierci: (wykład wygłoszony na IV (końcowym) posiedzeniu plenarnem XIII. Zjazdu Lekarzy i Przyrodników polskich w Wilnie, dnia 29 września 1929)*, [Vilnius] 1929.

*Wykaz Szkoły Głównej w letnim półroczu roku naukowego 1864/5*, Warsaw 1865.

*Z dziejów książki i bibliotek w Warszawie*, ed. Stanisław Tazbir, Warsaw 1961.

Władysław Zahorski, *Moje wspomnienia*, development, introduction Jolanta Sikorska-Kulesza, vol. 1, Warsaw 2018.

Władysław Zahorski, *Szymon Konarski. (Życie i czyny)*, Vilnius 1907.

Władysław Zahorski, *Zarys dziejów Cesarskiego Towarzystwa Lekarskiego w Wilnie 1805–1897*, Warsaw 1898.

Jadwiga Zanowa, *W służbie oświaty. Pamiętnik z lat 1900–1946*, Warsaw 1961.

*Западные окраины Российской империи*, ред. А. Миллер, А. Долбилов, Москва 2006.

Leszek Zasztowt, *Józef Mianowski – pomiędzy Polską a Rosją. Przegląd materiałów do biografii*, 'Nauka Polska Jej Potrzeby, Organizacja i Rozwój' 2002, vol. 11, pp. 109–130.

Leszek Zasztowt, *Józef Mianowski w humańskiej szkole bazylianów*, 'Przegląd Wschodni' 2004, vol. 9, z. 1 (33), pp. 131–147.

Leszek Zasztowt, *Kasa im. J. Mianowskiego – dorobek i znaczenie. W kręgu Tytusa Chałubińskiego i warszawskich społeczników*, 'Kwartalnik Historii Nauki i Techniki' 2010, no. 3–4, pp. 43–47.

Leszek Zasztowt, *Kresy 1832–1864. Szkolnictwo na ziemiach litewskich i ruskich dawnej Rzeczypospolitej*, Warsaw 1997.

Leszek Zasztowt, *Pierwszy okres działalności Kasy Mianowskiego. W kręgu pozytywistycznej tradycji instytucji społecznych zaboru rosyjskiego*, [in:] idem, *Europa Środkowo-Wschodnia a Rosja XIX–XX wieku. W kręgu edukacji i polityki*, Warsaw 2007, pp. 201–214.

Leszek Zasztowt, *Popularyzacja nauki w Królestwie Polskim 1864–1905*, Wrocław 1989.

[Leszek Zasztowt], *Sięgać do tradycji. Z dr. hab. Leszekim Zasztowtem sekretarzem Komitetu Kasy im. Mianowskiego rozmawia Magdalena Grzelecka*, 'Sprawy Nauki. Biuletyn Komitetu Badań Naukowych' 1999, no. 5 (49), May, pp. 5–6.

Leszek Zasztowt, *Wileńscy miłośnicy 'starożytności' w latach 1899–1914*, 'Kwartalnik Historii Nauki i Techniki' 1990, no. 2–3, pp. 259–283.

Leszek Zasztowt, *W kręgu pozytywistycznej tradycji instytucji społecznych zaboru rosyjskiego*, [in:] *Życie jest wszędzie ... Ruchy społeczne w Polsce i w Rosji do II wojny światowej*, ed. Anna Brus, Warsaw 2005, pp. 223–236.

Ewa Ziółkowska, *Petersburg po polsku*, Warsaw 2011.

Janusz Żarnowski, *Polska 1918–1939: praca, technika, społeczeństwo*, Warsaw 1999.

Janusz Żarnowski, *Struktura społeczna inteligencji w Polsce w latach 1918–1939*, Warsaw 1964.

Stefan Żeromski, *Sprawa Kasy Mianowskiego*, Warsaw 1929.

Janina Żurawicka, *Inteligencja warszawska w końcu XIX wieku*, Warsaw 1978.

# Annexes

### Document 1

Official description of service (drawn up on 12 November 1868) of the rector and full professor at the Warsaw Main School, permanent member of the Council of the Curator of the Warsaw Educational District, Active Member of the Medical Society, vice-president of the Society for the Encouragement of Fine Arts in the Polish Kingdom and president of the private board of the Hospital of the Infant Jesus, actual state councillor Józef son of Ignacy Mianowski.

The Russian State Historical Archive in St Petersburg (RSHA), *O utverzhdenii Ordinarnogo Professora Mianovskogo rektorom Varszawskoyj glavnoy szkoly* (18–23 Noyabria 1868), F. 733, op. 147, ed. chr. 752, k. 3–23. The original in the Russian language.

*Формулярный списокъ о службе (составленъ 12го Ноября 1868 г.) Ректора и Ординарного Профессора Варшавской Главной Школы, постоянного члена Попечитиельского Совета Варшавского Учебного Окрыга, Совещательного члена Медищинскаго Совета, Вице-Передседателья Общества Пощрения Художеств в Царстве Польцком и Председатиелья частного попиечительного Совета Варшавской Больницы Младеньца Иисуса, Действительного Статского Советника Осипа Игнатевича Мяновского.*

*– Из потомственных дворян Киевской губерни. – Нет имиения (родовое, благоприобретенное). Действительный статский советник Осип Игнатевич Мяновский. Ректор и Ординарный Профессор Варшавской Главной Школы. Постоянный член Попиечительского Совета Варшавского Учебного Округа, Совещательный Член Медищинскаго Совета, Вице-Председатель Общества Пощрения Художеств в Царстве Польском и Председатель в частном попечительном Совете Варшавской Больницы Младенца Иисуса. Шестидесяти пять лет. Римско-католического исповеданя. Кавалеръ Оденовъ Св. Анны Iй степени, Св. Станислава Iй степени и Св. Владимира IIIй степени. Имиеет знак отличя безпорочйной службы за XXV летъ и две темнобронзовыя медали: одну в память войны 1853–1856 годов на Андреевской ленте и другую в память усмиреня Польского мятежа 1863–1864 годовъ.*

*Жалованя: по должности*

*Ректора: 600 р.*

*Квартирных: 1500 р. По должности ординарного профессора 1500 р.*

*Пенсии за службу въ Империи 1681 р. 20 к.*

*Итого 5281 р. 20 к. В год.*

*По должности Ректора и Совещательного члена Медицинского Совета в V, а по должности Ординарного Профессора в VI классе; прочим же занимаемым имъ должностямъ классъ не присвоенъ.*

*По оконьчании въ 1827 году полного курса наукъ въ Императорском Виленском Университете 29 Июля 1828 г. Удостоен степени Доктора Медицины. В службу вступилъ и определенъ Помощником при Медицинской Клинике бывшего Императорского Виленского Университета, 1828 года Сентября первово дня... 1 Сентября 1828 г.*

*За отлично-усердную службу, Всемилостивейше награжденъ брилантном перестенямъ... 28 Декабря 1830 г.*

*Съ Февраля месяца 1831 г. По собствиенному желанию занимался пользованем больных воинских чинов въ Виленском госпитале, за что обявлено ему Высочайшее благоволение ... 2 Марта 1831 г.*

*Проподавал въ Виленском Университете курс физёлогии дла медицинских ученников 2го и 3го классов съ 1 Сентября 1831 г. По 26 Июня 1832 г.*

*Избран членом Императорского Виленского Общества... 13 Декабря 1831 г.*

*По закрытии Виленского Университета назначен помощником Профессора Медицинской Клиники въ Виленской Медико-Хирургической Академии ... 1 Сентября 1832 г.*

*За отлично-усердную службу въ бывшем Виленском Университете Всемилостибейше пожалован брилиянтовим перстнем ... 22 декабря 1834 г.*

*Утвержден въ чине Надворного Советника, со старшинством съ 1 Сентября 1833 года (Указ Правительцтвующего Цената) ... 15 Мая 1835.*

*За отлично-усердную службу, Всемилостивше пожалован брилиянтовым оперстнем ... въ Октябре 1835 г.*

*Признан почотным членом Императорской Ст. Петербурской МедикоХирургической Академии ... 23 Июня 1837 г.*

*По Высочайшему повеленю, отправлен был за границу дла усовершенствования въ медицинских науках, где находился съ 15 Августа 1837 г. По 15 Августа 1838 г.*

*Избран членом корреспондентом Королевского Берлинского МедикоХирургического Общества, Гуфеландовым называемого ... 12 Декабря 1837 г.*

*За примерение и неутомлимые труды въ составлении стати: "Observationes exactis medici rustituti clinici a 1834–1835 depromptae" къ изданному сочинению "Collectanea medico-chirurgica" обявлена ему особенная признательностъ всего Министерства Внутреннихъ Делъ въ продложенни Г-а Министра за No. 496 ... 7 Июня 1838 г.*

## ANNEXES

*По возвращении из заграницы назначен помощником профессора Медицинской Клиники и къ преподаванию физиологии въ Виленской Медико-Хирургической Академии ... 1 Сентября 1838 г.*

*Избран Пчетным членом Парижского Общества физических и химических наук ... 7 Апреля 1839 г.*

*По выбору конференции утвержден Г. Управляющим Министерством Внутренних Дел въ звании Ординарного Профессора Физиологии въ той же Академии ... 24 Января 1840 г.*

*Прозиводен за выслугу лет, въ Коллежсие Совиетники, со старшинством с 1 Сентября 1839 г. ... 4 Октября 1840 г.*

*Издал сочинение под заглавием "О переломах костией" ... 1839 г.*

*По Высочайшему повелению, определен въ Императорскую Ст. Петербурскую Медицо-Хирургическую Академию дла отдельного преподавания психиатрии и Главным врачем 2го Военного Сухопутного госпиталя по отделению внутренних болезней ... 19 Января 1842 г.*

*Съ розрешения Га Управлявшаго министерством поручено ему заведывать Акушерную женскою и детскою клиниками совокупно съ возложенною на него должносию по 2му Военно-Сухопутному Госпиталю ... 22 Августа 1842 г.*

*Высочайше утвержден Почетным членом Ст. Петербургского Совета детсих приютовъ ... 24 Октября 1842 г.*

*Производен, за выслугу лет, в Статские Советники со старшинством съ ... 1 Сентября 1843 г.*

*Съ Высочайшого Ея Императорского Величества разрешения назначенъ Директором Александро-Мар이инскофо Приюта ... 2го Сентября 1844 г.*

*Получилъ знак отличия безпорочной службы 25 летняго достоинства, при грамоте за No. 2252 ... 22 Августа 1844 г.*

*За отлично-усердную и ревностную службу Всемилостивейше пожалованъ Кавалером Ордена Св. Станислава 2й степении ... 14 Апреля 1845 г.*

*По поручению Га Военного Минситра отправлен дла осмотра по медицинской части Дунабурского и Виленского воинных госпиталей ... 3 Ноября 1845 г.*

*Съ Высочайшого разрешения уволенъ за границу на пять месацев, съ сохранениемъ получаемых им окладовъ с тем, чтобы во бремя путешествии осмотрел знаменитейшия практическия заведения въ Европе ... 27 Апреля 1847 г.*

*Воспользовался Высочайше дозволенным отпуском съ 11 Июня 1847 г.*

*Съ Высочайшого соизволения, сверх означенного пятимесячного отпуска, начавшагося съ 11 Июня позволено ему еще остатся за границей шесть недель, съ предоставлением за отсторочное время содержания с тем,* чтобы онъ употребил это время на посещение клиники лекций Парижских профессоров ... 3-0 Октября 1847 г.

Возврщился из путешествия ... 13 Декабря 1848 г.

За отлично-усердную и пщвностную службу, Всемилостивейше пожалован Кавалером Ордена Св. Анны 2й степени ... 11 Апреля 1848 г.

За таковую же службу объявлено ему Высочайшее благоволение ... 6 Декабря 1848 г.

По желанию Ея императорского Высочества Великой Княги Марии Николаевны, Гмъ Военным Министром командирован дла сопоровождения Ея Высочества въ Фаль ... 9 Июля 1849 г.

Возвратился к своим должностям ... 15 Августа 1849 г.

Произведенъ за отличе въ Действительные Статские Советники (Высочайший приказ по военному ведомству) ... 23 Апреля 1850 г.

Получил знак отличия безпорочной службы за XX летъ при грамоте No. 301 ... 22 Августа 1852 г.

Положением Военного Совета от 30 Ноября 1855 г. За выслугу более 25 летъ въ учебных должностяхъ назначено въ производительство емы пенсии по тысяч четыреста двадцать восеми рублей пятидесяти семи копеек серебром в год и бсего получаемого имъ тогда жалования, съ оставлением на службе Профессором и Главным Врачем въ 2м военносухопутном госпитале ... 5 Января 1856 г.

Получил темно-бронзовую медаль на Андреевской ленте в память войны 1853–1856 годовъ ... 26 Августа 1856 г.

По Высочайшему повелению командирован въ распоряжение Ея Императорскаго Высочецтва Государини Великой Книагини Марии Николаевны, дла сопровождения Ея Высочества въ заграничном вояже ... 25 Октября 1856 г.

Возвратился из заграницы ... 15 Декабря 1856 г.

За отлично-усердную и ревностную службу Всемилостивейше пожалован Орденом Св. Владимира 3й степени ... 17 Апреля 1858 г.

Съ Высочайшего соизволения командирован дла сопровождения Ея Императорского Высочества Госуфарини Великой Книагини Марии Николаевны въ заграничном бояже ... 29 Июля 1858 г.

Получил знак отличия безпоточной службы за XXV летъ ... 22 Августа 1858 г.

В награду долговременной и полезной службы Всемилостивейше пожалован золотыю табакеркою съ вензелевым изображением Имени Его Императорского Величества ... 3 Декабря 1860 г.

За выслугу узаконненых летъ, с разрешения Га Военного Министра уволенъ от службы при Императорской Медико-Хирургической Академии, съ

# ANNEXES

*предоставлением емы звания заслуженного Профессора и съ назначением ему пенсии по 1,861 п. 20 к. В год ... 25 Декабря 1860 г.*

*Избран Почетным членом тойже Академии ... 21 Марта 1861 г.*

*Поступил на службу въ Царство Польское и определенъ Ректором и Ординарным Профеоссором въ Варшавской Главной Школе съ жалованием по должности Ректора 600 р.с., по должности Ординарного профессора 1,500 р.с. и съ назначением квартирных по 1,500 р.с. в годъ ... 8 Ноября 1862 г.*

*Независимо от сего назначен Членом бывшего Совета Народного Просвещения в Царстве Польском, без жалования ... 8 Ноября 1863 г.*

*Независимо от сего назначен Членом бывшего Совета Народного Просвешченя въ Царстве Польцком без жалованя ... 8 Ноября 1862 г.*

*Избран Почетным Членом Варшавского Общества Врачей ... 1 Января 1863 г.*

*Назначен Председателем частного попиечутельского Совета Варшавской Больницы Младенца Иисыса, без жалования ... 29 Ноября 1863 г.*

*Получил темно-бронзовую медаль въ память усмирения Польского мятежа 1863–1864 годов ... 20 Мая 1865 г.*

*Государъ Императоръ по представлении Га Наместника в Царстве, принявъ во внимание засвидетельствование о немъ за время исправления имъ должности Ректора Варшавской Главной Школы в первые три года существования сего заведения, равно избрание его Общим Советом тойже Школы, по большинству голосов, вновъ въ эту должность, Высочайше соизволилъ утвердитъ его ректором означенной Шкилы на второе трехлетие ... 16 Ноября 1865 г.*

*За отлично-усердную и ревностную службу, Всемилостивейше пожалованъ Кавалером Ордена Св. Станислава 1й степени ... 26 Августа 1865 г.*

*Избран и утвержденъ на 1867 г. Въ должности Вице-Председателя Обшчества Поощрения Художествъ въ Царстве Польском ... 9 Июня 1867 г.*

*Во внимание отлично-усердной и равностной службы, Всемилостивейше пожалованъ Кавалером Ордена св. Анны 1й степени ... 10 Июня 1867 г.*

*По случаю упразднения б. Совета Народного Просвещения уволенъ от должности члена онаго Совета и назначен Постоянным членом Совета Попечителя Варшавского Учебного Округа без жалования ... 1 Июля 1867 г.*

*Избран и утвержден на 1868 год въ должности Вице-Председателя Общества Пощрения Художеств въ Царстве Польском без жалования ... 24 Апреля 1868 г.*

*Высочайшимъ приказомъ по Министерству Внутреннихъ Делъ, 24 Июля 1868 г. Назначенъ Совещательнымъ Членом Медицинского Совета, съ оставлением въ занимаемой должмости с. 1868 г., Мая 30.*

– *Был лу в походах против неприятеля [...]? Не был.*

– *Был ли в штрафах [...]? Не был.*

*Попечитель Варшавского Учебного Окрыга Ф. Витте.*

[*к. 24*]

*Утверждается: Ректоръ и Ординарный профессор Ваешавской Главной Школы – вновъ ректором цей школы по 16 Ноября 1871 г. /подпись/: М. Брадке.*

[*к. 4*]

*Был ли в отпусках? Въ отпусках былъ: въ 1856 г вакационного времени, на 28 дней, в 1863 и 1864 годах на летнее вакационное время, въ 1867 году по болезни, на три месяца, из коих на срок являлся.*

*Был ли въ отставках? Въ отставке был без награждения чином съ 25 Декабря 1860 г. По 8е Ноября 1862 г.*

*Холостъ или женатъ? Женат вторым бракомъ на дочери Статского Советника Александра Галлера девице Надеже. Жена Православного исповедания. Детей не имеетъ.*

### English translation:

*Official description of service (drawn up on 12 November 1868) of the rector and full professor at the Warsaw Main School, permanent member of the Council of the Curator of the Warsaw Educational District, Active Member of the Medical Society, vice-president of the Society for the Encouragement of Fine Arts in the Polish Kingdom and president of the private board of the Hospital of the Infant Jesus.*

*Age sixty-five years. Roman Catholic religion. Knight of the orders of St. Anne first grade, St. Stanislaus 1st grade and St. Vladimir 3rd grade.*

*Holder of Distinction award for impeccable service over 25 years and gtwo dark-bronze medals: one in commemoration of the 1853–1856 war on the Andreyeskaya line, the second in commemoration of the suppression of the Polish revolt 1863–1864.*

*Remuneration: for the position of*
*Rector: 600 roubles.*
*For accommodation: 1500 roubles.*
*For the position of full professor: 1500 roubles.*
*Pensions for service in the Empire: 1681 roubles 20 kopecks.*
*Total: 5281 roubles 20 kopecks per annum.*

*According to his position as rector and active member of the Medical Council he belongs to the 5th grade; and as a Full Professor, to the 6th; with the other position that he occupies, a grade is not awarded.*

ANNEXES

*On completing in 1827 a full course of studies at the Imperial University of Vilnius, he received on 29 July 1828 the degree of Doctor of Medicine. He commenced service and was designated as assistant at the Medical Clinic of the former Imperial University of Vilnius in the year 1828, the first day of September ... 1 September 1828.*

*For his excellent and conscientious service, he was graciously awarded a diamond ring ... 28 December 1830.*

*From February 1831 of his own volition, he cared for sick patients of various military ranks in the Vilnius Military Hospital, for which he received the Highest Acclaim ... 2 March 1831.*

*At the University of Vilnius, he delivered a course of lectures in physiology for 2nd and 3rd year medical students, from 1 September to 26 June 1832.*

*Elected member of the Imperial [Medical?] Society of Vilnius ... 13 December 1831.*

*After the closure of Vilnius University, he was designated as assistant to the professor of the Medical Clinic at the Vilnius Medical-Surgical Academy ... 1 September 1832.*

*For his excellent and conscientious service, he was graciously awarded a diamond ring ... 22 December 1834.*

*Confirmed in the rank of Court Councillor with seniority from 1 September 1833 (Decree of the Ruling Senate) ... 15 May 1835.*

*For his excellent and conscientious service, he was graciously awarded a diamond ring ... in October 1835.*

*Affirmed as Honorary Member of the Imperial Medical-Surgical Academy in St. Petersburg. 23 June 1837.*

*On the Highest Command was sent abroad to hone his skills in the medical sciences, where he resided from 15 August 1837 to August 1838.*

*Elected corresponding member of the Royal Medical-Surgical Society in Berlin, known as the Hufeland ... 12 December 1837.*

*For his exemplary and indefatigable work in preparing the article 'Observationes specificis medici rustituti clinici an 1834–1835 depromptae' for publication in the compilation 'Collectanea medico-chirurgica' he received expressions of especial gratitude of the entire Ministry of Internal Affairs, on the Honourable Minister's motion No. 496 ... 7 June 1838.*

*On his return from abroad, designated as assistant to the professor of the Medical Clinic and lecturer in physiology at the Vilnius Medical-Surgical Academy ... 1 September 1838.*

*Elected Honorary Member of the Paris Society of Physical and Chemical Sciences ... 7 April 1839.*

*On election by conference, affirmed by the director of the Ministry of Internal Affairs in the rank of full professor of physiology in the same Academy ... 24 January 1840.*

*Promoted to long-term service at the rank of collegial councillor with seniority from 1 September 1839... 4 October 1840.*

*Published a paper titled 'On bone fractures'... 1839.*

*On the Highest Command, appointed to the Imperial Medical-Surgical Academy in Petersburg separately to lecture in psychiatry and as Chief Surgeon of the Department of Internal Medicine of the 2nd Hospital of Land Forces ... 19 January 1842.*

*With the consent of the director of the Ministry, he was entrusted with the directorship of the Women's, Midwifery and Children's clinics in addition to his duties in the 2nd Military Hospital of Land Forces ... 22 August 1842.*

*By the Highest Will he was appointed honorary member of the Council of Children's Orphanages in St Petersburg ... 24 October 1842.*

*Appointed to long-term service at the rank of State Councillor with seniority ... 1 September 1843.*

*With the consent of His Imperial Majesty, appointed director of the Alexandro-Marian orphanage ... 2 September 1844.*

*Received honorary award for 25 years of impeccable service APRIL 4? CHECK with certificate no. 2252... 22 August 1844.*

*For exceptionally conscientious and assiduous service, he was most graciously granted the title of Knight of the Order of St. Stanislaus 2nd grade ... 14 April 1845.*

*At the behest of the Ministry of Defence, delegated to carry out inspections of medical services in the military hospitals of Dyneburg and Vilnius ... 3 November 1845.*

*With the consent of His Imperial Majesty, he was sent abroad for five months, retaining his salary, to investigate in his travels, the most renowned practical institutions in Europe ... 27 April 1847.*

*Made use of the leave granted to him by the emperor ... 11 June 1847.*

*With the granting by His Imperial Majesty of the abovementioned five-month leave, initiated on 11 January, he was allowed to remain abroad for a further six weeks, with a guarantee of pay during the time beyond the deadline, to attend the clinic to follow lectures by Paris professors ... 3 October 1847.*

*Returned from his travels ... 13 December 1848.*

*For exceptionally conscientious and assiduous service, he was most graciously granted the title of Knight of the Order of St. Anne 2nd grade ... 11 April 1848.*

*For this service, he was endowed with the highest favours ... 6 December 1848.*

*In accordance with the wish of Her Imperial Highness the Grand Duchess Maria Nikolayevna, he was seconded by the Minister of War to accompany Her Highness to the locality of Falaise (France) ... 9 July 1849.*

## ANNEXES

*Returned to his duties ... 15 August 1849.*

*For his services, promoted to Actual State Councillor (in accordance with the Highest Disposition of the Department of War) ... 23 April 1850.*

*Received Distinction award for impeccable service over 20 years with certificate no. 301 ... 22 August 1852.*

*On 30 November 1855 by decree of the Military Council, for service of over 25 years in pedagogic positions, received a retirement pension amounting to one thousand four hundred and twenty-seven roubles and fifty-seven kopecks in silver per annum, with the title of professor and senior surgeon in the 2nd Military Hospital of Land Forces ... 5 January 1856.*

*Received a dark-bronze medal on a St. Andrew's ribbon in commemoration of the 1853–1856 war ... 26 August 1856.*

*By the Highest Will he was seconded to accompany Her Imperial Highness Grand Duchess Maria Nikolayevna on a journey abroad ... 29 July 1858.*

*Received Distinction award for impeccable service over 25 years ... 22 August 1858.*

*In recognition of his long-standing and valuable service, graciously rewarded with a golden snuffbox engraved with a monogram with the name of His Imperial Majesty ... 3 December 1860.*

*In view of his long working record, released, with the consent of the Minister of War, from continuing service in the Imperial Medical-Surgical Academy, with the granting of the title of honorary professor and a retirement pension of 1861 roubles and 20 kopecks per annum ... 25 December 1860.*

*Elected honorary member of said Academy ... 21 March 1861.*

*Commenced service in the Polish Kingdom; appointed rector and full professor of the Main School in Warsaw with a salary of 600 imperial roubles for the position of rector, 1500 imperial roubles for his full professorship and 1500 imperial roubles for rent ... 8 November 1862.*

*Elected honorary member of the Warsaw Medical Society ... 1 January 1863.*

*Appointed president of the private board of the Warsaw hospital of the Infant Jesus, pro bono publico ... 29 November 1863.*

*Received dark-bronze medal in commemoration of the suppression of the Polish revolt, 1863–1864 ... 20 May 1865.*

*The Emperor, responding to the motion of the Viceroy in the Kingdom, taking into account the evidence regarding his person in carrying out the function of rector of the Main School in its first three years of existence and his re-election to that post by majority vote of the General Council, was absolutely sure in confirming his position as rector of said educational establishment for a successive three-year period ... 16 November 1865.*

*For his magnificent, assiduous, and self-sacrificing service he is graciously awarded the Order of St. Stanislaus 1st grade ... 26 August 1865.*

*Elected and confirmed for the year 1867 as vice-president of the Society for the Encouragement of Fine Arts in the Polish Kingdom ... 9 June 1867.*

*Considering his excellent and conscientious service, graciously appointed Knight of the Order of St. Anne 1st grade ... 10 June 1867.*

*In view of the liquidation of the former Council of Public Enlightenment he lost his place as member of the council and was appointed permanent member of the Council of the Warsaw Educational District pro bono publico ... 1 July 1867.*

*Elected and confirmed for the year 1868 as vice-president of the Society for the Encouragement of Fine Arts in the Polish Kingdom pro bono publico ... 24 April 1868.*

*By the Highest Disposition of the Ministry of Internal Affairs, on 24 July 1868 he was appointed consultant member of the Medical Council, the post to be back-dated to 30 May 1868.*

*– Did he take part in campaigns against the enemy? [...]? He did not.*

*– Did he have a criminal record [...]? No.*

*Head of the Board of the Warsaw Educational District, F[yodor] Witte*

*[k. 24]*

*It is confirmed: the rector and full professor of the Warsaw Main School is once again to be rector of said School until 16 November 1871. /signed/: M. Bradke*

*[k.4]*

*Did he take leave? He took leave: in 1856 in vacation time; for 28 days in 1863 and 1864 during summer vacations; in 1867 due to illness for three months, after which he returned to work on time.*

*Did he resign? He resigned without promotion from 25 December to 8 November 1862.*

*Bachelor or married? Married in his second marriage with the daughter of Actual Councillor Aleksandr Galler, Miss Nadiezhda. Wife's religion: Orthodox. No children.*

### Document 2

On the noble status of the Mianowski family.

*О дворянскомъ достоинстве рода Мяновского.*

*Fond 1405, op. 49, ech. 3752, k. 1–8. 10 февраля 1851 г. – 4 апр. 1851 г. (8 марта 1856 года в архив сдано) [k.1] Его Превосходительству, Господину Управляющему Министерством Юстиции Тайному Советнику и Кавалеру Платону Демьяновичу Илличевскому. Исполняющий должность Герольдмейстера Рапортъ Честь имею представить при семъ Вашему Превосходительству всеподданнейший докладъ Правительствующего*

## ANNEXES

*Сената по делу о дворянстве Мяновского съ краткою запискою въ 2-х экземплярах, выпискою из законов и подлинным делом. Исправляющий должноть Герольдмейстера В. /illegible/*

*[k.2] Исправляющий должность Герольдмейстера представилъ Вашему Превосходительству всеподданнейший докладъ Правительствующего Сената по дельу о дворянстве Мяновского съ краткою запискою въ 2-х экземплярах, выпискою из законов и подлинным деломъ. Из бумаг сих видно: Волынское Дворянское Депутатское Собраніе представило следующие документы о сопричеслении записанного въ число граждан Игнатія Мяновского къ роду его, Пётр – Адамъ (2) – Игнатій + Aleksandra (?) (3) – Анна + Николай (4) – Осипъ (5) – Семёнъ – Викентій (6) – Фавстинъ (7) – Игнатий (8) – Леонъ (9) – Станислав (10) 2 и 3 с сынами и внуками 9 и 10 утверждены герольдлею в дворянстве в 1848 г. Происхождение 4 от 3 и 8 от 4 доказывается метриками. Нач. Отд. Еврейский (?) [k.2 verso] Утверждённому в дворянстве: 1. Выписи метрических свидетельствъ Духовных Консисторій: Могилевской о крещении Николая 10 ноября 1793 г. отъ благородных Игнатія и Александры Мяновских и Луцко-Житомирской о рождении Игнатія в 1826 г. от дворянъ Николая и Анны Мяновскихъ. 2. Свидетельство Правящего должность Волынского Губернского Предводителя Дворянства данное дворянину Викентію-Семёну Игнатьеву [k. 3] сыну Мяновскому в том, что родной его брат Николай Игнатьевъ Мяновский по бывшем 5,6 и 7 ревизіям былъ писанъ въ число дворянъ и къ подушному окладу не принадлежалъ по 8-й же ревизіи, как не находившийся уже в живыхъ, нигде не записанъ, сынъ же его Николая Мяновского, Игнатий, родившийся въ 1826 году, оставшись въ малолетстве сиротою, по жительству въ Острогском уезде приписан тамошним Гражданским обществом въ [k.3 verso] число граждан, но как он, так и отец его Николай Мяновский не былъ лишен силою закона дворянского званія. 3. Копія съ определенія Волынского Дворянского Депутатского Собранія состоявшагося 6 Іюля 1850 года, коимъ оное Собраніе заключило: означенныя документы представить на разсмотреніе Правительствующаго Сената. Из имеющихся въ Правительствующем Сенате сведеніи оказалось, что Геролидія по разсмотреніи дела [k. 4] о дворянстве рода Мяновскихъ по определенію 28 Мая 1846 года утвердила определенія Волынского Дворянского Депутатского Собранія 16 Декабря 1802 и 16 Марта 1844 годовъ о внесеніи въ дворянскую родословную книгу Адама и Игнатія съ сыномъ Семёном Викентіемъ и сыновей сего последняго Леона Евзебія и Станислава Игнатія Мяновских въ отношеніи же Осипа и Николая и сыновей последняго Фавстина и Игнатия Мяновскихъ, то по [k. 4 verso] не именію въ*

*виду сведенiя въ какомъ разрядѣ бывшой польской шляхты записаны по той ревизiи въ число граждан города Острога, Герольдiя 159 ANEKS не постановляя о сихъ лицахъ рѣшительнаго опредѣленiя, предписала Депутатскому Собранiю пополнить дѣло по выше изясненнымъ замѣчанiямъ и въ дальнѣйшемъ ходѣ онаго поступить по установленному порядку, въ чемъ указъ [k. 5] посланъ 8 Iюля 1846 года. Правительствующiй Сенатъ, разсмотревъ дѣло сiе находитъ, что бывшая Герольдiя резолюцiею 28 Мая 1846 года утвердила опредѣленiя Волынскаго Дворянского Депутатскаго Собранiя, о внесенiи въ 1-ю часть дворянской родословной книги Адама и Игнатiя съ сыномъ Семеномъ Викентiемъ и сыновей сего послѣдняго: Леона Евгенiя и Станислава Игнатiя Мяновскихъ; что же касается до Осипа и Николая Игнатевыхъ и сыновей [k. 5 verso] послѣдняго Фавстина и Игнатiя Мяновскихъ, по не именiю тогда въ виду метрическаго свидѣтельства о происхожденiи Осипа отъ Игнатiя Мяновского и сведенiя, въ какомъ разрядѣ бывшей польской шляхты записанъ по ревизiи 1834 года Николай Мяновскiй, сыновья котораго, какъ усмотрѣла Герольдiя изъ дѣла, записаны по той ревизiи въ числе граждан города Острога, не постановляя о ихъ лицахъ рѣшительного опредѣленiя заключила: предписать Волынъскому Дворянскому Депутатскому Собранiю пополнить дѣло по вышеположеннымъ замѣчанiямъ и въ дальнѣйшемъ ходѣ онаго поступить по установленному порядку; о чемъ дала знать указомъ 8 Iюля 1846 года. Нынѣ Волынское Дворянское Депутатское Собранiе пополнивъ въ исполненiе этого указа бывшой Герольдiи, дѣло сiе, представляетъ на ревизiю Правительствующего Сената о сопричисленiи Игнатiя Николаева Мяновского документы изъ коихъ [k. 6] оказывается: 1, что законное хожденiе (происхожденiе?) Игнатiя въ 1793 году сына Николая, а отъ сего послѣдняго въ 1826 году сына Игнатiя доказывается метриками, завѣренными Могилевскою и Луцко-Житомирскою Духовными Консисторiями. 2, что Николай Игнатевъ Мяновский по 5, 6 и 7 ревизiямъ былъ писанъ въ число дворянъ и подушному окладу не подлежалъ, по 8-й же ревизiи, какъ умершiй, нигдѣ не записанъ, а сынъ его Николай, оставшись въ малолѣтствѣ сиротою, по жительству Волынской губернiи в [k. 7] Острогскомъ уѣздѣ приписанъ тамошнимъ Гражданскимъ Обществомъ въ число граждан, но какъ онъ Игнатiй, такъ и отецъ его Николай Мяновскiе не были лишены дворянского званiя силою закона, в чемъ удостовѣряется свидѣтельствомъ Предводителя Дворянства. Сообразивъ сiи обстоятельства съ 13 и 61 ст. и примѣч. къ послѣдней i X т. св. Зак. изд. 1842 г., и признавая опредѣленiе 6 Iюля 1850 года Волынскаго Дворянскаго Собранiя о признанiи Игнатiя [k. 7 verso] Николаева Мяновского достаточно доказавшимъ происхожденiе свое отъ признанного в 1846 году бывшею Герольдiею в дворянствѣ рода*

ANNEXES

*Мяновскихъ, правильнымъ и съ приведенными статьями закона соглас-
нымъ, положилъ: на исключеніе Игнатія Николаева Мяновского из подуш-
ного оклада и сопричисленіе его къ признанному въ 1846 году совнесеніем
въ 1-ю часть родословной книги, в дворянстве роду Мяновскихъ испросить
[k. 8] Высочайшее Его Императорскаго Величества соизволеніе всеподдан-
нейшимъ докладомъ. Заключеніе: Соглашаясь съ настоящимъ опредѣленіем
Правительствующаго Сената о возведеніи в дворянское достоинство
записаннаго въ числе граждан Игнатія Мяновского, 1-е Отдѣленіе пола-
галобы представленный исправляющимъ должность Герольдмейстера
всеподданнейший докладъ съ приложеніями внести установленнымъ поряд-
комъ на разсмотреніе Государственнаго Совета.*
/illegible/

**English translation**
*On the noble status of the Mianowski family.*

*10 February 1851 – 4 April 1851*
*(8 March 1856 placed in archives)*

*To His Excellency,*
*Director of the Ministry of Justice, Confidential Councillor and Knight*
*Platon Demyanovich Illichevsky.*

*Acting Heraldist*

*Report*

*I have the honour to present herewith to Your Excellency the full report of the
Governing Senate regarding the noble status of Mianowski, with a brief note in
two copies, extract from the laws and the original acts.*

*Acting heraldist W /illegible/*
*February the 6th day 1851*

*The acting heraldist presented Your Excellency with the full report of the
Governing Senate regarding the noble status of Mianowski, with a brief note in
two copies, extract from the laws and the original acts.*
*From these papers it transpires that: the Volhynia Diet of Nobles has presented
the following documents certifying that Ignacy Mianowski, registered as a citizen,
is a kinsman of his family:*

*Piotr – Adam (2) – Ignacy + Aleksandra (3) – Anna + Mikołaj (4) – Józef (5) – Siemion-Wincenty (6) – Faustyn (7) – Ignacy (8) – Leon (9) – Stanisław (10) 2 and 3 with sons and grandsons 9 and 10 are confirmed by the heraldry office to be of noble status as at the year 1848.*

*The lineage of 4 from 3 and 8 from 4 is evidenced by certificates of birth.*

*Head of Department Yevreysky (?) /illegible/*

*To him who is confirmed in nobility:*

> *1. Extracts from the certificates issued by the church consistories of: Mohylev, on the baptism of Mikołaj on 10 November 1793 from the noble Ignacy and Aleksandra Mianowscy; Lutsk and Zhytomir, on the birth of Ignacy in 1826 from the nobles Mikołaj and Anna Mianowsy.*
>
> *2. Certification by the acting Marshal of the Nobility issued to the nobleman Wincenty-Siemionow, son of Ignacy, Mianowski that his born brother Mikołaj, son of Ignacy, Mianowski was according to past reviews 5, 6 and 7 inscribed to the body of nobles and was not subject to the poll tax, according to review 8, as one longer among the living, while his, Mikołaj Mianowski's, son Ignacy, born in 1826, and in his infancy left as an orphan, by the fact of being domiciled in the county of Ostrog was registered by the Civic Association of that location as a citizen, but neither he nor his father Mikołaj Mianowski were legally denied their noble title.*
>
> *3. Copy of the decision by the assembly of the Volhynia Diet of Nobles, which took place on 6 July 1850, and which ruled: the above documents to be presented for the consideration of the Governing Senate.*

*From the information available from the Governing Senate it can be ascertained that the Heraldic Office, when appraising the question of the nobility of the Mianowski family, by a ruling of 28 May 1846 confirmed the decision of the Volhynia Diet of Nobles of 16 December 1802 and 16 March 1844 to inscribe in the noble family book Adam and Ignacy with their son Siemion-Wincenty, and the latter's sons Leon-Euzebiusz and Stanisław Ignacy Mianowski. However, in regard to Józef and Mikołaj, and the latter's sons Faustyn and Ignacy Mianowski, given the lack of information as to which tier of the former Polish nobility they are classified at according to the review in their registration as citizens of the city of Ostrog, the Heraldic Office, forgoing a binding decision with regard to those persons, instructed the Diet to supplement the case taking into account the above remarks and to do so in compliance with the designated procedure, the command having been issued on 8 July 1846.*

*Having appraised the case in question, the Governing Senate declares that the ruling of the former Heraldic Office of 28 May 1846 confirms the resolution of the Volhynia Diet of Nobles that Adam and Ignacy with his son Siemion-Wincenty, and the latter's sons Leon-Euzebiusz and Stanisław Ignacy Mianowski, be entered in the 1st part of the noble family book. Meanwhie, as regards Józef and Mikołaj, and*

ANNEXES

*the latter's sons Faustyn and Ignacy Mianowski, in the absence at the time of the possibility to have sight of certification of Józef's descent from Ignacy Mianowski, or of information as to which tier of former Polish nobility is Mikołaj Mianowski ascribed to in the review of 1834, which review classified his sons as citizens of the city of Ostrog, as the Heraldic Office dealing with the case observed, and not wishing to take a binding decision about these persons resolved to: instruct the Volhynia Diet of Nobles to supplement the case taking into account the above remarks and to do so in compliance with the designated procedure, the command having been issued on 8 July 1846.*

*As at this day the Volhynia Diet of Nobles, supplementing this case as required by the former Heraldic Office, moves that the Governing Senate incorporates in its review documents related to Ignacy son of Mikołaj Mianowski, which demonstrate: 1, that the correct lineage of Ignacy in 1793, son of Mikołaj, and in 1826 of his son Ignacy, is proven by certificates confirmed by the Mohylev and Lutsk-Zhytomir Church Consistories; 2, that Mikołaj, son of Ignacy, Mianowski was in reviews 5, 6 and 7 inscribed to the body of nobles and was not subject to the poll tax, according to review 8, being deceased, not registered anywhere, while his son Mikołaj was in his infancy left an orphan, and in view of his domicile in the Volhynia governorship and county of Ostrog was registered as a citizen by the local Civic Association; but neither he, Ignacy, nor his father Mikołaj Mianowski had their noble status removed by law, which is confirmed in the certification of the Marshal of the Nobility.*

*In consideration of these circumstances, and clauses 13 and 61 and comments in the last and tenth edition of Statutes published in 1842, and accepting the declaration of 6 July 1850 by the Volhynia Diet of Nobles that Ignacy son of Mikołaj Mianowski has sufficiently proved his lineage in the Mianowski family, declared in 1846 by the former Heraldic Office to be noble, with due correctness and in compliance with the legal clauses indicated, it is proposed: that Ignacy son of Mikołaj Mianowski be released from the obligation to pay the poll tax, and be included in the book of the noble Mianowski family, approved in 1846; and hereby humbly submitting this report we ask Your Imperial Highness for his uppermost consent.*

*Conclusion:*

*Agreeing with the resolution of the Governing Senate that Ignacy Mianowski, registered as a citizen, be raised to the ranks of nobility, the First Department proposes that the report and its annexes presented by the Acting Heraldist, be put before the Council of State for its consideration.*

Signature /illegible/

# Index of Names

Abicht Adolf   34, 36
Abrahamsohn Bernard   8
Aftanazy Roman   93
Aksakov Sergey T.   XIV
Alexander Bariatynski I.   XIX, 45, 87
Alexander I Romanov, tsar   16,17
Alexander II Romanov, tsar   XVI, XVII, 56,
   62, 81
Aleksandrowicz Jerzy (Alexandrowicz)   66
Anculewicz Zbigniew   89, 90, 93

Baal Szem Tow Izrael   7
Bacon Francis   63
Baerkman Jan Karol   36
Bairašauskaitė Tamara   35, 93, 101
Balińskis, family   26
Balińska Zofia (née Śniadecka)   21
Baliński Michał   21, 26, 27
Balzac Honoré, de   36
Balakirev Miliy A.   51
Barankiewicz   22
Baranowski Ignacy   69, 81, 82, 93
Baranowski Jan   68
Bariatynski, family   87
Barszczewska Alina   44, 93
Bazylow Ludwik   54, 57, 93
Bąbiak Grzegorz   XIII, 59, 69, 71, 93, 94, 98,
   101, 102
Bącewicz, doctor   66
Beaupré Józef Antoni   27
Beauvois Daniel   30
Bécu August   21, 23, 27, 32, 33
Bécu Jakub   30
Bécu Salomea   4, 21, 23, 25
Bécu, family   4, 23, 26
Bekhteriev Vladimir M.   50
Belke Gustaw   45, 46
Benni Karol   90
Berg Fyodor F.   XIX, 67, 70, 74, 76, 88
Białecki Antoni   58, 60, 61, 67, 74, 76, 81,
   87, 93
Bielecki Andrzej   2
Bieliński Józef (dr Szeliga)   28, 36, 40, 41,
   47, 48, 58
Bilozersky Vasil   XIV

Bludova Antonina D.   78
Bobrinsky Aleksey A.   5
Bobrinski, family   5
Bobrowski Michał   34
Bobrowski Tadeusz   20, 46, 51, 54, 55, 57, 93
Bogucki Józef Symeon   61, 94
Boholubow Andrzej   66
Bolesław z nad Dniepru (Bolesław upon
   Dnieper river)   7, 12
Borgia Cesare   85
Borodin Aleksandr P.   50
Borowczyk Jerzy   23, 94
Borowski Stanisław   57
Botkin Sergey P.   50
Brensztejn Michał   37, 94
Brudzewski Wojciech (Wojciech from
   Brudzew)   63
Brueghel Jan (Velvet)   49
Brykalska Maria   XII, XV, 73, 74, 75, 80, 94
Brzozowski Stanisław   24, 25, 85
Brzozowski Tadeusz   13
Brzozowski Karol   94
Bujalski, professor   51
Burke Edmund   XV

Casimir the Great, king   67
Chaborskis, family   13, 15
Chaborski Zenon   15
Chałubiński Tytus   67, 69, 82, 90, 103
Chimiak Łukasz   88, 94
Chłapowski Dezydery   29
Chmieleński Zygmunt   70
Chmielowski Piotr   19
Chodkiewicz, family   3
Chodźko Aleksander   21, 23
Choiński Henryk   27
Chreptowicz, family   22
Chrząszczewski Józef   13, 14, 15
Chwalewik Edmund   26, 94
Chwaściński Bolesław   85
Conrad Joseph   73, 77, 99
Copernicus Nicolaus   63
Cui César A.   51
Custine Astolphe, de   49
Cyłow N.I.   49

# INDEX OF NAMES

Czacki Tadeusz 9
Czapska Maria 31, 34, 87, 94
Czarniecki Stefan 14
Czartoryski Adam Jerzy 8, 9
Czech Jerzy XI
Czechowicz Szymon 26
Czepulis-Rastenis Ryszarda XVII
Czyż Anna Sylwia 32, 94

Daszyński Ignacy 92
Długosz Jan 64
Dmowski Roman 92
Dolgoruky, prince 37
Drucki-Lubecki Ksawery, prince 53, 101
Dubowik Henryk 3, 95, 103
Dunin-Borkowski Jerzy Sewer 2
Duninówna Helena 95
Dutkiewicz Walenty 58
Dzierżawski Bolesław 30, 95

Eisenbletter Aleksander 44
Elgot Jan 63
Epsztajn Tadeusz 2, 95
Erdelyi Michael, von 38, 39, 47
Estreicher Karol 80
Estreicher Stanisław 80

Falkowski Juliusz 13, 95
Feduszka Jacek 30, 95
Feliński Zygmunt Szczęsny 44, 55, 59, 65, 95
Fiszer Ludwik 95
Fiszer Otto 67
Fita Stanisław XII, 95
Fleischmann, author 39
Fonberg Ignacy 36
Formiconi Paolo 87, 100
Frederiks Platon 74
Fredro Aleksander 35

Gałęzowski Seweryn (Gałęziowski) 13, 16, 41, 47, 69, 78
Garbačova Volha V. 30
Gerson Wojciech 79
Giełgud Antoni 29
Gintrowski Przemysław XI
Girsztowt Polikarp 66, 67, 69
Głębocki Henryk 78, 96
Godlewski Mścisław 90

Gogol Nikolai 36
Gołąbek Józef XIV, 96
Gorecki Antoni 21
Goszczyński Seweryn XI, XIX, 13, 14, 15, 16, 19, 20, 35, 73, 78, 79, 91, 103
Gozdawa-Giżycki J.M. (Wołyniak) 3, 4, 6, 7, 8, 9, 10, 11, 12, 18
Grabowskis, family XV, 15
Grabowski Antoni 13
Grabowski Michał XIV, 13, 14, 19, 20, 28, 35, 47, 78
Grecenstein G.M. 51
Gromov J.W. 37
Groza Augustyn 14
Groza Pius 14
Grzegorz of Sanok 63
Gulczyński Eugeniusz 30
Günters, family 41
Gurvich Herman Bernard (Hirsz-Ber) 7
Gutowski Bartłomiej 32, 94

Halicki Gabryel 11
Haller Adolf Ferdinand 57
Haller Nadezhda 57
Hewelke Otton 30, 95
Hirszfeld Ludwik 69, 125
Hoene-Wroński Józef XIII
Holewiński Władysław 65, 67, 90
Hołowiński Ignacy XIV, 27, 54, 55
Hoyer Henryk 69
Hromowicz Józef 11, 13
Hryckiewicz Aleksander 44
Hryniewiecki Klemens 12
Hübbenet, von (probably Kristian Jakovlevich Gubenet) 81
Hube, wife of Przecławski 57
Hübner Piotr XII, 96
Hufeland Christoph Wilhelm 42, 111
Hugo Victor 36
Hulak Mykola XIV
Hus Jan 63

Ilgiewicz Henryka 34, 96
Iwanowski Ignacy 27, 55, 57
Iwański Jan 15

Jadwiga of Anjou, queen 63
Jakubielski, prelate 54

## INDEX OF NAMES

Jałowiecki Mieczysław   62
Janikowski Andrzej   66
Janion Maria   91, 97
Jankowski Edmund   67, 68, 82, 83, 94, 97, 98
Jankowski Jan   23
Jankowski Władysław   8, 102
Janowiczowa Brygida (*née* Kaszycówna)   22
Janowski Ludwik   27, 43, 97
Janowski Maciej   97
Janowski Władysław   30, 95
Janusz of Mianowo   2
Januszewskis, family   XIX, 3, 4, 33
Januszewska Hersylia (*née* Bécu)   3, 4, 21,
    32, 33, 98
Januszewski Teofil   3, 4, 21, 23, 31, 32, 33, 98
Januszkiewicz Eustachy   21
Jaroszewicz Józef   21
Jedlicki Jerzy   XVII, 95, 97, 99
Jelskis, family   22
Jurgiewicz Norbert   20

Kampe Joachim   7
Karieyev Nikolai I.   82
Karnicki Justyn (Justynian)   79
Kaszewski Kazimierz   67, 87
Kasznica Józef   65, 67
Katkov Mikhael   78
Kavelin Aleksandr A.   46, 47
Kelles-Krauz Kazimierz   97
Khomiakov Alexey S.   XIV
Khoraninov, Councillor of the estate   37
Kicka Natalia   69
Kieniewicz Hieronim   86
Kieniewicz Katarzyna   86
Kieniewicz Stefan   XIII, XIX, 3, 20, 24, 38,
    43, 44, 45, 56, 57, 60, 61, 69, 70, 71, 81,
    85, 86, 95, 97
Kierbedź Stanisław   27, 57, 85, 86
Kijas Artur   4, 57, 97
Kireyevsky Ivan V.   XIV
Kizwalter Tomasz   101, 102
Kleiner Juliusz   23
Kłągiewicz Benedykt   30, 37
Koberdowa Irena   70
Kochański Wiktor   67, 69
Kołbuk Witold   6, 14
Konarski Szymon   XVI, 33, 38, 44, 45, 46, 93,
    98, 103

Kondratowicz Ludwik   19
Koniecpolskis family   1, 5
Konopka Stanisław   73, 97
Konstantin Mikolayevich Romanov   62
Korczyński Janusz   2
Korsak Julian   21
Korycki Tomasz   15
Korzeniewski Jan   42
Korzeniewski Józef   36, 42
Korzeniowskis family   13
Korzeniowska (*née* Bobrowska) Ewa   77
Korzeniowski Apollo   73, 76
Kosmulski Leon   19
Kossak Juliusz   79
Kostecki Herakliusz   6
Kostomarov Mykola (Nikolay)   XIV
Kotzebue Paweł J., von   XIX, 88
Kowalewski Józef   67, 68, 72
Kozak Stefan   XIV, 98
Kozakiewicz Stanisław   44
Kozłowski Eligiusz   95
Kozłowski Jerzy   51
Kraszewski Józef Ignacy   87
Kraushar Aleksander   61, 69, 90, 93, 98
Krechowieckis family   13, 15
Krechowiecki Jan   7, 13, 14
Kridl Manfred   28
Kronenberg Leopold   71, 90
Kronenberg Stanisław   90
Krylov Iwan   36
Krzywicki Kazimierz   59, 71, 73, 87, 97
Krzywoszewski Bronisław   75
Kukolnik Nestor   37
Kulecka Alicja   88, 98
Kulish Panteleymon   XIV
Kulakovskiy Genrik Kazimirovich   51
Kurtz Karol   71
Kuzak Rafał   30, 98
Kwapiński Stanisław   75, 76

Laënnec Réne   38
Le Brun Aleksander   68
Leiboschütz (Lejboszyc)   22
Lens, french language teacher   13
Leonow Iwan   36
Leontiev Pawel   81
Lermontov Mikhail   36
Lesiński Teofil   66

124 INDEX OF NAMES

Leuchtenberg Maria Nikolaevna 53
Leuchtenberg Maximilian 53
Lewicki Pachomij 9
Lewiński Emilian 12
Lichocka Halina 43
Lieven Karl, von 34
Limanowski Bolesław 46, 98
Linde Samuel Bogumił 88
Linnaeus Carl 63
Lityński Bartłomiej 12, 17, 18
Liwski Edmund 18
Lomachevsky Asinkrit I. 46
Lorentz Stanisław 26, 98
Lubczański Julian 12
Lubomirski Franciszek Ksawery 5, 71
Lubomirski Jan Tadeusz XV
Lubomirskis family 5
Łopacińskis family 41
Łopalewski Tadeusz 19, 98
Łowicki Maciej 28, 38, 47, 48, 98
Łubieńskis family 53, 87
Łubieński Roger 53, 98
Łubieński Tomasz Pomian 53, 98

Machiavelli Niccolo 86
Maciejowski Wacław Aleksander 88
Majer Józef 74
Majewski Karol 70, 71
Malczewski Antoni 35
Malewski Czesław 2, 99
Malewski Szymon 11, 34
Malinowski Leszek Jan 95, 103
Małecki Antoni 58
Marcinkiewicz-Żaba Jan 35
Marcinkowski (inspector) 9
Markus (Stanisław Markusfeld?) 66
Massalski Józef 23
Mateusz of Mianowo 2
Mendelssohn Moses 7
Mérimée Prosper 36
Metzel Ludwik 8
Méyet Leopold XIX, 1, 10, 20, 26, 27, 28, 30, 33, 98, 99
Meysztowicz Aleksander 2
Mianowski Aleksandra (wife of Ignacy Mianowski, mother of Aleksandra, Józef the second, and Szymon Wincenty) 4

Mianowski Aleksandra neé Bécu (Olesia, first wife of Józef) 3, 23, 27, 28, 29, 30, 31, 32
Mianowski Anna (wife of Mikołaj, brother of Józef the second) 4
Mianowski Antonina (wife of Mikołaj, the professor) 3
Mianowski Lidia (Protopopow, adoptive daughter of Józef) 57
Mianowski Nadezhda neé Haller (Nadzieja, Hope, Maria, second wife of Józef) 57, 90, 114
Mianowski neé Micewicz Antonina (mother of Józef) 2
Mianowski Adam (brother of Ignacy – father of Mikołaj, Józef the second, and Szymon Wincenty) 4
Mianowski Aleksander (hydrotechnical engineer) 2
Mianowski Aleksander (son of Mikołaj, court counselor) 3
Mianowski Antoni Wincenty (court writer of the Main Court of the Warsaw Town) 2
Mianowski Faustyn (son of Mikołaj and Anna) 4, 118, 119
Mianowski Henryk (military doctor) 2
Mianowski Ignacy (father of Józef) 2, 4, 5
Mianowski Ignacy (father of Mikołaj, Józef the second, and Szymon Wincenty) 4, 17, 20, 28, 105, 117, 118
Mianowski Ignacy (son of Mikołaj and Anna) 119
Mianowski Jan (son of Józef and Aleksandra neé Bécu) 32
Mianowski Józef (the second) 3
Mianowski Józef (doctor from Kuyavian Brześć) 2
Mianowski Józef (older, Tępa Podkowa – Blunt Horseshoe coat of arms, lawyer) 3
Mianowski Konstanty (son of Mikołaj, brother of Aleksander, court councilor) 3
Mianowski Leon (son of Szymon Wincenty) 4, 118
Mianowski Mikołaj (brother of Józef the second and Wincenty Szymon, son of Ignacy and Aleksandra) 3, 4, 118

# INDEX OF NAMES

Mianowski Mikołaj (professor and rector in Vilnius)  2, 3

Mianowski Piotr (father of Ignacy and Adam, grandfather of Mikołaj, Józef the second and Szymon Wincenty)  4, 118

Mianowski Stanisław (author)  2, 99

Mianowski Stanisław (son of Szymon Wincenty)  4

Mianowski Szymon Wincenty  4, 118

Mianowski Wincenty Szymon (younger brother of Józef the second, and Mikołaj, son of Ignacy and Aleksandra)  4

Michał of Żorniszcze  3

Micińska Magdalena  XVII, 99

Mickiewicz Adam  XX, 21, 23, 35, 52, 64

Mierzyński Antoni  75

Nicolas I Romanov, tsar  XVII, 46, 53, 56

Nicolas II Romanov, tsar  52

Mikuliński Gracyan  9, 12

Mikulski Józef  28, 29

Milewski Ignacy Kapica  2

Miriam Karol Edward  36

Mirkowicz Fiodor J. (Mirkovitsch)  45

Mładanowski Rafał Despot vel Mładanowicz  7

Morawski Stanisław  22, 33

Morawski Stanisław  34, 99

Mościcki Henryk  99

Muchliński Antoni  27

Mussorgsky Modest P.  51

Nachman of Bratslav  7

Najder Zdzisław  73, 77, 99

Naryszkins (Naryshkins), family  87

Natanson Jakób  90

Natanson Józef  65

Natanson Ludwik  69

Nazimov Vladimir I.  46

Nehring Władysław  14

Neugebauer Ludwik  66, 69

Newlińskis, family  14, 15

Niedzielski, doctor  54

Nowosilcow Mikołaj  33

Nusbaum Henryk  73, 99

Nusbaum-Hilarowicz Józef  94, 99

Odyniec Antoni Edward  21, 23, 26, 27, 28

Oleśnicki Zbigniew  64

Orlov-Davidov, family  87

Orłowski Bolesław  85

Otzolig  66

Paderewski Ignacy Jan  92

Papłoński Jan  67, 80

Paucker Anna Katharina  57

Pawlicki Stefan  73, 77

Pavlov Ivan P.  50

Pelikan Wacław  20, 33, 34, 37, 41, 66

Pierejesławski-Jałowiecki Mieczysław  52

Pigoń Stanisław  12, 96

Piłsudski Józef  92

Piotr of Bnin  63

Piotr o f Mianowo  2

Pirogov Nikolai I.  50, 51

Piskurewicz Jan  XII, 96, 99, 100

Plater Filip  9

Plater, countess  77

Platers, family  22

Plebański Józef  65

Poczobut Marcin  24

Podczaszyński Bolesław  26

Podoski Mikołaj  11

Pogodin Mikhail P.  XIV

Poprzęcka Maria  79

Porcyanko Konstanty  34

Potemkin Grigory A.  5

Potocki, family  7, 10, 87

Potocki Zofia  8

Potocki Franciszek Salezy  6

Potocki Stanisław Szczęsny  5, 6, 8

Poznański Karol  58, 100

Prockiewicz Zygmunt  11

Prus Bolesław (Głowacki Aleksander) XVIII

Przecławski Jan Emanuel  57

Przezdziecki Aleksander  79

Przezdzieckis, family  22

Przyborowski Walery  70

Przystański Stanisław  66, 90

Pushkin Alexander  36

Puzynina z Günterów Gabriela (Puzynina *née* Günter)  33, 35, 41, 45, 46, 100

Rachuba Andrzej  7

Radziszewska, Mrs  20

Radziwiłłowicz Rafał  51

Radziwiłłs, family  22, 87

# INDEX OF NAMES

Radziwiłłówna Barbara 79
Rastawiecki Edward 79
Regnier Anicenty 27
Remak Robert 43, 47
Remy Johannes XIV, 44, 46, 100
Richter (August Gottlob?) 39
Rimsky-Korsakov Nikolai A. 51
Rodziewicz Ignacy 44
Rosental Nitel (aka Tryntroch) 44
Rovere Giovanni, della 85
Róziewicz Jerzy 34, 42, 100
Rudomino Jan 9
Ruprecht Karol 71
Rymkiewicz Feliks 34, 36, 48
Rzewuski Henryk 54

Samoylov Aleksandr N. 5
Samoylov, family 5
Sandler Samuel 75
Santoni Giuseppe 85, 100
Sarnecki Ignacy 14
Sawicz Franciszek 44
Schiller-Walicka Joanna 67, 72, 73, 80, 81,
      82, 100, 101
Sebastiani August 39, 47
Selinger Julia 74
Sienkiewicz Henryk XVIII, 90
Sienkiewicz Karol 21
Sierotwiński Stanisław 14
Siewruk Ludwik 36
Simmler Józef 79
Skibowski Leon 9, 10, 11, 12, 13, 15, 17, 18
Słowackis, family 21, 27, 54
Słowacki Juliusz XVII, XIX, 4, 23, 26, 27, 28,
      28, 30, 31, 32, 33, 35, 53
Smuglewicz Franciszek 26, 51
Sołtys Karolina 35, 101
Soszyński Jacek XII, 96
Spasowicz Włodzimierz 71
Spitznagel Fred 23
Spitznagel Ludwik 21, 23
Sternhartz Natan 7
Suchodolski Bogdan 96
Suchodolski January 79
Szaszkiewicz Floryan 9
Szczepański Jerzy 53
Szenic Stanisław 2, 101
Szevchenko Taras XIV

Szokalski Wiktor 69
Szperl Józef Ludwik 68, 102
Szpoper Dariusz 2
Szujski Józef 56, 58, 60, 87
Szukiewicz Wandalin 26
Szumakowicz Józef 13
Szumowski Władysław 41
Szwarc Andrzej 68, 74
Szweykowski Zygmunt XII, 102
Szymański F. 74
Szymański Marcely 30
Shyrynski (Szyryński), prince 54
Śniadeckis, family 21, 26
Śniadecka Ludwika 31, 34, 94
Śniadecki Jan 27
Śniadecki Jędrzej 24, 25, 26, 30, 33, 34, 36,
      38, 41, 42, 43, 47, 94, 102
Świętochowski Aleksander XII, XV, XVIII,
      73, 74, 75, 80, 94

Taczanowski Edmund 70
Tarkowski Fortunat 14
Tarkowski Hieronim 14
Tarkowski Mikołaj 54, 102
Tazbir Janusz 54
Tazbir Stanisław 103
Tocqueville Alexis de XV
Tokarz Wacław 30
Tolstoy Dmitry A. 78, 81, 87, 88
Tomaszewski Jan 14
Tomicki Piotr 64
Traugutt Romuald XVI
Trąba Mikołaj 63
Trembecki Stanisław 8, 102
Troćkiewicz Zygmunt 13
Trynkowski Ludwik 27, 44
Turkułł Ignacy 57
Tustanowski Felicjan 27
Twardowski Józef 20, 33, 93
Tymanowicz Justynian 12
Tyszkiewicz Konstanty 27
Tyszkiewiczes, family 22
Tyszyński Aleksander 27
Tyzenhauzes, family 22

Urusova Aleksandra 53, 54
Uvarov Sergey S. 45, 46, 53, 54
Uvarova Catherine *née* Razumovska 53

# INDEX OF NAMES

Valuyev Pyotr A.   XIX, 87, 88
Vishlenkova Elena A.   42

Walicki Andrzej   XIII, 95, 102, 103
Wasilewski Zygmunt   XI, 103
Werner Ferdynand   66
Weysenhoffs, family   22
Wielopolski Aleksander   XI, XV, XVI, 58, 59, 67, 70, 71, 72, 78
Wiercińska Janina   79, 103
Więckowska Helena   41
Wisznicki Mikołaj   5
Witte Fyodor   67, 68, 80, 114
Wittgenstein of the Bariatynskis Leonilda   45
Wittgensteins, family   41
Władysław, Mazovian Prince   2
Wodzianowska Irena   54, 103
Woeleck Aleksander   34
Wojciechowski Stanisław   92
Wojniłłowiczes, family   22
Wolfram Emil   69
Wolfram Jan   67
Wołonczewski Maciej   27
Wołowski Jan   65
Woronin M.N.   85
Woronina M.M.   85

Wróblewski Mikołaj   11
Wrześniowski August   90
Wrzosek Adam   73, 87, 97
Wyhowski, family   5
Wyleżyński Jan Nepomucen   9, 11

Zahorski Jan   44
Zahorski Władysław   34, 43, 44, 45, 103
Zaleski Józef Bohdan   XIX, 13, 14, 15, 19, 20, 35
Zaleski Julian   13
Zaleski Kazimierz   90
Zaliwski Józef   46, 98
Załuziański Adam   63
Zamoyski Jan   64
Zamoyski Stanisław   79
Zasztowt Leszek   IX, XII, 9, 13, 26, 38, 45, 65, 79, 96, 103
Zathey Hugo   15
Zatthier Nazariusz   12, 17
Zawadzki, publisher   33, 40
Zawadzki Józef   30, 95
Zbyszewski, brothers   14
Zeiszner Ludwik   66
Ziemowit, Mazovian Prince   2
Ziółkowska Ewa   52, 104
Żyliński Wacław   54

# List of Figures

Fig. 1. Joseph Mianowski. Source: 'Kłosy' 1879, no. 708, p. 56

Fig. 2. Uman. Church of the Assumption of the Blessed Virgin Mary (1826). Source: https://perlyny-ua.narod.ru/cherkaska/uman/uman2.html

Fig. 3. Uman. Market. Source: National Museum, Cracow. Collection 3rd – rare acquisitions 2861. (Portfolio Ukraine). Source: http://www.pinakoteka.zascianek.pl/Orda/Orda_Ukraina_R1.htm

Fig. 4. Tadeusz Czacki (1765–1813). Portrait by Józef Pitschmann (1758–1834). Source: https://commons.wikimedia.org/wiki/File:J%C3%B3zef_Franciszek_Jan_Pitschmann,_Portret_Tadeusza_Czackiego.jpg

Fig. 5. Seweryn Goszczyński (1801–1876). Source: Museum of Literature Collection/East News, https://culture.pl/pl/tworca/seweryn-goszczynski

Fig. 6. Michał Grabowski (1804–1863). Source: Musej odnijeji wulyzi, Kiev

Fig. 7. Józef Bohdan Zaleski (1802–1886). Source: https://commons.wikimedia.org/wiki/File:Portret_J%C3%B3zefa_Bohdana_Zaleskiego.jpg

Fig. 8. Vilnius, Vilnius University. Source: Vilnius album. Polona. Public domain

Fig. 9. Vilnius, Dominican street. Source: Vilnius album. Polona. Public domain

Fig. 10. Vilnius, the War Governor's Palace, and the Astronomical Observatory. Source: Vilnius album. Polona. Public domain

Fig. 11. Portrait of Jędrzej Śniadecki (1768–1838). Source: National Museum in Warsaw. Public domain

Fig. 12. Michał Baliński (1794–1864). Source: from the collection of the the the Polish Academy of Sciences Archives in Warsaw, reference number XV-79-001

Fig. 13. Prince Adam Jerzy Czartoryski (1770–1861). Source: from the collection of the National Library in Warsaw, reference number G.5992, POLONA. Public domain

Fig. 14. August Bécu (1771–1824), father of Aleksandra Mianowska. Source: from the collection of the Polish Academy of Sciences Archives in Warsaw, ref. A MR. XV-57-001

Fig. 15. Salomea Słowacka (1792–1855), mother of Juliusz Słowacki, stepmother of Aleksandra Mianowska née Bécu. Source: Wikimedia Commons

Fig. 16. Aleksandra Mianowska née Bécu (1803–1832). Source: https://commons.wikimedia.org/wiki/File:Aleksandra_Mianowska.jpg

Fig. 17. Hersylia Januszewska (1805–1872) née Bécu, sister of Aleksandra Mianowska. Source: https://commons.wikimedia.org/wiki/File:Hersylia_%C5%81ucja_Januszewska.jpg

Fig. 18. Teofil (ca. 1798–1865) and Hersylia (1805–1872) Januszewscy, on the steps of the manor house in Ubień. Source: National Museum in Warsaw. Public domain

# LIST OF FIGURES

Fig. 19. Juliusz Słowacki (1809–1849). Source: from the collection of the Polish Academy of Sciences Archives in Warsaw, reference number XLI-102-001

Fig. 20. Adam Mickiewicz (1797–1855). Source: https://de.m.wikipedia.org/wiki/Datei:Wa%C5%84kowicz_Adam_Mickiewicz.jpg

Fig. 21. Wacław Pelikan (1790–1873). Source: from the collection of the National Digital Archives of Poland

Fig. 22. Szymon Konarski (1808–1839). Source: from the collection of the Polish Academy of Sciences Archives in Warsaw, reference number XXI-199-001

Fig. 23. Church of St. Alexander at Plac Trzech Krzyży (the Three Crosses Square) in Warsaw. Source: Mazovian Digital Library. Public domain

Fig. 24. Krakowskie Przedmieście in Warsaw, in the background Staszic Palace, first half of the 19th century. Source: Mazovian Digital Library. Public domain

Fig. 25. Kazimierzowski Palace at Krakowskie Przedmieście in Warsaw (university old campus), second half of the 19th century. Source: author's collection

Fig. 26. Church of the Visitation Sisters of the Protection of St. Joseph, Spouse of the Immaculate Mother of God, Mary. Source: Mazovian Digital Library. Public domain

Fig. 27. Hotel Europejski, Saski (Saxon) Palace in the background. Source: Mazovian Digital Library. Public domain

Fig. 28. Oboźna Street with university buildings. Source: 'Kłosy' 1882, no. 881, p. 317

Fig. 29. Tsar Alexander II (1818–1881), King of Poland. Source: 'L'Illustration' 1855, no. 629, p. 1

Fig. 30. Main School building. Photographed on the 50th anniversary of its founding. Source: Marek Kwiatkowski, Wspomnienie dawnej Warszawy, Wydawnictwo Naukowe PWN, Warszawa 1993, p. 45, https://commons.wikimedia.org/wiki/File:Budynek_Szko%C5%82y_G%C5%82%C3%B3wnej_kampus_centralny_UW.jpg

Fig. 31. Margrave Aleksander Wielopolski (1803–1877). Source: 'Kłosy' 1877, no. 655, p. 41

Fig. 32. The interior of the Main School Library. Source: 'Kłosy' 1865, no. 308, p. 77

Fig. 33. Reading room for students at the Main School. Source: 'Kłosy' 1868, no. 154, p. 320

Fig. 34. Column room with a collection of plaster figures in the former Main School Museum Building. Source: 'Tygodnik Ilustrowany' 1866, no. 338, p. 124

Fig. 35. Professors of the Main School. Tableau presented to J. Mianowski on the occasion of his name day in 1867. Source: "Tygodnik Ilustrowany" 1903, No. 23, p. 450

Fig. 36. Rector and deans of the Main School. Source: https://de.m.wikipedia.org/wiki/Datei:Rektor_i_Dziekani_Szko%C5%82y_G%C5%82%C3%B3wnej_Warszawskiej,_(Rysowa%C5%82_Tegazzo,_z_fotografij_Trzebieckiego)_(58086).jpg

LIST OF FIGURES

Fig. 37. Lecturers of the Faculty of Medicine at the Warsaw Main School. From the left: Aleksander Le Brun (dean), Józef Mianowski (rector), Władysław Tyrchowski (2nd dean), below: Polikarp Girsztowt, Antoni Kryszka, Tytus Chałubiński, Wiktor Szokalski, below: Teofil Wisłocki, Adam Gliszczyński, Ludwik Neugebauer, Hipolit Korzeniowski. Romuald Pląskowski, below: Henryk Hoyer, Michał Pilecki, Henryk Łuczkiewicz, Ludwik Hirszfeld, below: Włodzimierz Brodowski, Witold Jodko-Narkiewicz, Ferdynand Werner, Józef Rose, Ignacy Baranowski, below: Piotr Seifman, Feliks Nawrocki, Herman Fudakowski, Bronisław Hoynowski. Source: 'Kłosy' 1868, no. 131, p. 5 photo.

Fig. 38. Professors of the Warsaw Main School: Julian Kosiński, Teodor Dydyński, Ignacy Baranowski, Władysław Holewiński, Walenty Miklaszewski. Source: From the collection of the Polish Academy of Sciences Archives in Warsaw, reference number ZF, XIII-63

Fig. 39. Tytus Chałubiński (1820–1889). Source: From the collection of the Polish Academy of Sciences Archives in Warsaw, reference number ZF. XIV-1

Fig. 40. Winter Palace in St. Petersburg, first half of the 19th century. Source: from the collection of the Polish Academy of Sciences Archives in Warsaw, reference number XLI-104-001

Fig. 41. Imperial Public Library in St. Petersburg (now Russian National Library). Source: https://commons.wikimedia.org/wiki/File:Russian_National_Library_building.jpg?uselang=de

Fig. 42. St. Petersburg University. Source: https://commons.wikimedia.org/wiki/File:Saint_Petersburg_University.jpg

Fig. 43. Grand Duchess Maria Nikolaevna Leuchtenberg (1819–1876), daughter of Nicholas I. Source: https://commons.wikimedia.org/wiki/File:Maria_Nikolayevna_von_Leuchtenberg_by_Winterhalter_(1857,_Hermitage).jpg

Fig. 44. Zygmunt Szczęsny Feliński, Archbishop of Warsaw. Source: https://commons.wikimedia.org/wiki/File:Portret_arcybiskupa_Zygmunta_Szcz%C4%99snego_Feli%C5%84skiego.jpg

Fig. 45. Stanisław Kierbedź (1810–1899). Photograph made in the Warsaw atelier of Jan Mieczkowski from around 1865. From the collection of the National Library in Warsaw, reference number F. 88341/W. Source: POLONA. Public domain

Fig. 46. Józef Mianowski's epitaph in the post-piary church of Our Lady of Grace. Source: https://commons.wikimedia.org/wiki/File:Pomnik_J%C3%B3zefa_Mianowskiego_ods%C5%82oniony_w_dniu_14_b.m._w_ko%C5%9Bciele_po-Pijarskim_w_Warszawie_(79234).jpg

Fig. 47. Bust of Józef Mianowski, marble, by Ludwik Pyrowicz, 1903. In the collection of the Museum of the University of Warsaw, photograph by Łukasz Kamiński

LIST OF FIGURES

Fig. 48. The church of Santa Maria delle Grazie in Senigalla, next to which is the Cimitero delle Grazie – cemetery, where the tomb of Józef Mianowski is located. Photograph by Jaroslaw Rubin

Fig. 49. Grave inscription. Photograph by Jaroslaw Rubin

Fig. 50 and 51. Józef Mianowski's tomb in Senigalla. Photograph by Jaroslaw Rubin

# Figures

Fig. 1    Joseph Mianowski. Source: 'Kłosy' 1879, no. 708, p. 56.

Fig. 2　　Uman. Church of the Assumption of the Blessed Virgin Mary (1826). Source: 19th century illustration, Uman Regional Museum.

Fig. 3
Uman. Market. Source: National Museum, Cracow. Collection 3rd – rare acquisitions 2861.

Fig. 4　　Tadeusz Czacki (1765–1813). Portrait by Józef Pitschmann (1758–1834). Source: Wikimedia Commons.

Fig. 5    Seweryn Goszczyński (1801–1876). Source: Museum of Literature Collection/East News.

FIGURES 137

Fig. 6      Michał Grabowski (1804–1863). Source: Musej odnijeji wulyzi, Kiev.

Fig. 7　　Józef Bohdan Zaleski (1802–1886). Source: Wikimedia Commons.

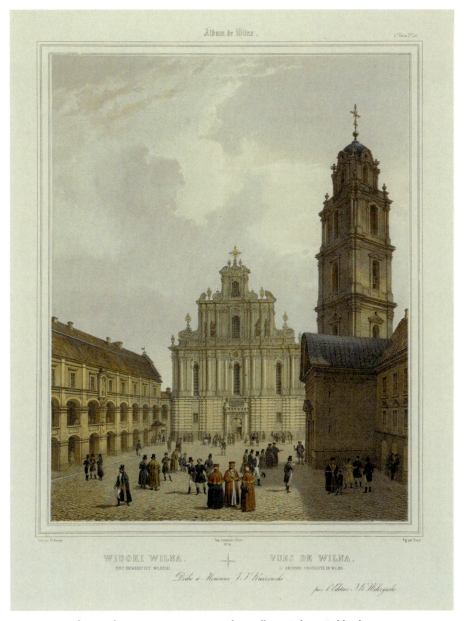

Fig. 8    Vilnius, Vilnius University. Source: Vilnius album. Polona. Public domain.

Fig. 9    Vilnius, Dominican street. Source: Vilnius album. Polona. Public domain.

FIGURES 141

Fig. 10  Vilnius, the War Governor's Palace, and the Astronomical Observatory. Source: Vilnius album. Polona. Public domain.

Fig. 11  Portrait of Jędrzej Śniadecki (1768–1838). Source: National Museum in Warsaw. Public domain.

FIGURES 143

Fig. 12 Michał Baliński (1794–1864). Source: from the collection of the the Polish Academy of Sciences Archives in Warsaw, XV-79-001.

Fig. 13
Prince Adam Jerzy Czartoryski (1770–1861). Source: from the collection of the National Library in Warsaw, G.5992, POLONA. Public domain.

Fig. 14
August Bécu (1771–1824), father of Aleksandra Mianowska. Source: from the collection of the Polish Academy of Sciences Archives in Warsaw, A MR. XV-57-001.

Fig. 15
Salomea Słowacka (1792–1855), mother of Juliusz Słowacki, stepmother of Aleksandra Mianowska née Bécu. Source: Wikimedia Commons.

Fig. 16
Aleksandra Mianowska née Bécu (1803–1832). Source: Wikimedia Commons.

Fig. 17
Hersylia Januszewska (1805–1872) née Bécu, sister of Aleksandra Mianowska. Source: Wikimedia Commons.

Fig. 18
Teofil (ca. 1798–1865) and Hersylia (1805–1872) Januszewscy, on the steps of the manor house in Ubień. Source: National Museum in Warsaw. Public domain.

FIGURES

Fig. 19　　Juliusz Słowacki (1809–1849). Source: from the collection of the Polish Academy of Sciences Archives in Warsaw, XLI-102-001.

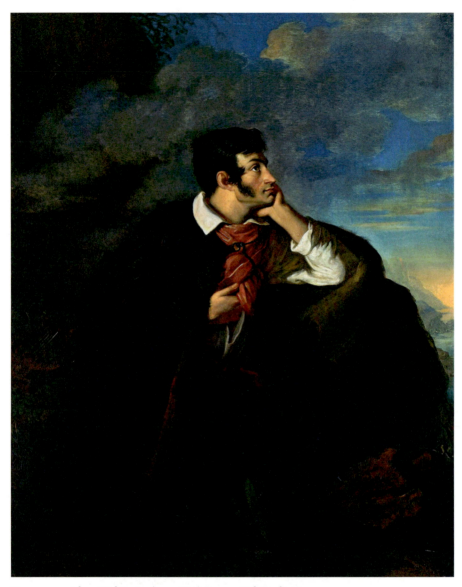

Fig. 20    Adam Mickiewicz (1797–1855). Source: Wikimedia Commons.

Fig. 21   Wacław Pelikan (1790–1873). Source: National Digital Archives of Poland.

Fig. 22　　Szymon Konarski (1808–1839). Source: from the collection of the Polish Academy of Sciences Archives in Warsaw, XXI-199-001.

FIGURES 151

Fig. 23    Church of St. Alexander at Plac Trzech Krzyży (the Three Crosses Square) in Warsaw. Source: Mazovian Digital Library. Public domain.

Fig. 24    Krakowskie Przedmieście in Warsaw, in the background Staszic Palace, first half of the 19th century. Source: Mazovian Digital Library. Public domain.

Fig. 25    Kazimierzowski Palace at Krakowskie Przedmieście in Warsaw (university old campus), second half of the 19th century. Source: author's collection.

Fig. 26    Church of the Visitation Sisters of the Protection of St. Joseph, Spouse of the Immaculate Mother of God, Mary. Source: Mazovian Digital Library. Public domain.

Fig. 27  Hotel Europejski, Saski (Saxon) Palace in the background. Source: Mazovian Digital Library. Public domain.

Fig. 28    Oboźna Street with university buildings. Source: 'Kłosy' 1882, no. 881, p. 317.

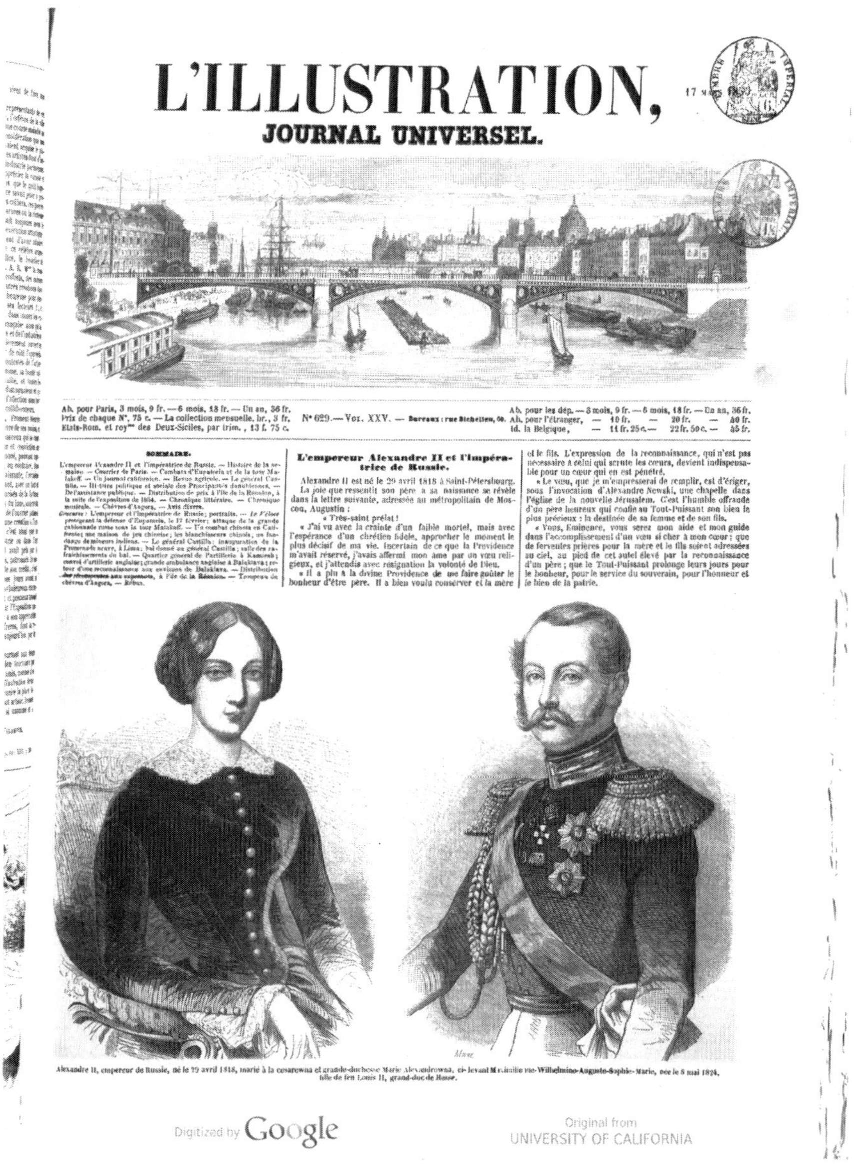

L'ILLUSTRATION,

JOURNAL UNIVERSEL.

Ab. pour Paris, 3 mois, 9 fr. — 6 mois, 18 fr. — Un an, 36 fr.
Prix de chaque N°, 75 c. — La collection mensuelle, br., 3 fr.
Etats-Rom. et roy^mes des Deux-Siciles, par trim., 13 f. 75 c.

N° 629. — Vol. XXV. — Bureaux : rue Richelieu, 60.

Ab. pour les dép. — 3 mois, 9 fr. — 6 mois, 18 fr. — Un an, 36 fr.
Ab. pour l'étranger, — 10 fr. — 20 fr. — 40 fr.
Id. la Belgique, — 11 fr. 25 c. — 22 fr. 50 c. — 45 fr.

SOMMAIRE.

L'empereur Alexandre II et l'impératrice de Russie. — Histoire de la semaine. — Courrier de Paris. — Combats d'Eupatoria et de la tour Malakoff. — Un journal californien. — Revue agricole. — Le général Castilla. — Histoire politique et sociale des Principautés danubiennes. — De l'assistance publique. — Distribution de prix à l'île de la Réunion, à la suite de l'exposition de 1854. — Chronique littéraire. — Chronique musicale. — Chèvres d'Angora. — Avis divers.

*Gravures :* L'empereur et l'impératrice de Russie; portraits. — *Le Véloce* protégeant la défense d'Eupatoria, le 17 février; attaque de la grande cabionnade russe sous la tour Malakoff. — Un combat chinois en Californie; une maison de jeu chinoise; les blanchisseurs chinois; un fandango de mineurs indiens. — Le général Castilla; inauguration de la Promenade neuve, à Lima; bal donné au général Castilla; salle des rafraîchissements du bal. — Quartier général de l'artillerie à Kamiesh; convoi d'artillerie anglaise; grande ambulance anglaise à Balaklava; retour d'une reconnaissance aux environs de Balaklava. — Distribution des récompenses aux exposants, à l'île de la Réunion. — Troupeau de chèvres d'Angora. — Rébus.

**L'empereur Alexandre II et l'impératrice de Russie.**

Alexandre II est né le 29 avril 1818 à Saint-Pétersbourg.

La joie que ressentit son père à sa naissance se révèle dans la lettre suivante, adressée au métropolitain de Moscou, Augustin :

« Très-saint prélat !

« J'ai vu avec la crainte d'un faible mortel, mais avec l'espérance d'un chrétien fidèle, approcher le moment le plus décisif de ma vie. Incertain de ce que la Providence m'avait réservé, j'avais affermi mon âme par un vœu religieux, et j'attendis avec résignation la volonté de Dieu.

« Il a plu à la divine Providence de me faire goûter le bonheur d'être père. Il a bien voulu conserver et la mère et le fils. L'expression de la reconnaissance, qui n'est pas nécessaire à celui qui scrute les cœurs, devient indispensable pour un cœur qui en est pénétré.

« Le vœu, que je m'empresserai de remplir, est d'ériger, sous l'invocation d'Alexandre Newski, une chapelle dans l'église de la nouvelle Jérusalem. C'est l'humble offrande d'un père heureux qui confie au Tout-Puissant son bien le plus précieux : la destinée de sa femme et de son fils.

« Vous, Eminence, vous serez mon aide et mon guide dans l'accomplissement d'un vœu si cher à mon cœur; que de ferventes prières pour la mère et le fils soient adressées au ciel, au pied de cet autel élevé par la reconnaissance d'un père; que le Tout-Puissant prolonge leurs jours pour le bonheur, pour le service du souverain, pour l'honneur et le bien de la patrie.

Alexandre II, empereur de Russie, né le 29 avril 1818, marié à la cesarewna et grande-duchesse Marie Alexandrowna, ci-devant Maximilienne-Wilhelmine-Auguste-Sophie-Marie, née le 8 mai 1824, fille de feu Louis II, grand-duc de Hesse.



Fig. 29 Tsar Alexander II (1818–1881), King of Poland. Source: 'L'Illustration' 1855, no. 629, p. 1.

Fig. 30   Main School building. Photographed on the 50th anniversary of its founding. Source: Marek Kwiatkowski, Wspomnienie dawnej Warszawy, Wydawnictwo Naukowe PWN, Warszawa 1993, p. 45, Wikimedia Commons.

Fig. 31   Margrave Aleksander Wielopolski (1803–1877). Source: 'Kłosy' 1877, no. 655, p. 41.

Fig. 32　　The interior of the Main School Library. Source: 'Kłosy' 1865, no. 308, p. 77.

Fig. 33　　Reading room for students at the Main School. Source: 'Kłosy' 1868, no. 154, p. 320.

Fig. 34　　Column room with a collection of plaster figures in the former Main School Museum Building. Source: 'Tygodnik Ilustrowany' 1866, no. 338, p. 124.

Fig. 35    Professors of the Main School. Tableau presented to J. Mianowski on the occasion of his name day in 1867. Source: "Tygodnik Ilustrowany" 1903, No. 23, p. 450.

# FIGURES

Fig. 36     Rector and deans of the Main School. Source: Wikimedia Commons.

Fig. 37　Lecturers of the Faculty of Medicine at the Warsaw Main School. From the left: Aleksander Le Brun (dean), Józef Mianowski (rector), Władysław Tyrchowski (2nd dean), below: Polikarp Girsztowt, Antoni Kryszka, Tytus Chałubiński, Wiktor Szokalski, below: Teofil Wisłocki, Adam Gliszczyński, Ludwik Neugebauer, Hipolit Korzeniowski. Romuald Pląskowski, below: Henryk Hoyer, Michał Pilecki, Henryk Łuczkiewicz, Ludwik Hirszfeld, below: Włodzimierz Brodowski, Witold Jodko-Narkiewicz, Ferdynand Werner, Józef Rose, Ignacy Baranowski, below: Piotr Seifman, Feliks Nawrocki, Herman Fudakowski, Bronisław Hoynowski. Source: 'Kłosy' 1868, no. 131, p. 5 photo.

Fig. 38    Professors of the Warsaw Main School: Julian Kosiński, Teodor Dydyński, Ignacy Baranowski, Władysław Holewiński, Walenty Miklaszewski. Source: From the collection of the Polish Academy of Sciences Archives in Warsaw, ZF, XIII-63.

Fig. 39  Tytus Chałubiński (1820–1889). Source: From the collection of the Polish Academy of Sciences Archives in Warsaw, ZF. XIV-1.

Fig. 40   Winter Palace in St. Petersburg, first half of the 19th century. Source: from the collection of the Polish Academy of Sciences Archives in Warsaw, XLI-104-001.

Fig. 41   Imperial Public Library in St. Petersburg (now Russian National Library). Source: Wikimedia Commons.

Fig. 42   St. Petersburg University. Source: Wikimedia Commons.

Fig. 43    Grand Duchess Maria Nikolaevna Leuchtenberg (1819–1876), daughter of Nicholas I. Source: Wikimedia Commons.

Fig. 44    Zygmunt Szczęsny Feliński, Archbishop of Warsaw. Source: Wikimedia Commons.

Fig. 45   Stanisław Kierbedź (1810–1899). Photograph made in the Warsaw atelier of Jan Mieczkowski from around 1865. From the collection of the National Library in Warsaw, reference number F. 88341/W. Source: POLONA. Public domain.

Fig. 46   Józef Mianowski's epitaph in the post-piary church of Our Lady of Grace.
Source: https://commons.wikimedia.org/wiki/File:Pomnik_J%C3%B3zefa_
Mianowskiego_ods%C5%82oniony_w_dniu_14_b.m._w_ko%C5%9Bciele_po-
Pijarskim_w_Warszawie_(79234).jpg.

Fig. 47  Bust of Józef Mianowski, marble, by Ludwik Pyrowicz, 1903. In the collection of the Museum of the University of Warsaw, photograph by Łukasz Kamiński.

Fig. 48    The church of Santa Maria delle Grazie in Senigalla, next to which is the Cimitero delle Grazie – cemetery, where the tomb of Józef Mianowski is located. Photograph by Jaroslaw Rubin.

FIGURES

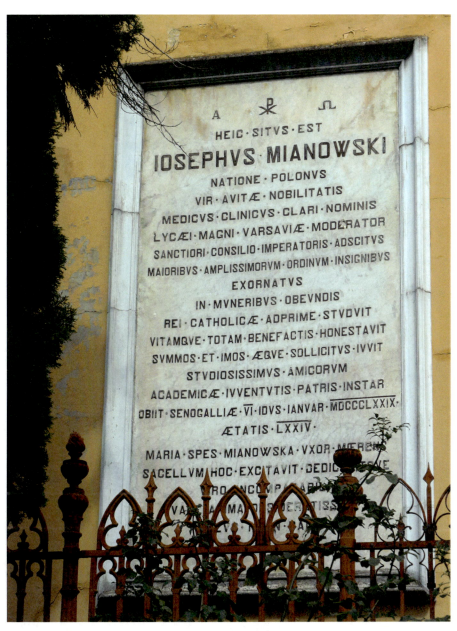

Fig. 49    Grave inscription. Photograph by Jaroslaw Rubin.

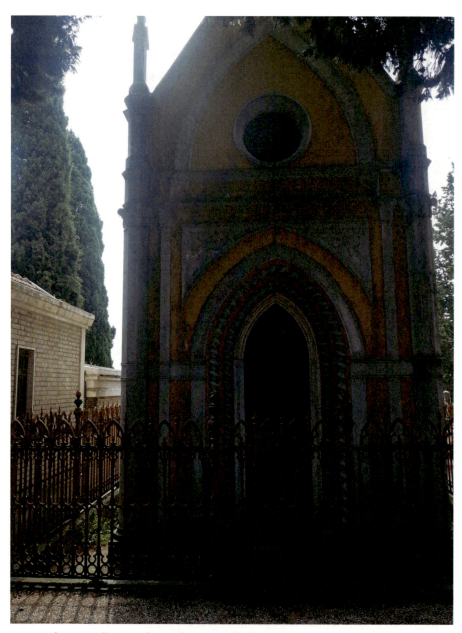

Fig. 50 and 51    Józef Mianowski's tomb in Senigalla. Photograph by Jaroslaw Rubin.